I0900974

IMAGES
of America

TUSCAN SPRINGS

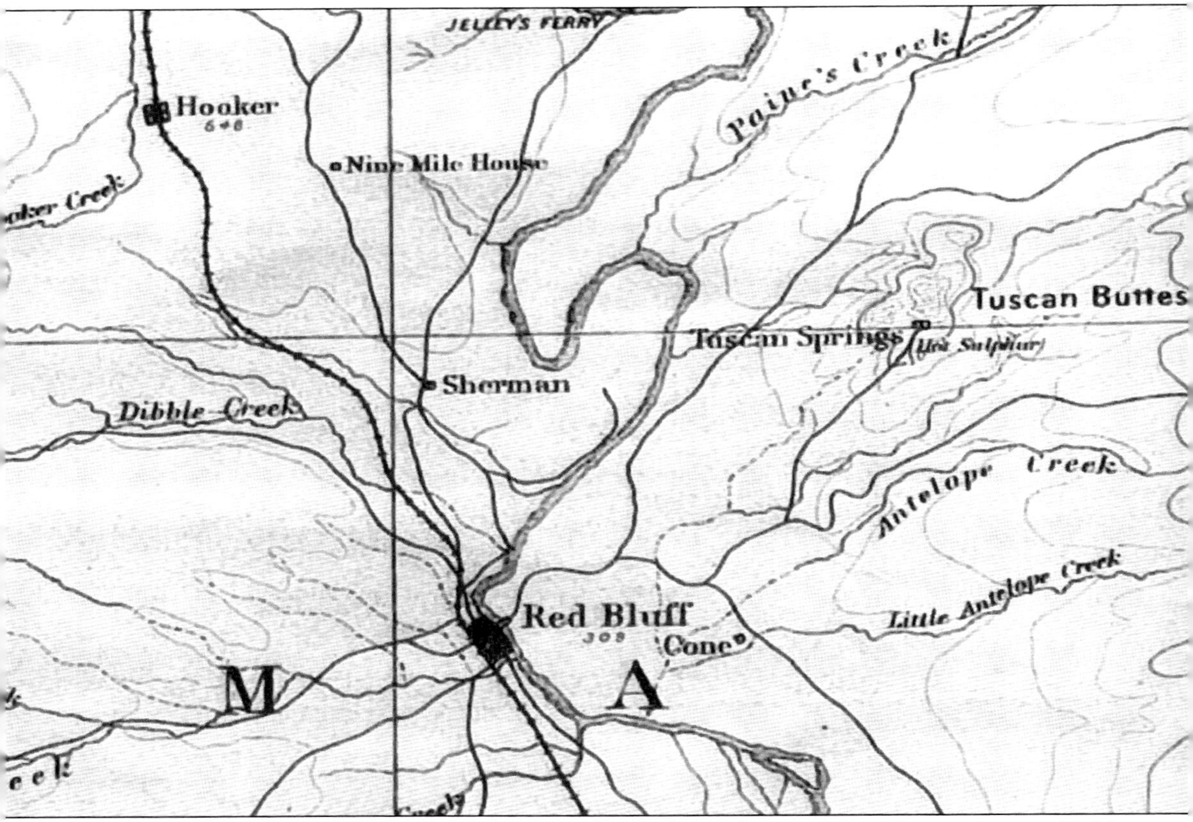

An 1882 survey map of Tehama County, California, shows the location of Tuscan Springs. Hidden in an extinct volcanic crater and surrounded by rocky buttes nine miles northeast of Red Bluff, the collection of mineral water springs was, if not the first, among the earliest hot springs resorts in the new state of California. The same year this survey was done, a massive downtown fire in Red Bluff destroyed many of the local businesses, including a shop owned and operated by Edgerton Byron Walbridge. A former telegraph operator from Iowa, Walbridge also lost his next business venture, a hotel, to fire in 1885, which led him to purchase the struggling Tuscan Springs resort in 1887. He constructed a magnificent Victorian hotel and steered the unique attraction to unprecedented heights of world-renowned success. (Courtesy Tehama County Library.)

On the Cover: In its heyday at the turn of the 20th century, the famous Tuscan Springs mineral water resort offered a grand three-story, 126-room hotel, complete with verandas all around, two kitchens, two dining rooms, parlors, and rooms for gambling. The resort also featured numerous cottages, stables, a saloon, steam and plunge baths, swimming pool, bowling alley, post office, ample hunting, and even a man-made lake, fully stocked with fish, ducks and sailboats. Its main attraction, though, was the more than 50 mineral water springs, each of which was said to cure numerous maladies—from cancer to the common cold. (Courtesy Tehama County Museum.)

IMAGES
of America

TUSCAN SPRINGS

Bryon Burruss

ARCADIA
PUBLISHING

ISBN 978-1-4671-3122-3

Published by Arcadia Publishing
Charleston, South Carolina

Printed in the United States of America

Library of Congress Control Number: 2013945928

For all general information, please contact Arcadia Publishing:
Telephone 843-853-2070
Fax 843-853-0044
E-mail sales@arcadiapublishing.com
For customer service and orders:
Toll-Free 1-888-313-2665

Visit us on the Internet at www.arcadiapublishing.com

For Mom and Dad, with a lifetime of love.
This is yours.

Contents

Foreword

One of the greatest joys of living in rural Northern California is learning of the obscure and often fascinating histories of its hidden treasures. Typically, these tales are passed down through generations of local families, but details can be difficult to authenticate.

When it comes to the rise and fall of Tuscan Springs, Red Bluff author Bryon Burruss has done the legwork and offers here the most thorough account of the events that led to the development and eventual abandonment of Tehama County's most unusual resource.

Beyond simply recounting the hard facts of Tuscan Springs, Burruss weaves together newspaper clippings, promotional materials, historical and societal context, and an abundance of photographs into a truly compelling story. The facts are there, but he has made the tale very readable.

One can only hope the author will apply his gift for storytelling to other North State yarns and preserve them for generations to come.

—Chip Thompson
editor, *Red Bluff Daily News*

ACKNOWLEDGMENTS

This book would not have been possible without the archives and helpful staff of the Tehama County Library, in particular, as well as the Tehama Museum, the Kelly-Griggs House Museum, and the Tehama County Genealogical & Historical Society. Each of them is severely underfunded and desperately in need of volunteers. Please consider offering your time to help them preserve the fascinating history of Northern California and encourage an interest in our heritage so that more books like this can be created before it all fades away.

I would especially like to thank Robert and Richard Neher, the current owners of Tuscan Springs, who have helped solve many mysteries over the years; Dan Masey for access to his collection and knowledge; Richard Burill, the author of numerous books on Ishi, for advice; *Red Bluff Daily News* editor Chip Thompson; Lamar Bayles and his photographic heritage; Red Bluff Fire Department history addict Larry Shnell; Arcadia acquisitions editor Jared Nelson for his knowledge and patience; and Joe H., without whom this book would never have happened.

Unless otherwise specified, images in this book are reprinted courtesy of the Tehama County Library. In most other cases, photographs are provided courtesy of the following: the author's collection (Author); Robert and Richard Neher (Neher); the Tehama County Museum (TCM); the Kelly-Griggs House Museum (KGHM); Dan Massie (Massie); Lamar Bayles (Bayles); the Meriam Library, California State University, Chico (CSUC); and Northern California Title Company (NCT).

INTRODUCTION

What is the chief end of man?—to get rich. In what way?—dishonestly if we can; honestly if we must.

—Mark Twain (1835–1910)

As the 20th century loomed ahead and railroad tracks stitched across the country like sutures on the wounds of the Industrial Revolution and the coming Civil War, a new and deadly epidemic was sweeping across the United States, leaving millions in its wake. "Neurasthenia Americana" caused varied and vague symptoms but was generally marked by chronic fatigue, sleeplessness, muscle pains, headaches, lack of motivation, and feelings of inadequacy. It was brought on, according to Dr. George M. Beard in the *Boston Medical and Surgical Journal* (1869), by such 19th-century developments as steam power, the periodic press, telegraph service, the sciences, and even the "mental activity of women."

For relief, Americans turned to the hundreds of available patent medicines, homeopathy, phrenology, osteopathy, alcohol (and if that did not work, temperance), and even electrical shock treatments, but any relief was temporary at best.

Then, a small Northern California community stumbled upon a wondrous elixir that not only eradicated all traces of the dreaded new disease but also apparently cured every other illness known to man; it would also, incidentally, help put the fledgling city of Red Bluff on the map.

It is safely tucked in a long-extinct crater and tightly embraced by ragged, towering buttes. Sheltered from wind and weather, the hidden home of this magical potion might as well have been torn from the pages of a fairy tale. Set against a backdrop of oak, pine, and polished lava amid the contented trill of birds and the aroma of rich earth, saltwater, and wild herbs—far from the city lights, its evening stars smolder like sapphire embers.

It is only a casual horse trot northeast of Red Bluff, yet the purveyors of its liquid miracle would find scandal, heartbreak, and ruin on the road to Tuscan Springs.

The story of this famous health resort is the story of Red Bluff, which is the story of California; one tale cannot be fully told without the others, and they all begin with an accident near Sacramento in 1848.

The discovery of gold at Sutter's Mill began the largest mass movement of people since the Crusades as crazed settlers crowded into the virgin territory, bringing with them the new philosophy that no obstacle can possibly stand in the face of providence and a little bit of luck—or at least the right pickaxe.

John A. Sutter saw it all coming.

He predicted the inevitable land boom and its need for lumber and began harvesting timber, envisioning himself as baron of a West Coast lumber empire. Undeterred by the Mexican-American War, which raged between 1846 and 1848, and the fact that California was not even American property, Sutter commissioned James W. Marshall to build a water-powered sawmill in Coloma. His plans were progressing exactly as anticipated until Marshall found flakes of gold in the mill's tailrace. Sutter tried desperately to keep the discovery a secret for fear that it would ruin all his plans, but there was no stopping the news, and settlers soon flooded in from all over the world in a rabid race for riches.

It turned out that Sutter was right in all respects. There was a lumber empire to be built, and the owners would become filthy rich for the foreseeable future; however, he was also correct in his fear of ruin. As soon as word got out, all of his employees immediately ran off to find their own slices of the golden pie, and when the forty-niners arrived, squatters took over his land, and vandals stole his crops and cattle. He was finished.

One of the first people to visit Marshall's discovery was Maj. Pierson B. Reading, a Bear Flag Revolt and Mexican-American War veteran and the first white settler in Shasta County (1845). He quickly returned to his land, Rancho Buena Ventura (what would later become Redding and Cottonwood), to look for gold of his own. He gathered a company consisting of, in his words, "three white men, seven Delewares, one Walla Walla, one Chinook, and sixty Sacramento Valley Indians" and began prospecting along the Trinity River near Shasta County. By July, the company had found the end of the rainbow in the headwaters of the river, a strike which yielded $80,000 in its first six weeks.

Prospectors then rushed toward Shasta and Trinity Counties from the overcrowded sites around Coloma, and by the time California became the 31st state in 1850, every city near the mother lode had become a boomtown, with new settlements sprouting at every fork in the road.

Despite his great success, Reading soon abandoned his Trinity claim to a band of belligerent Oregonians who protested his association with Indians.

Some years later, the Southern Pacific Railroad routed it tracks through an area in Reading's land grant known as Poverty Flats, where it placed a depot in a community originally recorded as Reading. It redubbed the settlement Redding, according to Alice B. Reading, the last descendant of the major, "to please a railroad land agent, B.B. Redding." Area residents protested the new name and convinced the state legislature to change it back to Reading in 1873, but the railroad never recognized the change, and the act was repealed in 1880.

The major had run several steamboats from Cottonwood upriver to his new settlement over the years with the intention of establishing it as the head of navigation on the Sacramento River, the last stop for steamboats traveling up the waterway. This designation would guarantee untold fortune to the businesses and residents of whatever community could attain it, making it the main connection between the products and markets of the Bay Area and the mines and forests of the North State. As a result, false cities, or "paper towns," were recorded all along the river by settlers in the hopes that one of them might eventually gain that title.

One such aspiring community near the river would later be called Reed's Creek; about 40 miles south of Redding, William Myers constructed its first true building—a log cabin for his family. The Myers were the only white residents of the new settlement until businessman Meredith Meador moved into their home and opened the first blacksmith shop and roadside inn.

In 1852, a regular stagecoach service was established between Sacramento and Redding, and E.G. Reed moved his family to the community to run a stage station. He built a frame house on the south end of town and opened a stable and hotel.

A severe winter in 1853 rendered the single track-worn road from Reed's Creek to Shasta County impassable, making it impossible to take a load of supplies directly from Sacramento to Redding in one unbroken trip. This immediately made Reed's Creek a large transient gathering place. It was during that time that another important permanent resident joined the community, a trader named M.L. Cavert. Cavert found good money in having the steamboats deliver to Reed's Creek the goods he sold to the mining communities, and other traders soon followed his lead.

Myers, Cavert, and Reed laid out a plan for a town adjacent to Reed's Creek, closer to the Sacramento River, called Red Bluffs. To grow the community quickly, Myers began selling and even giving away land to entice prospective settlers on the promise that the river would be made permanently navigable for steamboats. The new town began to fill up, and work started on improving the river and adding landings.

Reed's Creek was abandoned by 1855, and, in 1856, the enveloping county of Tehama was organized. At first, the county seat was in the city of Tehama, but when Red Bluffs finally established itself as head of navigation, its good citizens made a raid on Tehama, absconding with all the county records and declaring their city the new county seat.

The western population boom was bolstered again when more gold was discovered in Idaho in 1860, increasing the already impossible demand for fast lumber for mining projects, homes, businesses, and fuel.

Another boost came when the first transcontinental railroad was completed in 1869 and when the Central Pacific Railroad established a depot in Red Bluff (the name long since shortened from Red Bluffs) in 1872 . But cheaper, quicker, and more reliable supply transportation was still needed—especially when much of the timber came from mountain areas inaccessible to the trains. That was the same year that Charles F. Ellsworth, a woodsman from Maine, began building the Empire Flume (later called the Sierra Flume) through Tehama County. The first flume west of the Sierras promised the fast and fairly trouble-free transportation of lumber.

At a construction cost of $5,000 per mile, the flume was completed in 1873. Ellsworth, however, was never able to admire his finished project, having fallen from the top of the flume to his death during final construction. This, and the fact that many thought the project was doomed to fail, caused the flume to be popularly called "Ellsworth's Folly." But soon, thousands of feet of lumber per hour were racing from the forests to the new communities.

These were the developments that were simmering when a visiting physician of an inquisitive mind and a restless spirit stopped at E.G. Reed's new hotel around 1854. Born March 5, 1808, Dr. John Allen Veatch—a surgeon, surveyor, and scientist with an abiding wanderlust that kept him moving and exploring throughout his life—was the eldest of eight children born to a Kentucky frontier family. He showed a very early fascination with medicine, which he began to study as a young adult, and relocated to Louisiana at 21, where he taught school. In 1834, the family moved to Texas, where he later married. He and his wife had two sons before her death in 1844.

At six feet, four inches tall and more than 200 pounds, the auburn-haired, blue-eyed doctor was an imposing character, serving as a volunteer soldier during the Mexican-American War (for which he also recruited both of his sons) and acting as a field surgeon from 1846 to 1848. After the war, he moved to San Antonio and remarried. However, the marriage did not go well, and he eventually took his sons with him to the newly acquired US territory called California, following the forty-niners in the 1850s. It was during this time that he found his way to Red Bluffs.

While visiting the fledgling community, Veatch heard some very interesting tales of a well-hidden area not far from the settlement where the Native American tribes of the region bathed in natural hot springs that they considered to have remarkable healing qualities. These tribes were most likely the Yana (best known for its most famous member, Ishi), whose southwestern border extended to Tuscan Springs (eastern Tehama County), and the Nomlaki, who mostly populated western Tehama County, though other visitors might have included the neighboring Wintu, Konkow (Maiduan), Patwin, and Yuki peoples. The stories had it that the land was so sacred to the Indians that it was considered neutral territory, and even warring tribes would lay down their spears and arrows and bathe together there on peaceful terms.

Nonetheless, any area as remote as Lick Springs, as it was then called, could be very dangerous for white settlers as Indian raids and violence—sometimes even murders—were common occurrences throughout the county. But hot springs had been an increasingly popular fixation in other parts of the country, especially on the East Coast, for many years, and no such retreats had yet been developed in the young California. The springs also perfectly suited Veatch's lifelong fascination with aquatic botany and mineralogy. The opportunity to investigate such a relatively unexplored site and find whatever secrets the "miraculous" waters might hold would be invaluable. And, of course, there was always the possibility that where there were minerals, there might also be gold.

At some point between his stay at Reed's hotel and January 8, 1856, Veatch did discover a form of metaphorical gold—"white gold," as it might have been called—when he became the first person in America to find borax, at Lick Springs, which he optimistically renamed Tuscan

Springs after the borax-containing fumaroles of Tuscany, Italy. He sent away a sample to a San Francisco lab for verification and then wrote to the Borax Company of California on June 28, 1857, to record his claim.

The significance of his discovery lay in the many applications of the white powder at that time. Though the average person did not even know what borax was, it was widely used by manufacturers for cleaning, disinfecting, water softening, food preservation, gold extraction, and as an enamel additive, among many other applications. But since its only sources were outside of America, it was a very expensive ingredient, and its discovery could certainly be nearly as good as real gold to the right person.

The testing labs told Veatch that there simply were not high enough levels of the money-making mineral in the waters of Tuscan Springs for commercial use, but that did not stop two men from convincing the good doctor it could be done anyway. Unfortunately, these men did not know the first thing about mineral extraction.

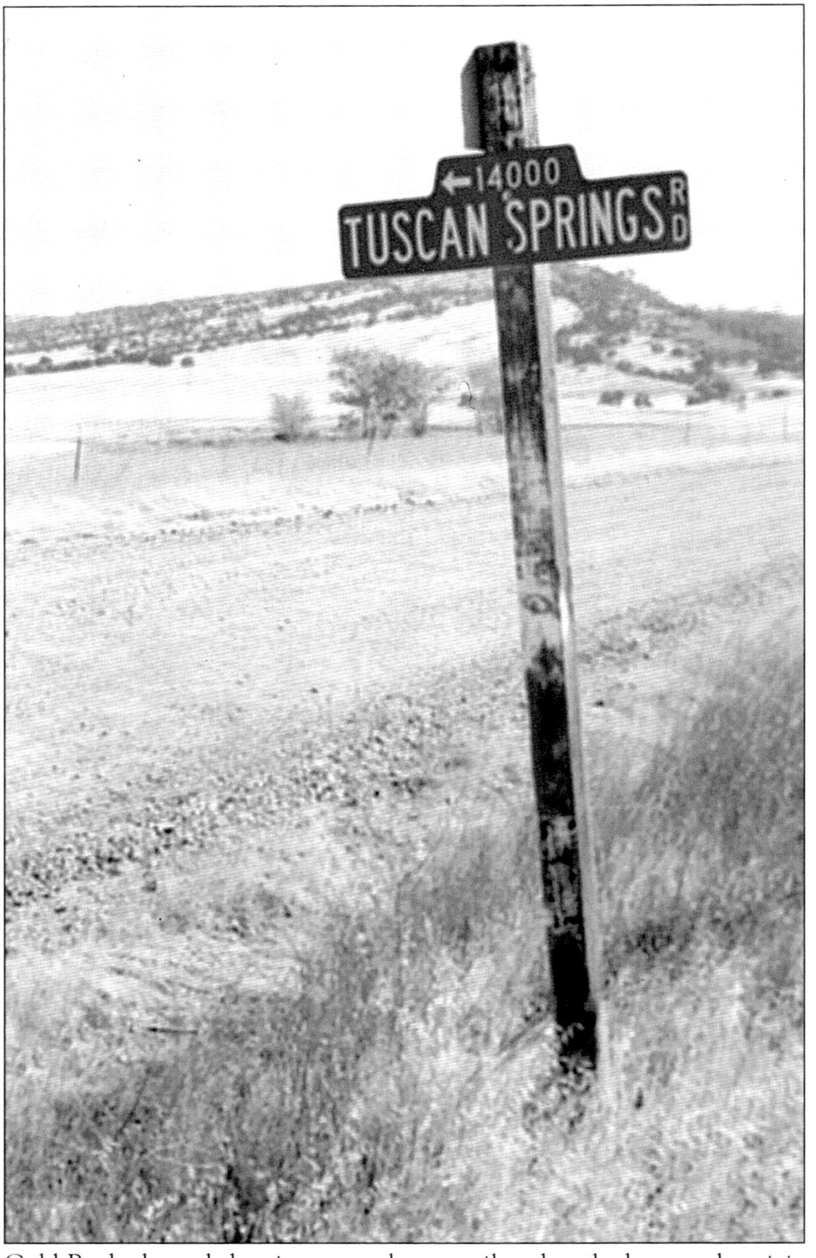

From the Gold Rush through logging, steamboats, railroads, telephones, electricity, and the dawn of the 20th century, the famous Tuscan Springs (1856–1916) was intimately connected to the settlement of California and the development of Red Bluff, Tehama County, and Northern California. Today, the only hint of its location is this lone street sign off Highway 99E, near Dairyville. The gravel road was created by the Texas Company (Texaco) in 1928 to transport drilling equipment in search of oil and natural gas on the land. A rugged, rocky trail snakes north from this sign for more than a mile, through numerous gates and past free-range cows and steers, before finally revealing the ruins. Since the land is on private property, interested persons should always request permission from the owners before visiting. (Author.)

One

Once Upon a Time

In 1856, two enterprising judges—Baldwin and Burnett—convinced Dr. Veatch to let them attempt extracting massive amounts of borax from the waters of Tuscan Springs (the three men would split the proceeds). Veatch explained to the pair how the process usually worked, left the project in their hands, and disappeared to explore other interests. The judges spent enormous amounts of time and money building troughs to run the waters two miles from the springs and 200 feet up a hill, where it would drip through piles of greasewood. The brush would collect the mineral, and the water would continue downhill, accumulating in large pigpens. The pigs would pack the ground, making it waterproof, so the liquid would evaporate, leaving acres of bonus salt for harvest. Whether the scheme failed because the borax would not stick to the slick greasewood or because they could not get the water to run uphill is unclear, according to the January 9, 1861, *Sacramento Union*.

Veatch returned later in 1856, listed the land for sale, and was off on his next adventure, taking up with Col. Joel Lewis, a bear hunter from Sacramento, in pursuit of a mountain of "a white pulverulent substance . . . a rivulet of water which was totally unfit to drink, and of an Irishman who knew of a borax lake," according to the *American Druggist and Pharmaceutical Record*. The mountain turned out to be a small bank of sulfur, and the borax lake was just a pond of salt; only the Irishman was real.

However, during his journey, Veatch did happen upon borax crystals in 200 acres of water in Lake County, California, and forged another partnership—this time with another scientist—to extract the mineral, producing the first commercial borax in America.

Within four years, flooding ruined the operation, and the project was abandoned, but Veatch was already gone again—surveying Carros Island in 1858, curating conchology from 1858 to 1861, and joining the Rush to Washoe in the Comstock Lode by 1862.

Meanwhile, back in Tehama County, Tuscan Springs was under new ownership.

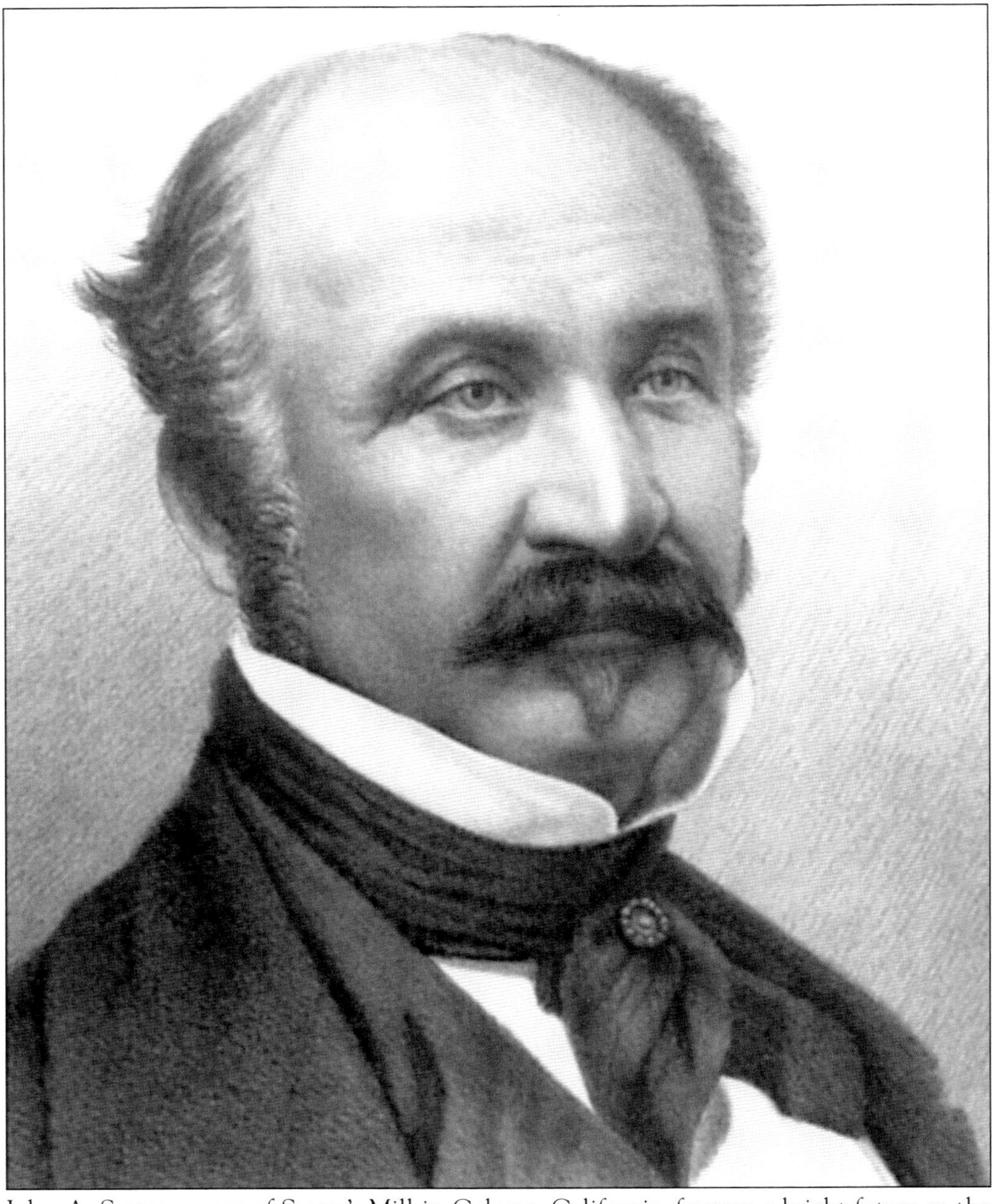

John A. Sutter, owner of Sutter's Mill in Coloma, California, foresaw a bright future as the baron of a West Coast lumber empire once the Mexican-American War was over and the land was the property of the United States. However, when John W. Marshall discovered gold in the mill's tailrace on January 24, 1848, Sutter feared his plans would be ruined and desperately tried to suppress the news. Word did get out, though, and Sutter's employees quit to search for gold, while squatters took his land and stole all his crops and cattle. Sutter deeded what was left of his land to his son and moved to Hock Farm, California, with the rest of his family. In later life, he relocated to Pennsylvania, largely (and coincidentally) for the therapeutic mineral waters of Lititz Springs.

Carpenter James W. Marshall (right) was one of Sutter's most trusted employees when he discovered the gold at the mill he was building for Sutter. Marshall left Coloma when the area turned into chaos with the flood of prospectors, but he returned later in life to try his hand at prospecting. The venture left him bankrupt. In the end, the mill (below) was never used for its intended purpose, and neither man ever profited from the discovery of gold there. The person in the photograph below is not Marshall but a photographer's assistant asked to stand in to show the scale of the building in 1853.

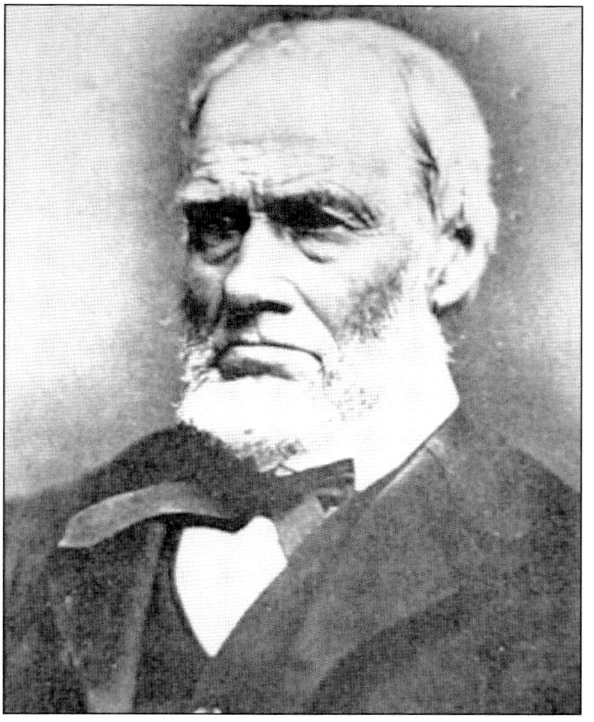

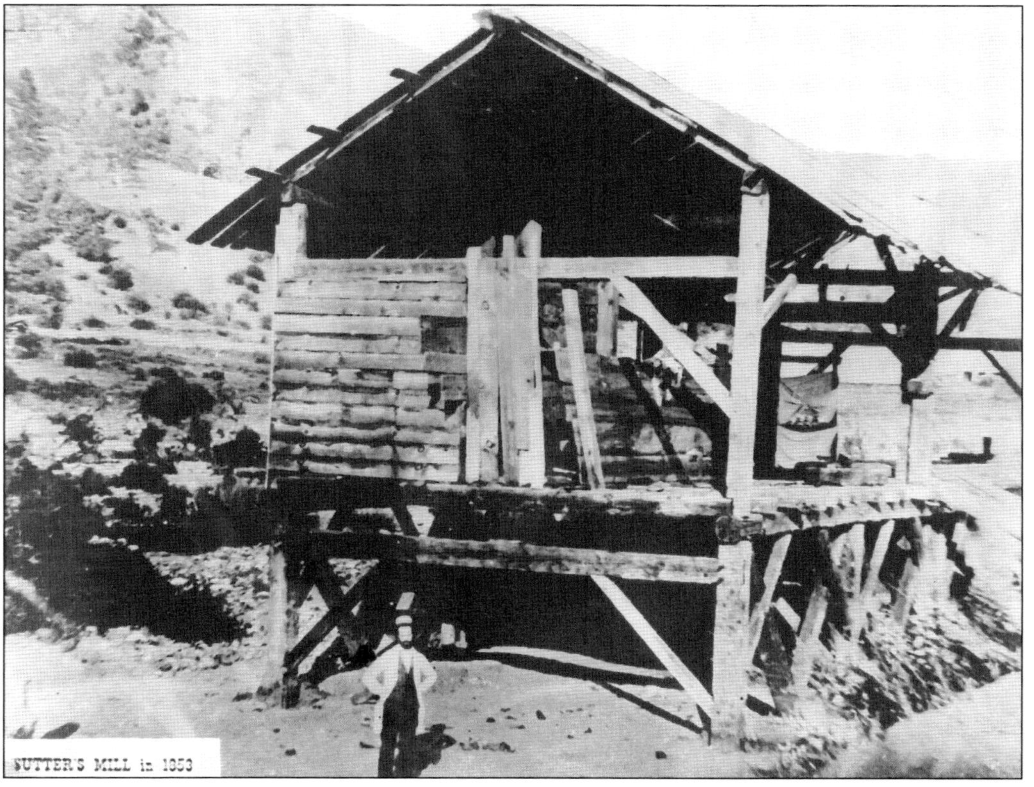

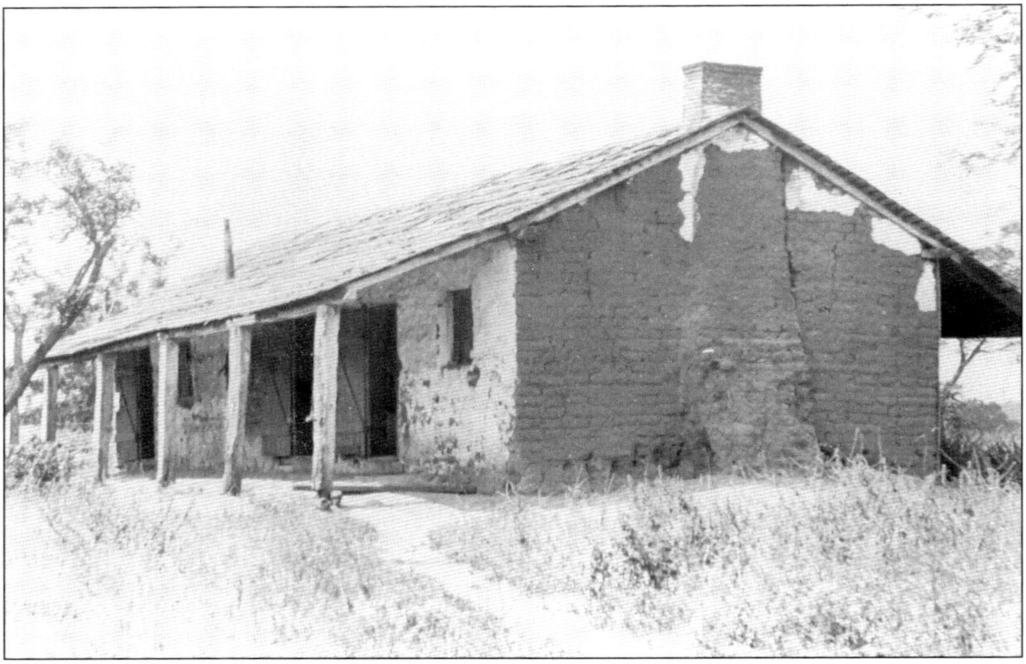

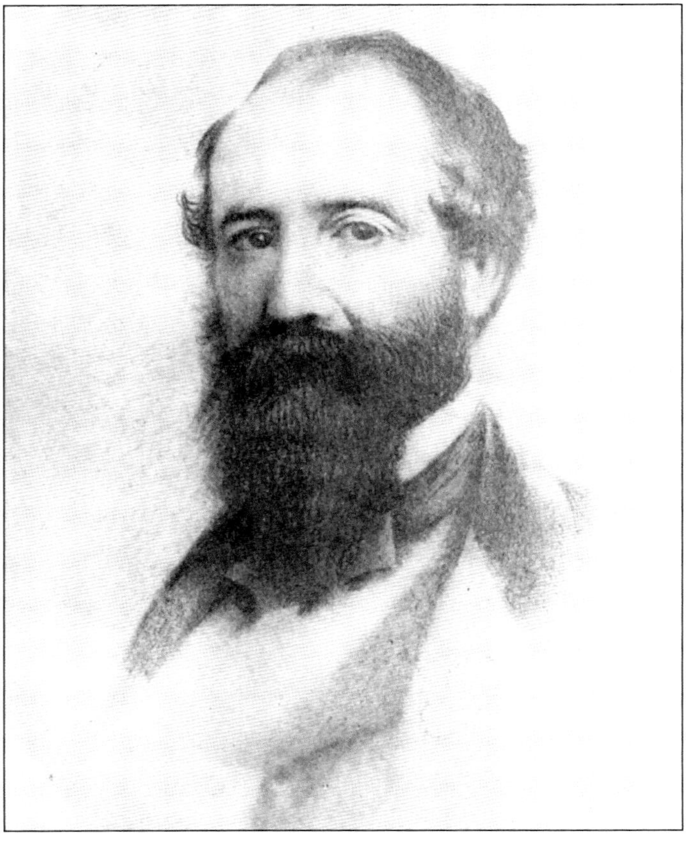

Pierson B. Reading (left) was a veteran of the Mexican-American War and recipient of a 26,632-acre land grand known as Rancho Buena Ventura ("Good Fortune") in what is now Shasta County, California. He was also among the first to visit Sutter's Mill a short time after the gold discovery, which inspired him to return to his land and prospect along the Trinity River. His party made a big strike just months later, prompting a second gold rush. His adobe (above), built in 1847 near Cottonwood Creek, was the first home constructed by a European in Shasta County, marking the beginning of white settlement in the area. (Left, sketch by Helen Tanner Brodt; above, courtesy Shasta Historical Society.)

A gold-panner like most settlers of the period, Dr. John Allen Veatch may have been looking for that elusive metal when he ventured out to Lick Springs sometime between 1854 and 1856. What he found instead was something nearly as valuable: borax, a widely used mineral formerly available only outside of the United States. He renamed the area Tuscan Springs after springs in Italy. Efforts to extract the borax were fruitless, but Veatch did go on to discover the first commercially viable source of the mineral in Lake County, California. The sizable crystal pictured below is an example of borax from the waters of Tuscany, Italy. (Right, courtesy Cindy Brown; below, courtesy Leon Hupperichs.)

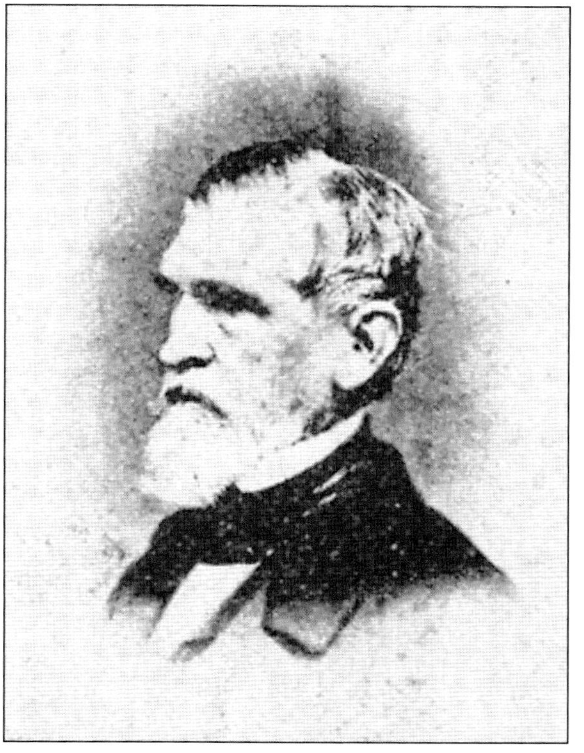

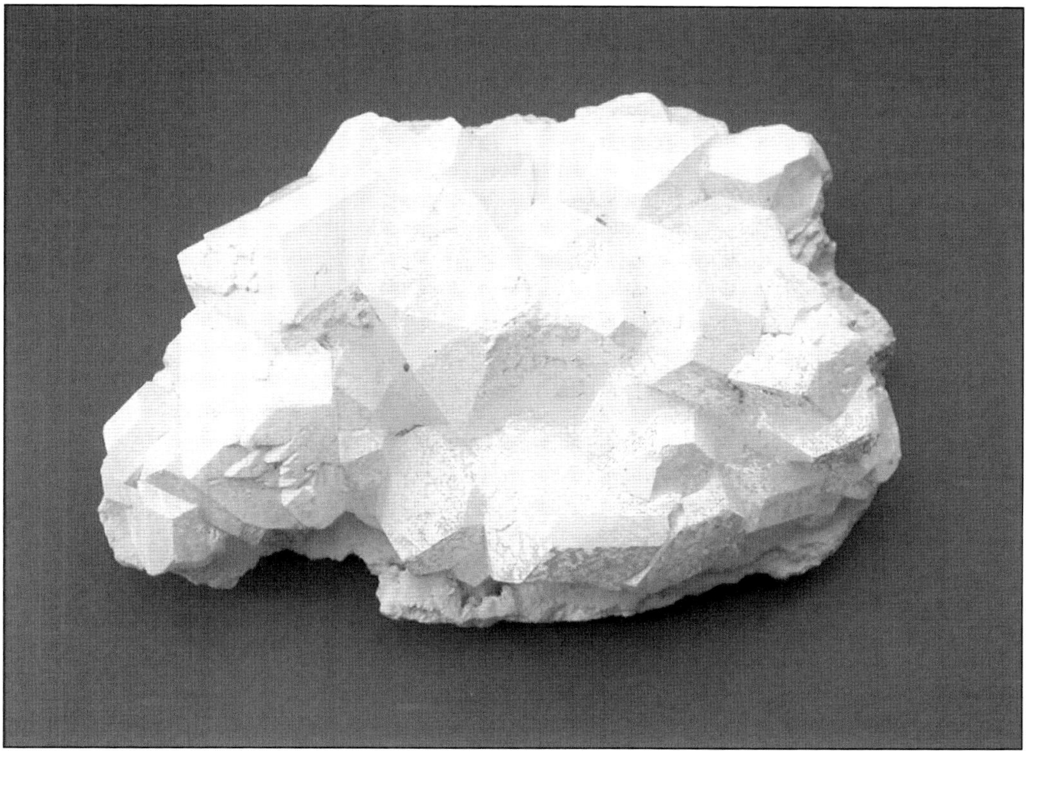

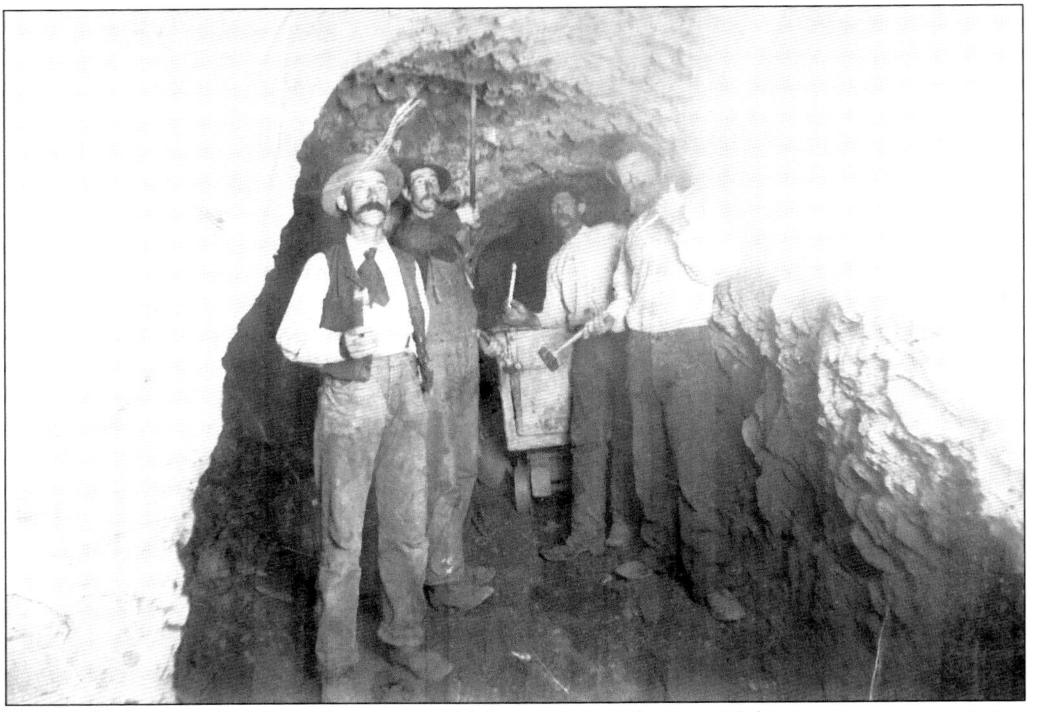

One of the most profitable professions in California during the later 19th century was not mining for gold but providing supplies to those who did. This fact was well understood by newspaper publisher Samuel Brennan, who, after quickly setting up a prospecting-supply shop, marched around the streets of San Francisco with store leaflets, shouting, "Gold! Gold from the American River!" The photograph above shows miners digging a gold shaft in Shasta County around 1898. Below, at a nearby gold-mining camp, ore would be run from the shaft to the crushing machine on the track where the two men are standing on the right.

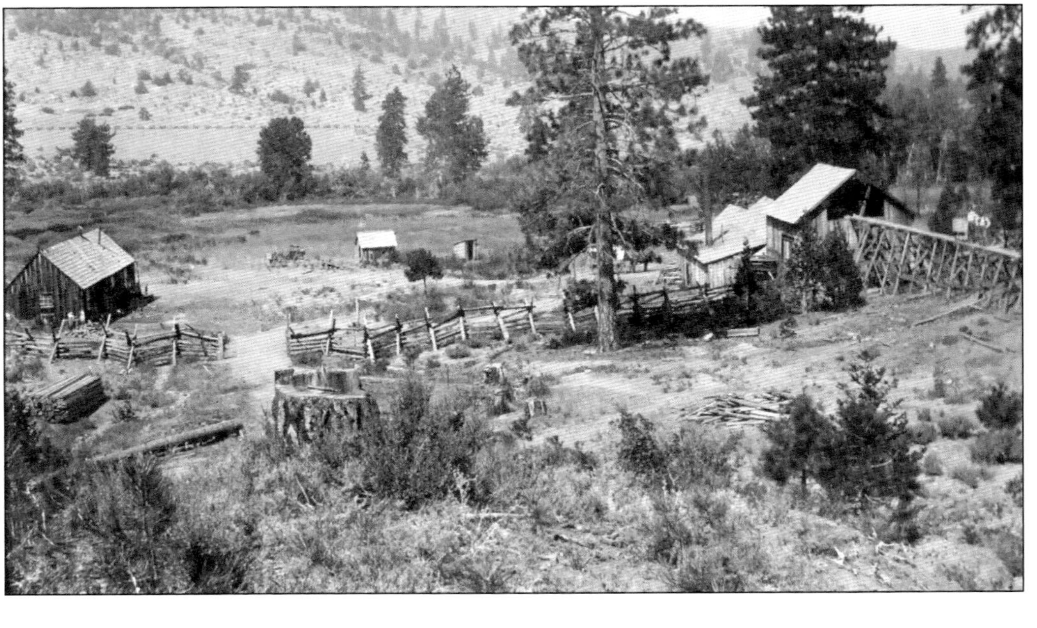

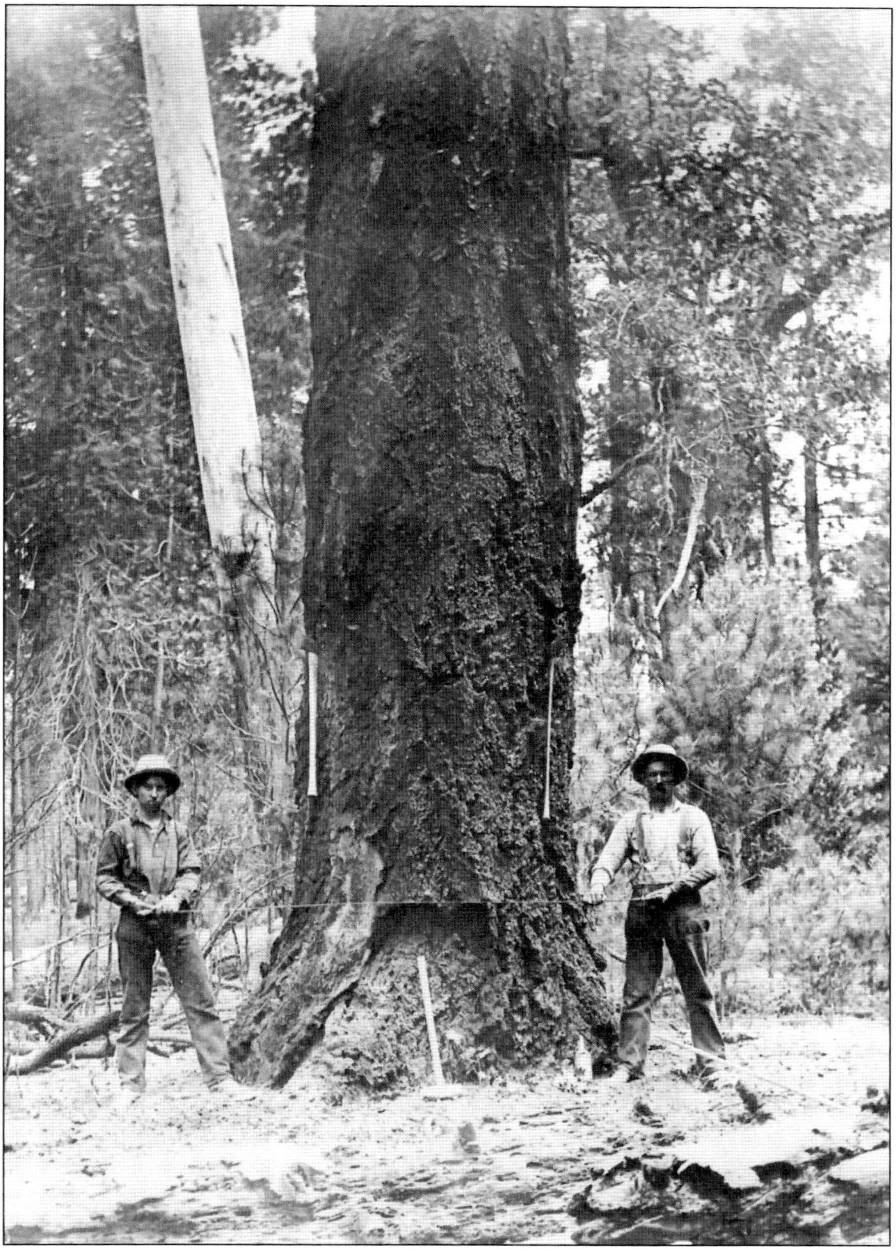

Loggers Dyas (left) and Doc Shelton (Dyas's father) prepare to fell a massive tree in the forests of Shasta County around 1900. Yet another gold rush to Idaho in 1860, along with the North's need for pine resin and turpentine during the Civil War (1861–1865), prompted the construction of roads between that territory and California (through Tehama County) and opened up what must have seemed an unlimited supply of previously inaccessible timber. In 1876, the Sierra Flume & Lumber Company began buying up all the smaller lumber companies in the North State—including the Empire, Blue Ridge, and Butte Flume & Lumber companies—to become the largest lumber production company in the world. This incredible expansion was one factor that led to its bankruptcy in 1878, when it was sold to the Sierra Lumber Company.

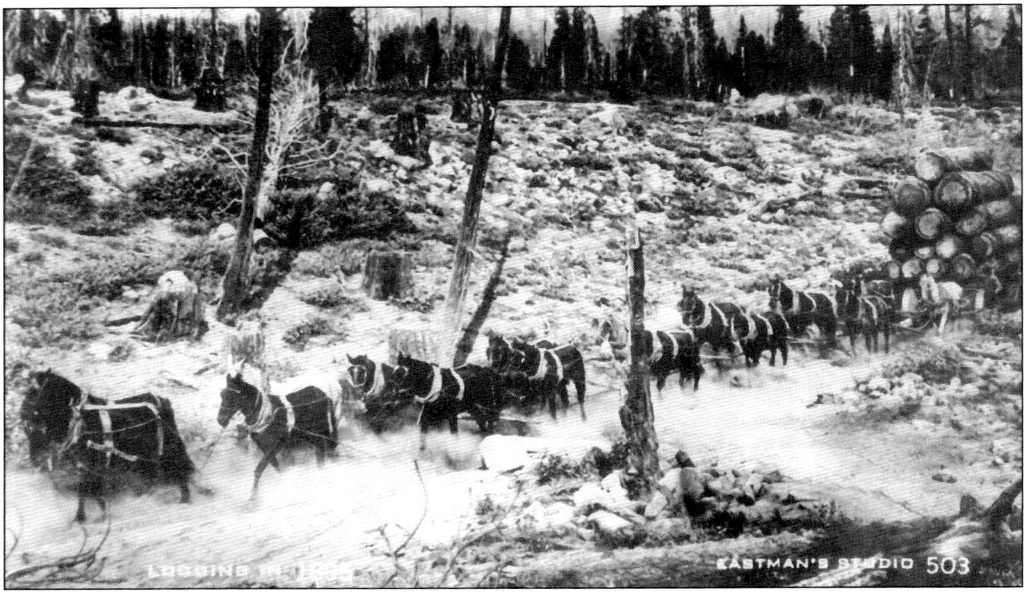

As John A. Sutter foresaw, the most lucrative and steady income in late-1880s California was lumber, without which there would have been no homes, businesses, steamboats, stagecoaches, rail tracks, or steam-powered trains. In remote areas that were inaccessible to the railroads, and even after the flumes arrived, timber often had to be moved the old-fashioned way—by a 16-horse team (above). Not long after the invention of the steam engine came the Dolbeer Donkey (below), which would drag timber attached to a cable short distances through a forest 10 times faster than a team of oxen.

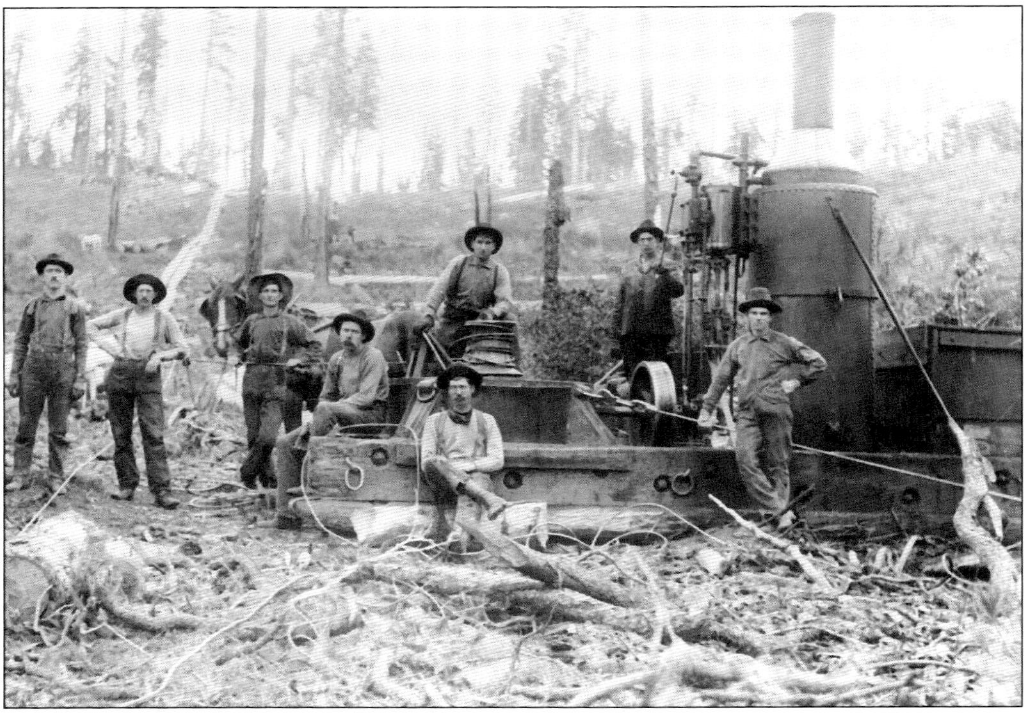

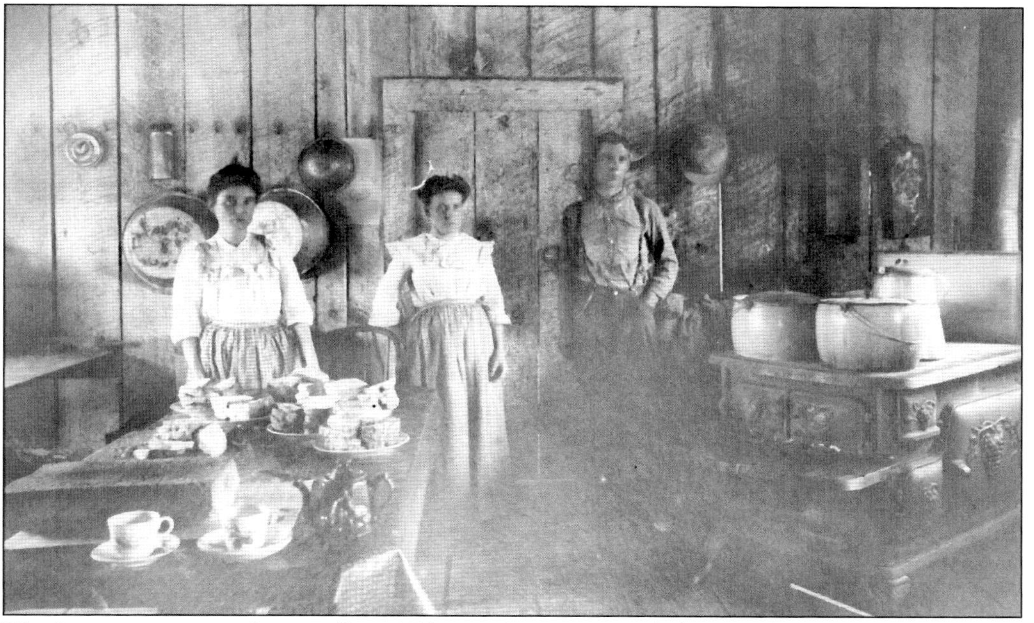

The logging camps at Lyonsville in Tehama County provided most of the lumber needed to build all incarnations of the Tuscan Springs hotel. Near century's end, the logs and rough-cut lumber from Lyonsville would be sent down the Sierra Lumber Company's flume for finishing at its mill in Red Bluff. In the photograph above, cooks pause from hard work preparing dinner to fuel Lyonsville camp workers. The women are unidentified, but the man is Jim Moore. The photograph below shows the workers enjoying the final product as they take a well-deserved rest for chow in the 1890s.

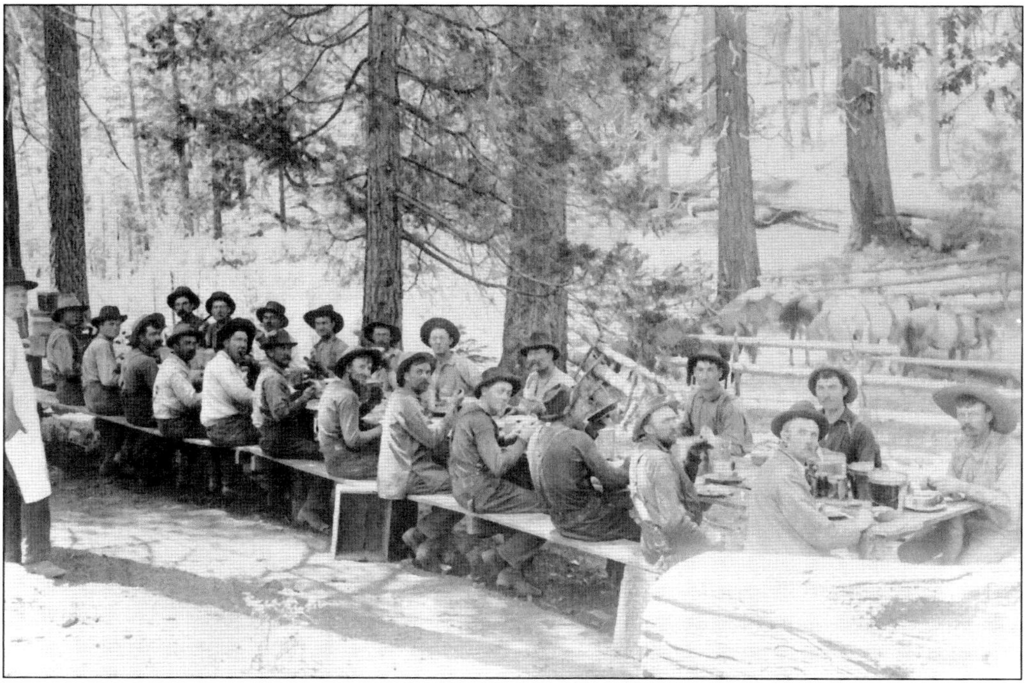

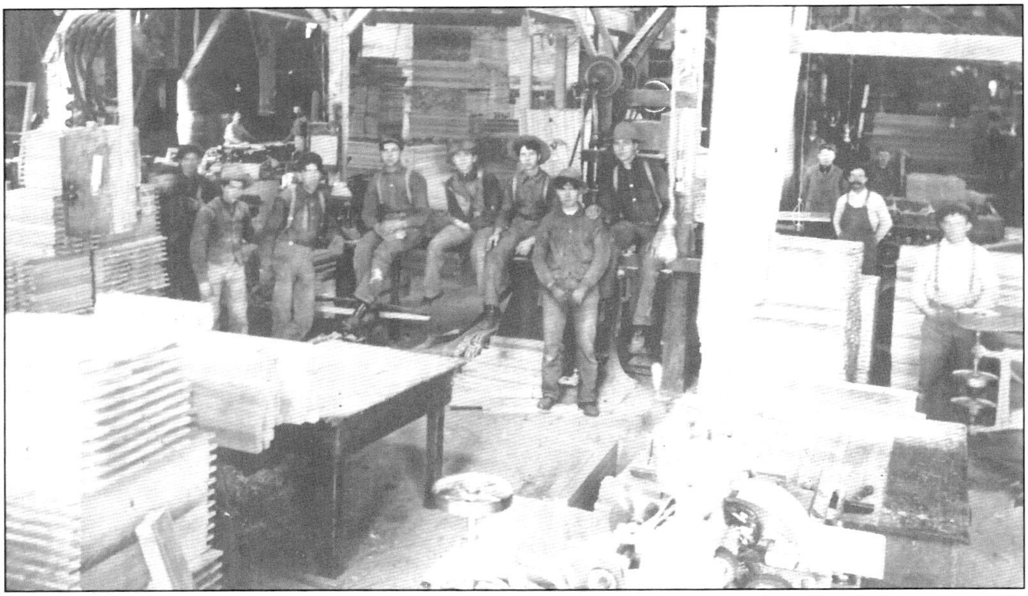

The Diamond Match Company bought the Sierra Lumber Company's Red Bluff mill, but eventually abandoned it in 1911, leaving Tehama County in need of building supplies. The Judd Creek Mill, seen above, near Mount Lassen on Antelope Creek (land previously in Yana territory), was constructed in 1914. Owner A.E. Engebretsen arranged with Diamond to send lumber to Red Bluff using a section of its flume. However, the arrangement only last a few months before the trestles near Finley Lake collapsed, never to be rebuilt. When the mill closed, it marked the end of lumber production there until 1952. Below, workers take a break at the Sierra Mill in Red Bluff.

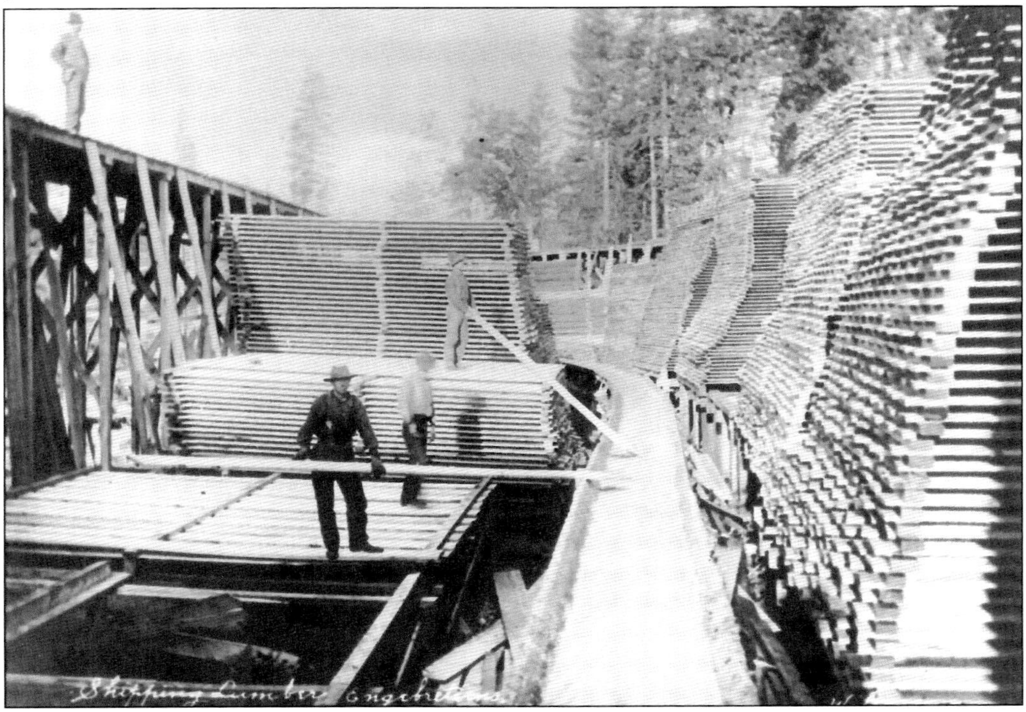

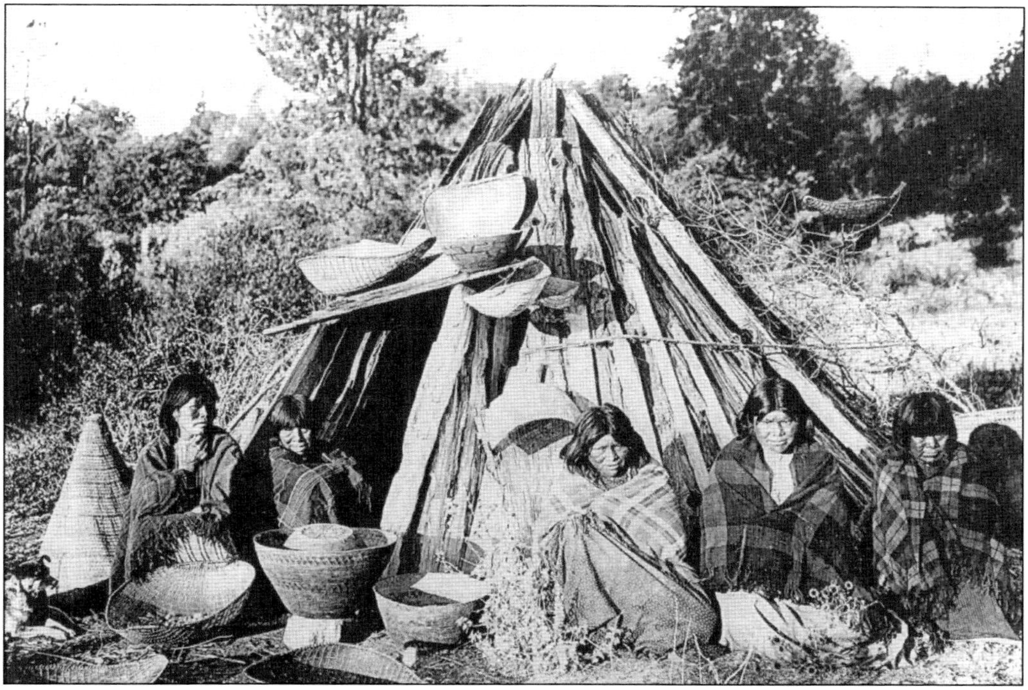

Above, unidentified Nomlaki women are gathered outside a hut. The Nomlaki were the predominant tribe in what would become western Tehama County when the white settlers came in the 1840s, though they were bordered by the Yuki on the west, the Wintu on the north, the Konkow on the east, the Patwin on the south, and the Yana/Yahi on the east and northeast. Reportedly, the Nomlaki and Yana were often in conflict. The map below, which approximates one drawn with the help of Ishi, shows the portions of Tehama County (gray area at the right) at Tuscan Springs within Yana territory. (Below, author.)

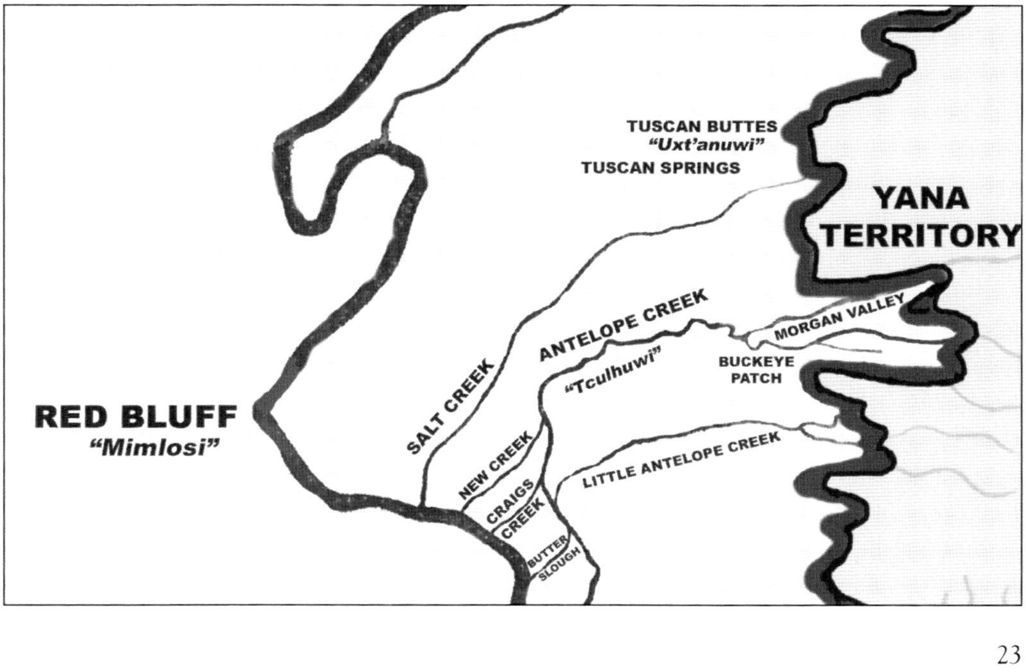

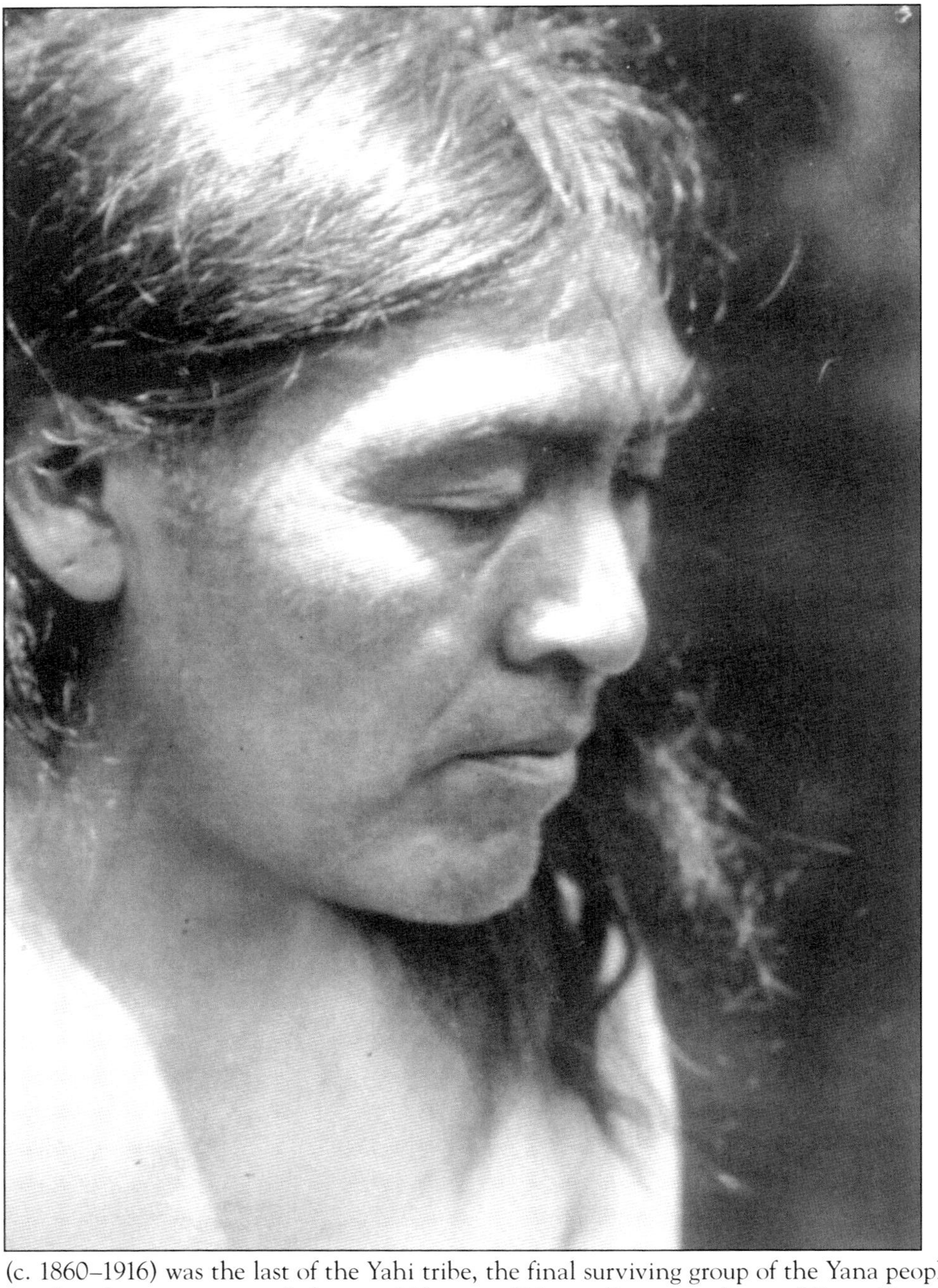

Ishi (c. 1860–1916) was the last of the Yahi tribe, the final surviving group of the Yana people, who lived in the eastern part of what would become Tehama County and part of Butte County. In 1911, at about the age of 49, he emerged, alone and emaciated, from the woods near Oroville, California, leaving his homeland in the foothills of Mount Lassen (known to the Yahi as Wa ganu p'a). Ishi also knew the Tuscan Springs area and referred to the surrounding buttes as Uxt'an üwi (possibly meaning "big sugar pines upstream"). It is very likely that the Yana/Yahi made frequent use of the mineral waters at Tuscan Springs until the mid-1850s. Ishi died of tuberculosis in 1916, a year that also marked a great tragedy at Tuscan Springs.

Two

All This Happened, More or Less

While Red Bluffs continued to grow from steamboat trade and the lumber industry, no one knew exactly what to do with Tuscan Springs. On May 31, 1856, the property was sold to Meredith Meador, a businessman, civic leader, later justice of the peace, and possibly the first to see the area's potential.

But, whether for lack of profit or ongoing threats from the Indians, the enterprise was ultimately not to his liking, and Meador ran variations of the following advertisement from 1857 to 1862: "Watering Place For Sale—Proprietor of this valuable property desirous of disposing of the same in order that he may engage in some business more congenial to his tastes, and for which by habit and disposition, he is better qualified. Will sell or lease the entire concern at a bargain." Capt. James Maxey and John Lytle leased the land and made improvements; however, it seemed no more suited to their predilections than to Meador's, and within a year, it was leased to Dr. O.S. Allen and S.D. Parker.

"Determined to Sell!" Meador reminded newspaper readers in 1861. "Persons wishing to invest would do well to apply immediately . . . Recollect, a *bargain* can be got on this property." Meador had no more luck with real estate than with his other ventures, including dealings with Dr. Allen and, later, a Dr. William D. Olendorf, who arrived in California in 1850 and eventually found his way to Red Bluffs. By all accounts, Olendorf disliked being a doctor, which kept him away from home during the day and often required he stay with patients overnight.

In 1862, a financial arrangement went sour, and Olendorf sued Meador for $1,496.81. Meador could not pay, and Tuscan Springs was sold at a sheriff's sale to Olendorf and Allen. By 1864, Allen had left Red Bluff, and Olendorf found running a resort even less fun than being a doctor. It took him two more years, but he finally unloaded the property to an elderly patent medicine salesman from Tennessee.

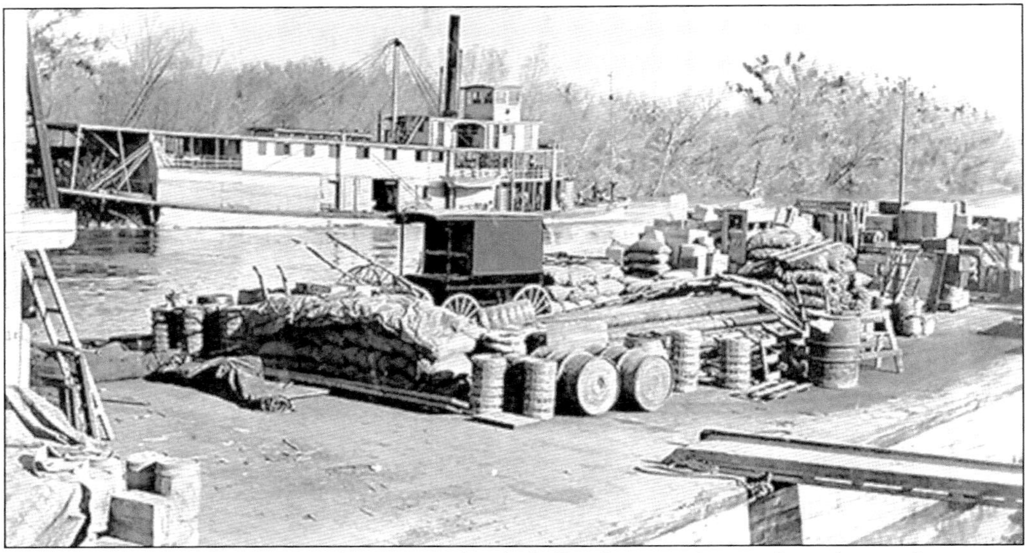

The steamboats were the key to the success of Red Bluff and Tuscan Springs from the very beginning. Becoming head of navigation made the fledgling community the crucial hub between the waters of San Francisco Bay and the mines and forests of Northern California. At times, up to 20 steamers were working the river simultaneously, carrying goods and passengers and towing barges full of supplies back and forth. Above is a dock filled with supplies awaiting pickup or delivery; below is the steamer *Red Bluff*, built in Sacramento in 1894, as goods are about to be loaded.

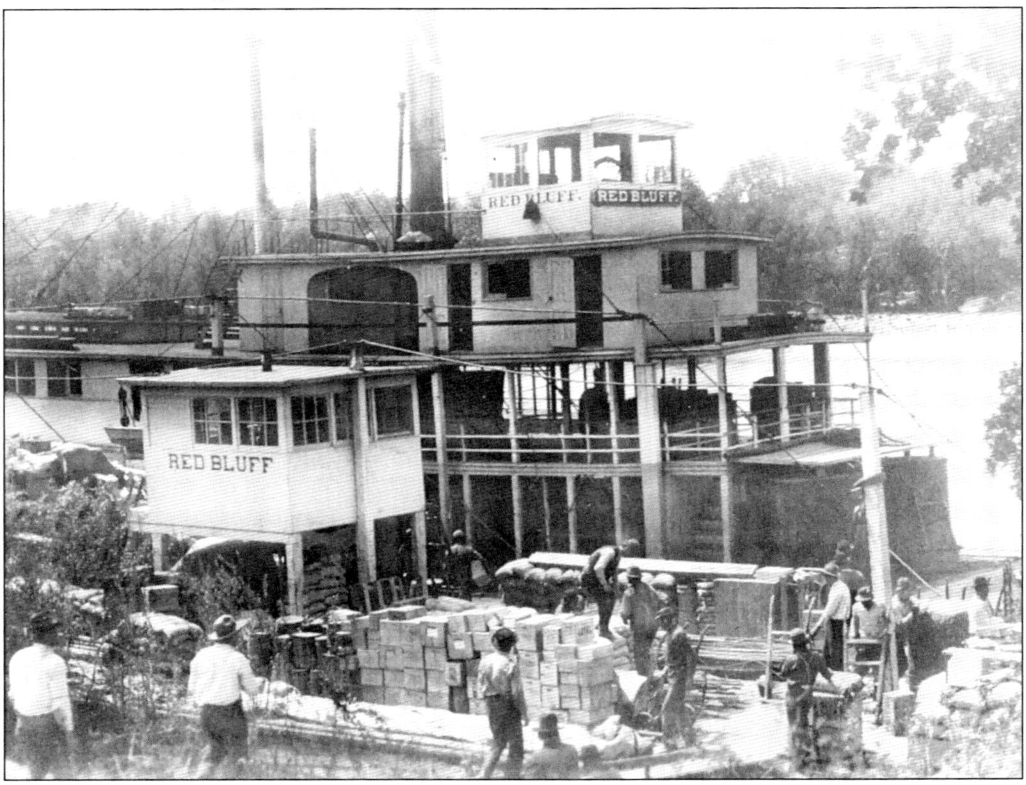

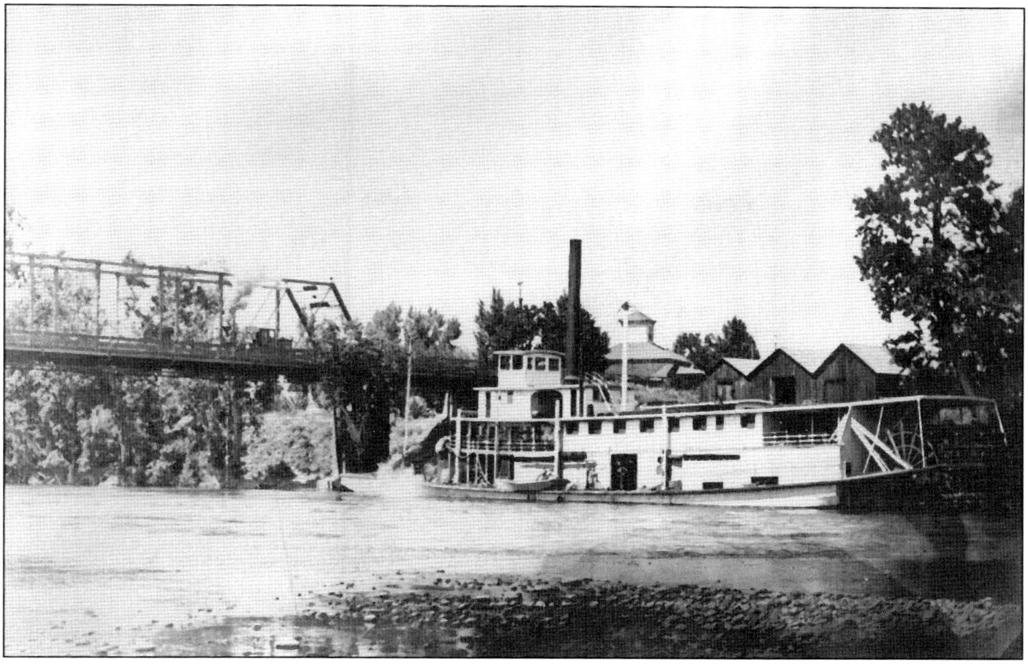

The image above, from less chaotic days, is an interesting moment in time, as noted by author Mary Lee Grimes, showcasing the four elements to which Red Bluff and Tuscan Springs owed their early prosperity: the Centennial Free Bridge, the railroad (crossing the bridge), the steamboats, and the lumber mill (just behind the steamer). Below is the 157-foot snag boat *Seizer*, built in 1881, which kept navigation open and safe for steamboat traffic.

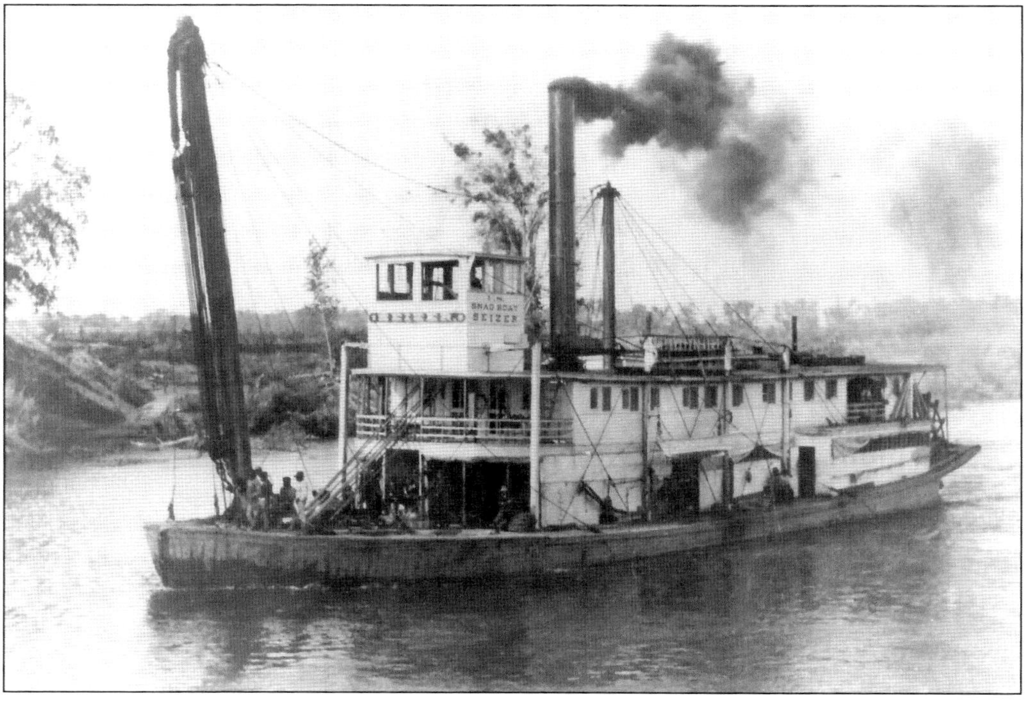

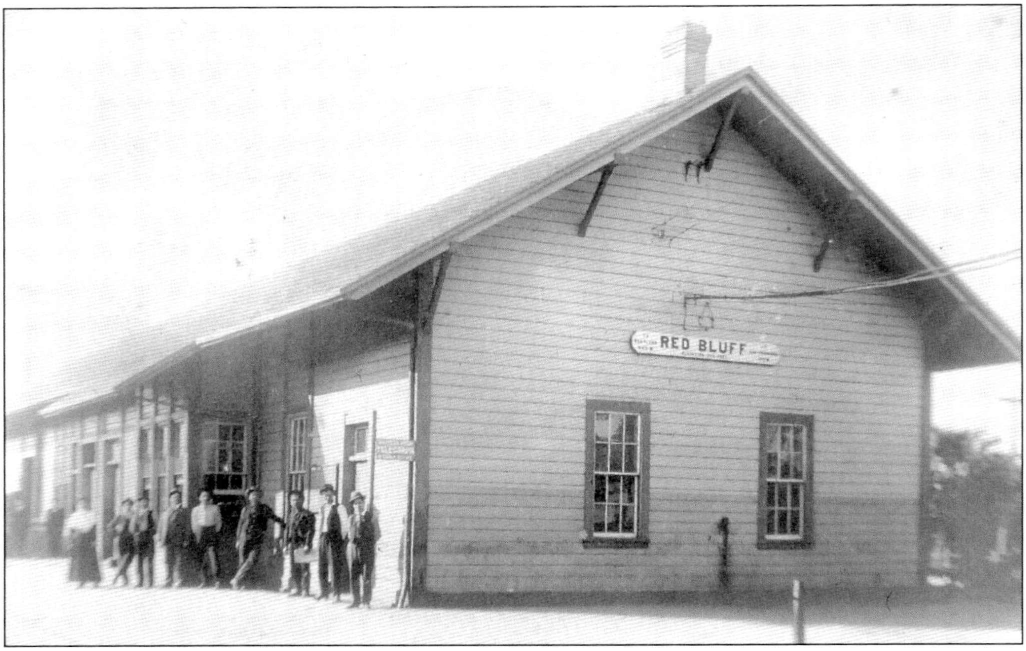

The Central and Union Pacific Railroads completed their portions of the Transcontinental Railroad to San Francisco in 1869, finally opening the West Coast to the rest of the country. Soon after, the Central Pacific Railroad built tracks to Red Bluff, where it set a depot in 1871 (above) before completing its line to Redding the following year. The company eventually purchased the California-Oregon Railroad and changed its name to Southern Pacific in 1886 (below). By the 1920s, the railroads had eliminated all need for the familiar steamboats along the Sacramento River, and they gradually disappeared.

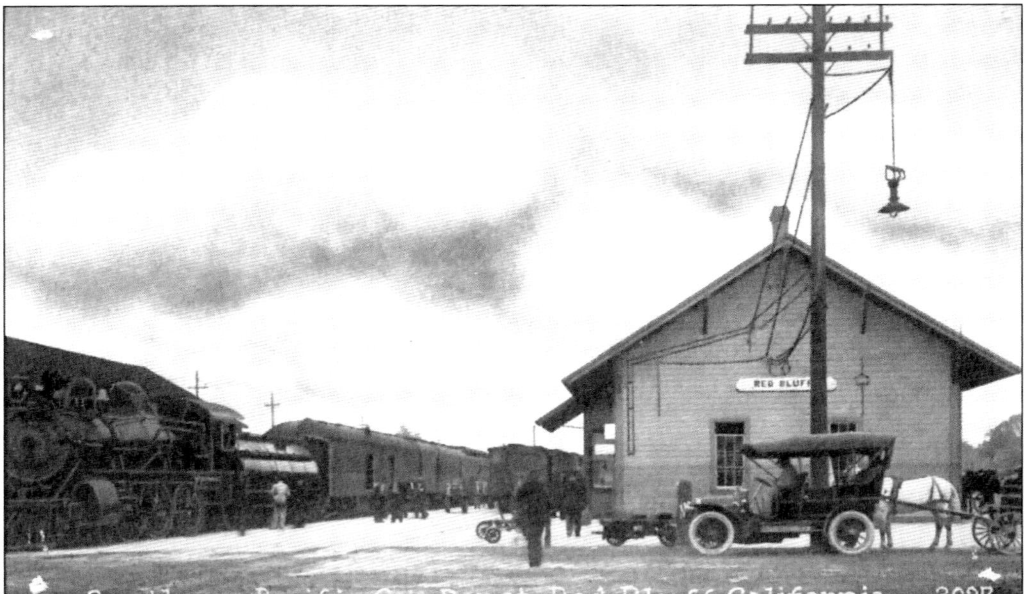

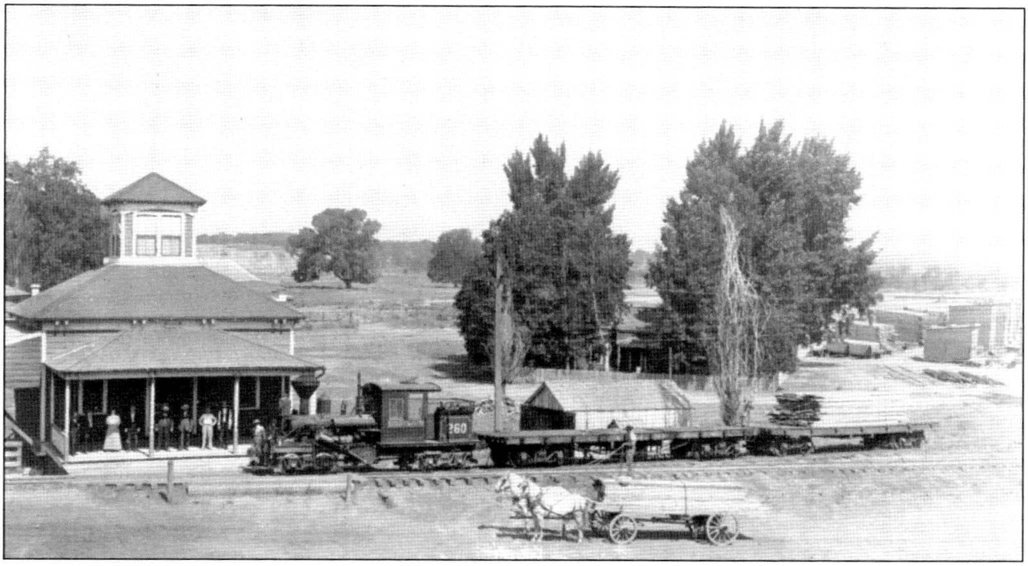

The Sierra Lumber Company constructed a mill on the east bank of the Sacramento River in Red Bluff shortly after the completion of the Centennial Bridge in 1876. Special arrangements had been made with the city to have the bridge built to accommodate a narrow-track rail system with which to transport lumber (pictured above and below). Consequently, Sierra closed its mill in Sesma and rerouted its flume to the Red Bluff riverbank. There, lumber would be loaded onto its small trains and delivered to the Central Pacific depot on the west side of the river. Sierra sold everything in 1907 to the Diamond Match Company.

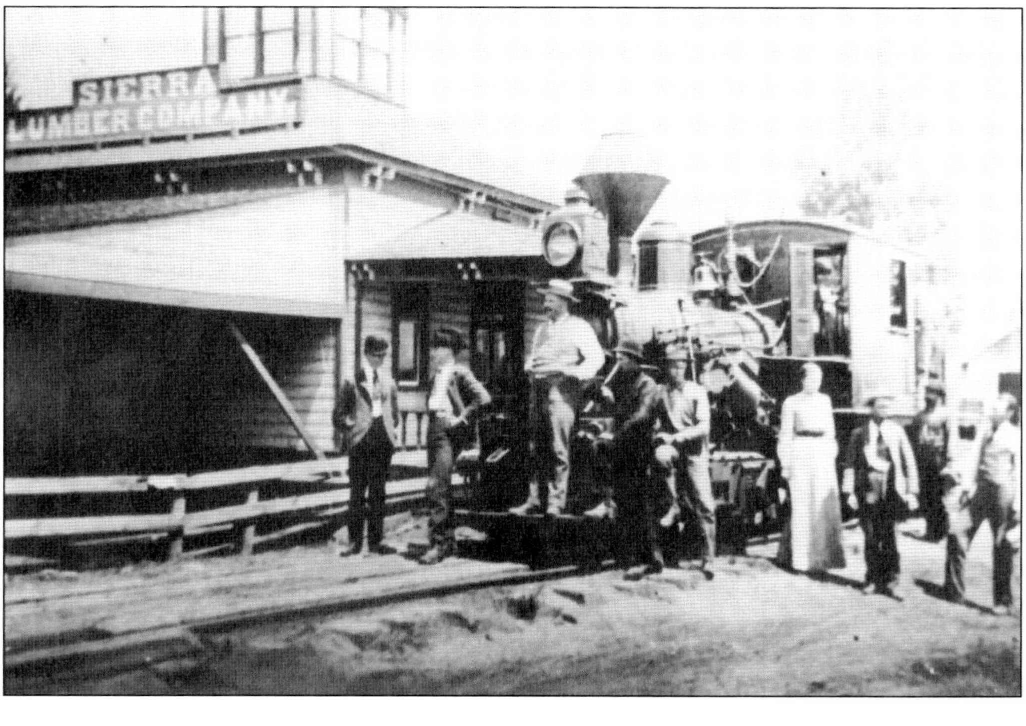

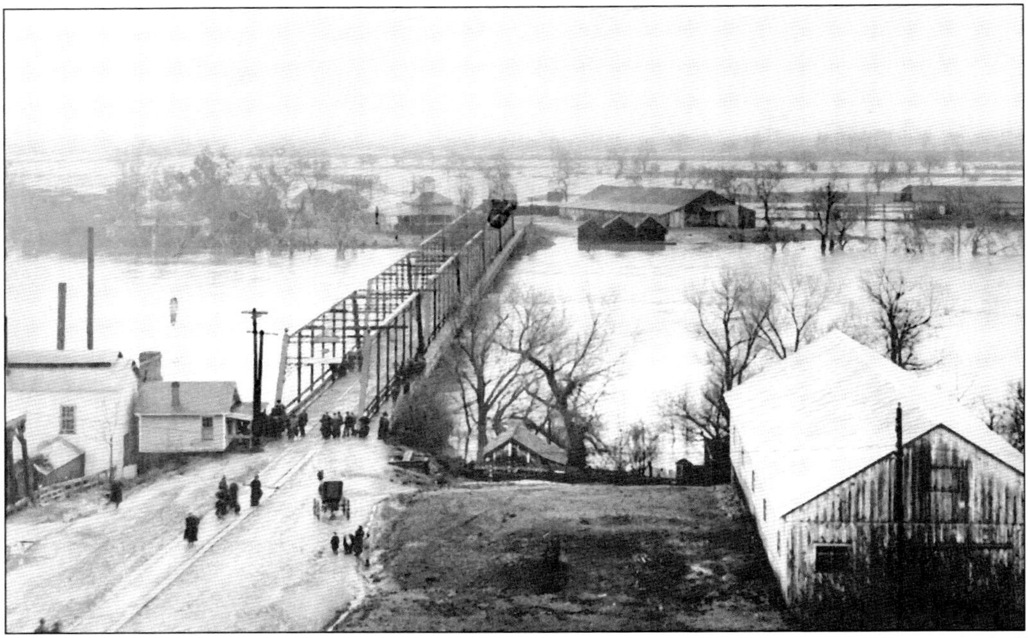

The Diamond Match Company kept the lumber coming until persistent flooding in Red Bluff —like the great flood of 1909 (above)—made it impractical to continue. Pictured above is the Centennial Bridge, from the Red Bluff side, looking toward Chico. The photograph below shows a steamer about to cross under the Centennial Free Bridge. Built in 1876, it was the first bridge across the Sacramento River in Northern California. The structure eliminated the need for ferries, conveniently connected Red Bluff to the communities to the east, and provided another route to Tuscan Springs. Notably, this structure had walkways on its outer sides and bore a memorable sign stipulating that anyone crossing faster than a walk would be fined $5 (approximately $108 in 2014).

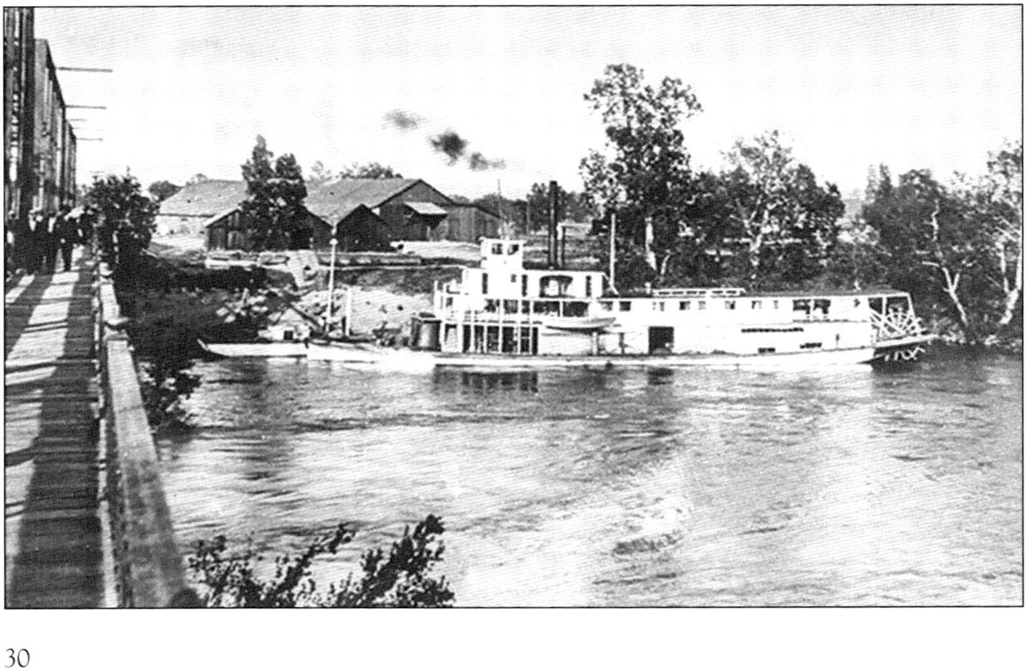

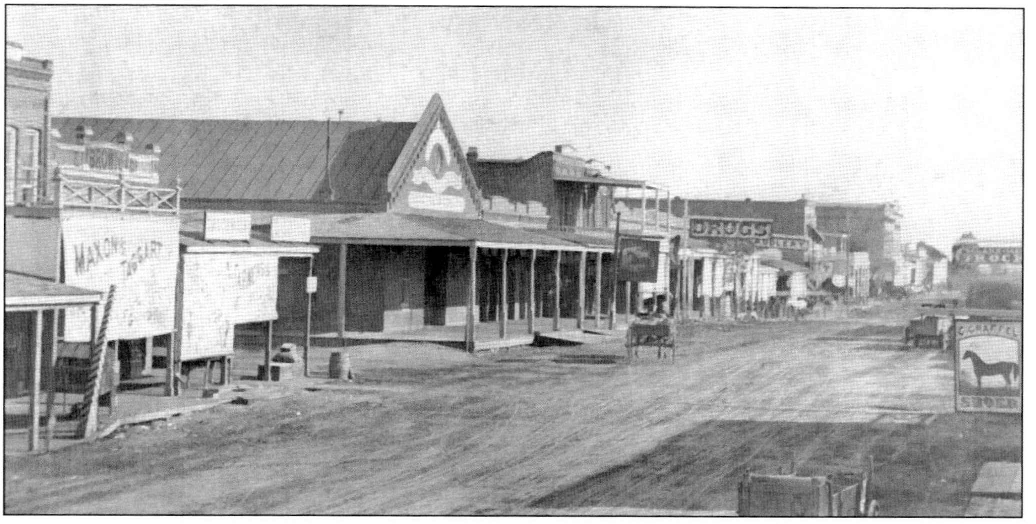

James R. Freeman's Fashion Livery & Feed Stables, with the triangular roof near the center of the photograph above, was located on the southeast corner of Main and Walnut Streets in Red Bluff and provided stage service between the city and Tuscan Springs from the resort's earliest years. This photograph was probably taken in the 1870s. The image below is a close-up of the same establishment but was shot sometime after phone service and electricity came to Tehama County in 1888. Edgerton Walbridge would build the Tuscan Springs Livery Stables a few years later just a few blocks away. (Both, author.)

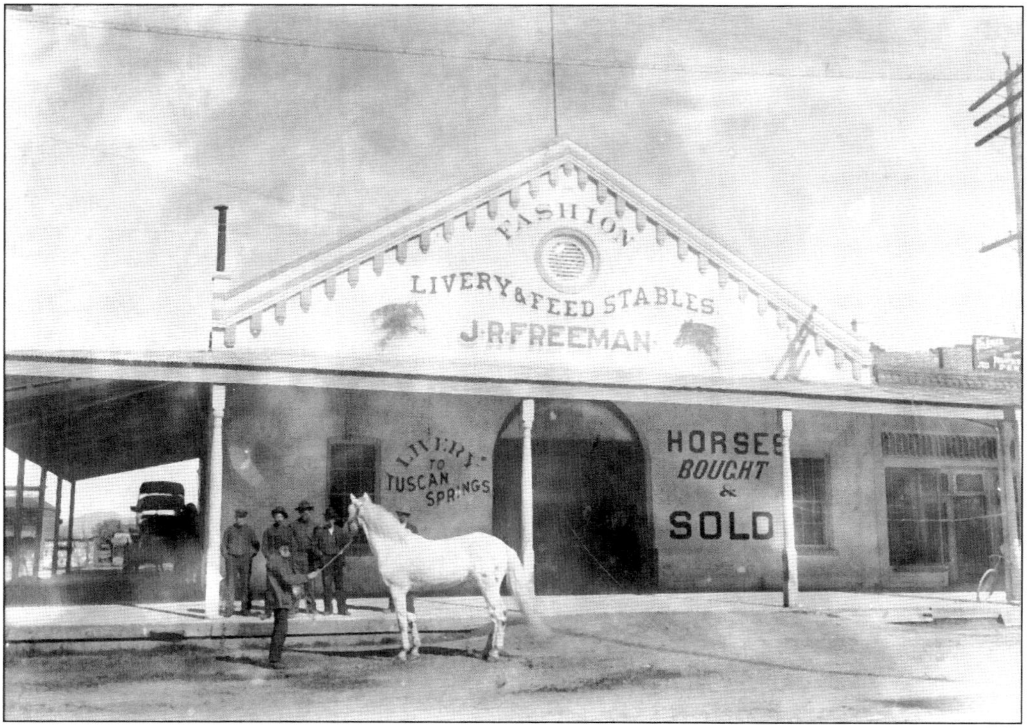

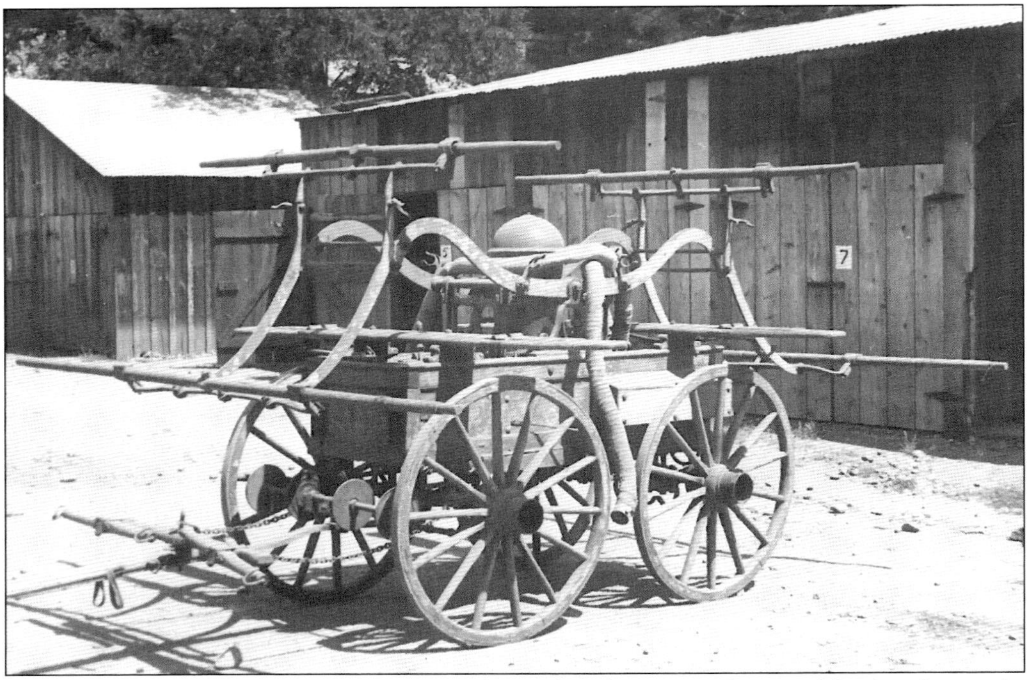

Both of these photographs are of an 1849 Lafayette hand-pump truck, one of the first fire trucks in California when it was purchased by the City of San Francisco. It was later sold to the City of Sacramento before being sold to Red Bluff in 1877. In those days, trucks did not carry water or have engines to pump it. Instead, firefighters would drop a hose into the nearest body of water and pump the device like a handcar to siphon water onto a fire. The device was kept by Red Bluff until 1906, when it was sold for $100 to the City of Weaverville, where it may still be seen today.

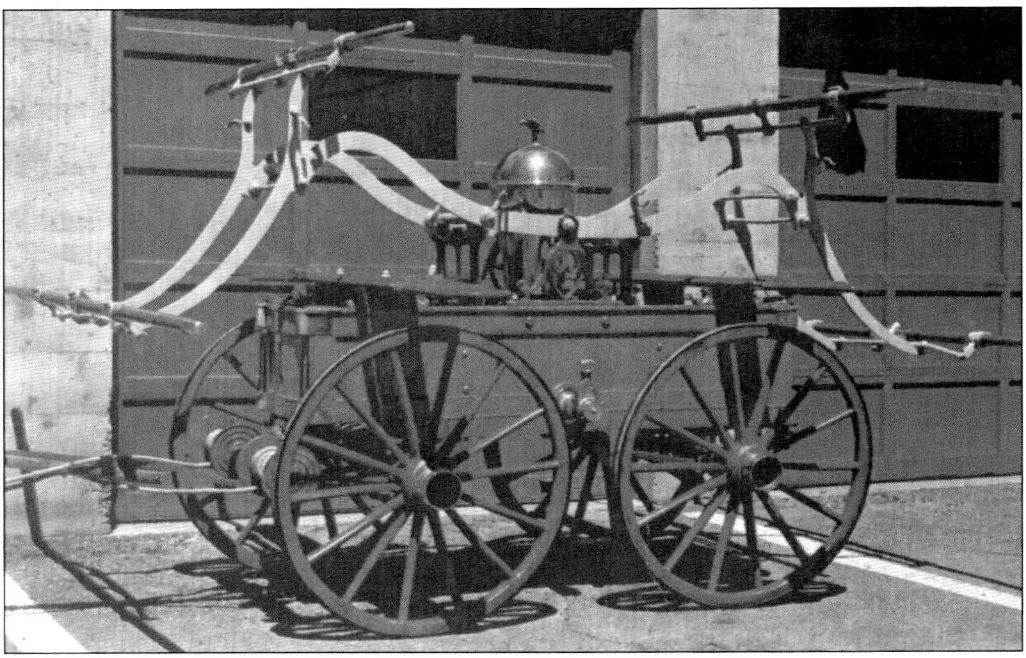

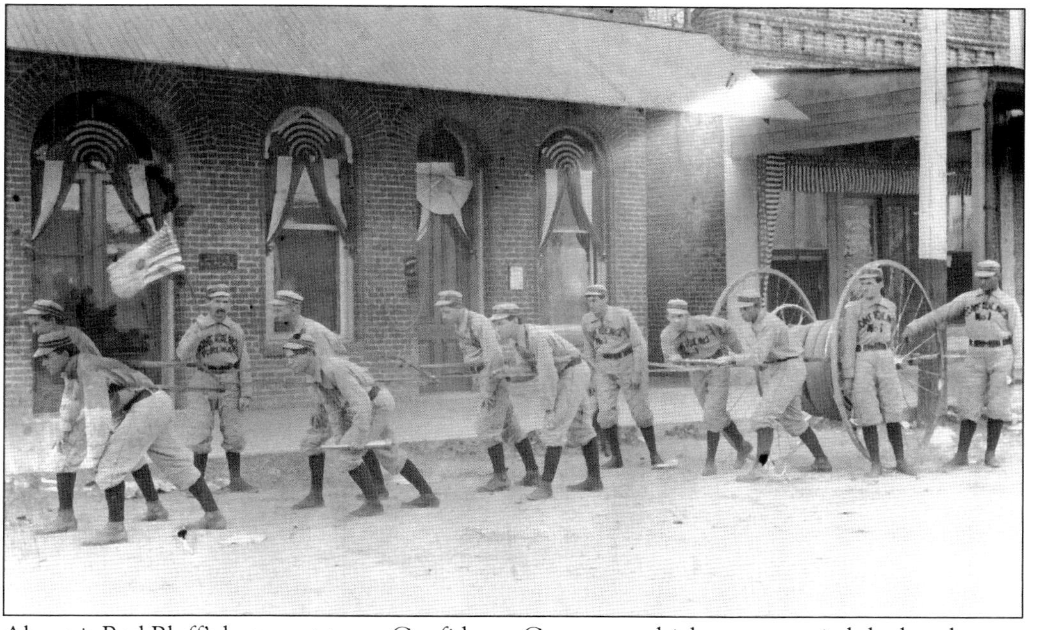

Above is Red Bluff's hose cart team, Confidence Company, which accompanied the hand-pump truck to fires. The team was probably involved in fighting the 1882 downtown fire that burned Walbridge's shop as well as the 1885 blaze that decimated the Union Hotel. Below is the more efficient steamer pump truck, which siphoned at a greater quantity and force through a steam engine. This truck might have responded to the fires at Tuscan Springs in 1899 and 1916. However, most of the damages from both fires occurred in the first 30 minutes, and the trip to the springs at full gallop took around an hour.

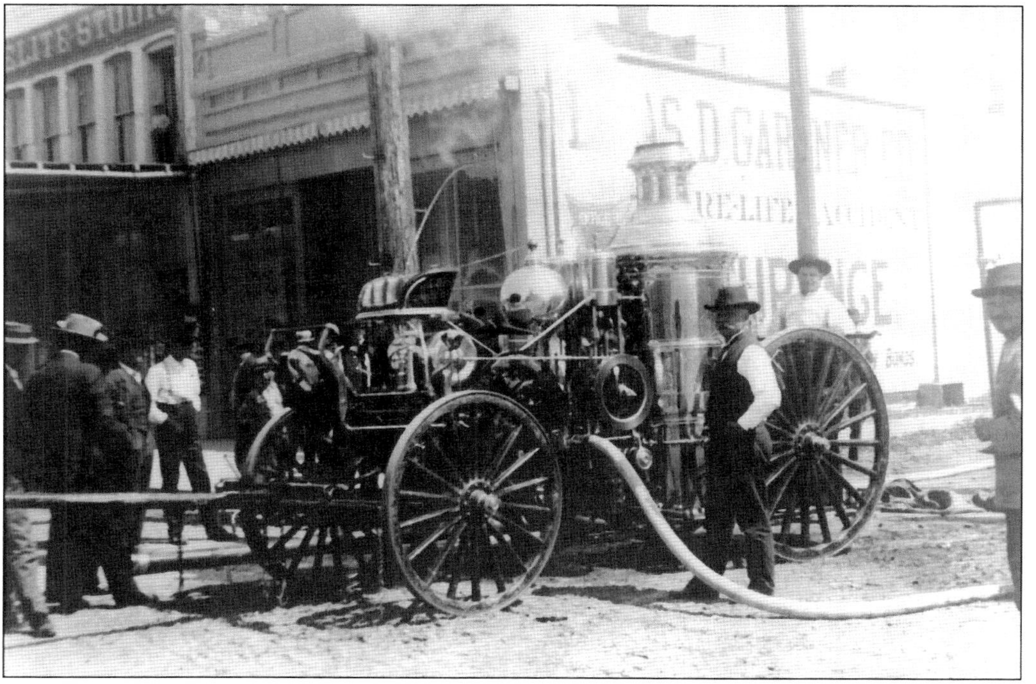

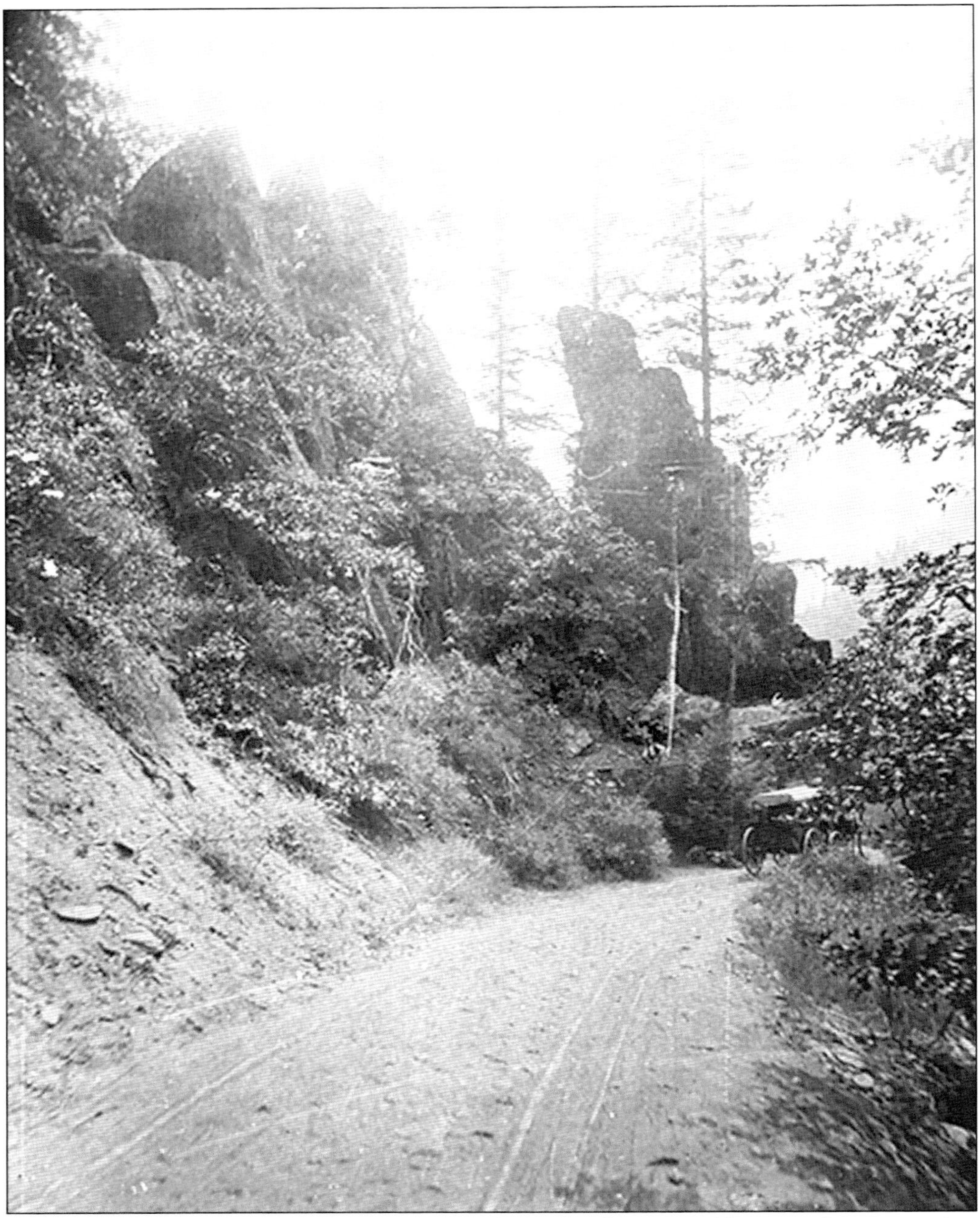

If not the actual wagon trail, this road certainly bears a striking resemblance to the passage that led to Tuscan Springs. Like the newfangled automobile peeking around the bend, the advances of the 20th century were just around the corner and arriving faster than expected. In the 1870s came the railroad, the flumes, the first fire department, water service (in Red Bluff), and gas lighting. The 1880s and 1890s heralded automobiles, electrical power, and the first phone services. Meanwhile, in the 1860s, with the help of a salty patent medicine salesman, Tuscan Springs was about to find just what it had been lacking: stability.

Three

Somewhere in La Mancha

Before buying Tuscan Springs in 1866, Maj. Jefferson Calhoun Bradley peddled patent medicines in downtown Red Bluff. Born in Tennessee in 1802, he fought in the Mexican-American War, came to California in 1849, found minor income panning gold on Reading's Trinity River, married Mary Owens in 1859, and relocated to Tehama County in 1861.

Purchasing the springs at age 65, Bradley was not the energetic businessman his predecessors may have been, but neither was he careless—what he lacked in innovation, he made up for in old-fashioned customer service.

When patrons began grumbling that the temporary buildings were ragged and uninviting. Bradley saved the funds and constructed a 68-room hotel, the first permanent building on the site. When the railroad established a Red Bluff depot in 1871, Bradley arranged for a coach to meet the train daily, and after a three-hour ride, guests were welcomed at the hotel entrance with a large complimentary lunch.

Whatever plans Bradley ultimately had for the resort, however, came to an end on August 27, 1875, when he suddenly died, reportedly the victim of a pistol duel. The widowed Mary Bradley continued to own the resort for 12 more years, a period that saw the introduction of such innovations as the Centennial Bridge, the telephone, gas engines, automobiles, phonographs, and lightbulbs.

Business may have dropped off by June 1876; the resort was offering half-price rooms to servants and children under 10, and the stage was only running on Tuesdays and Saturdays. By 1887, Mrs. Bradley had spent more than 20 years at Tuscan Springs. Her advancing age, along with the death of her son in a sawmill accident in 1885, may have made the prospect of leisurely retirement more attractive. She decided to sell lock, stock, and barrel to a popular young entrepreneur with a knack for business and—as it later turned out—an unfortunate relationship with fire.

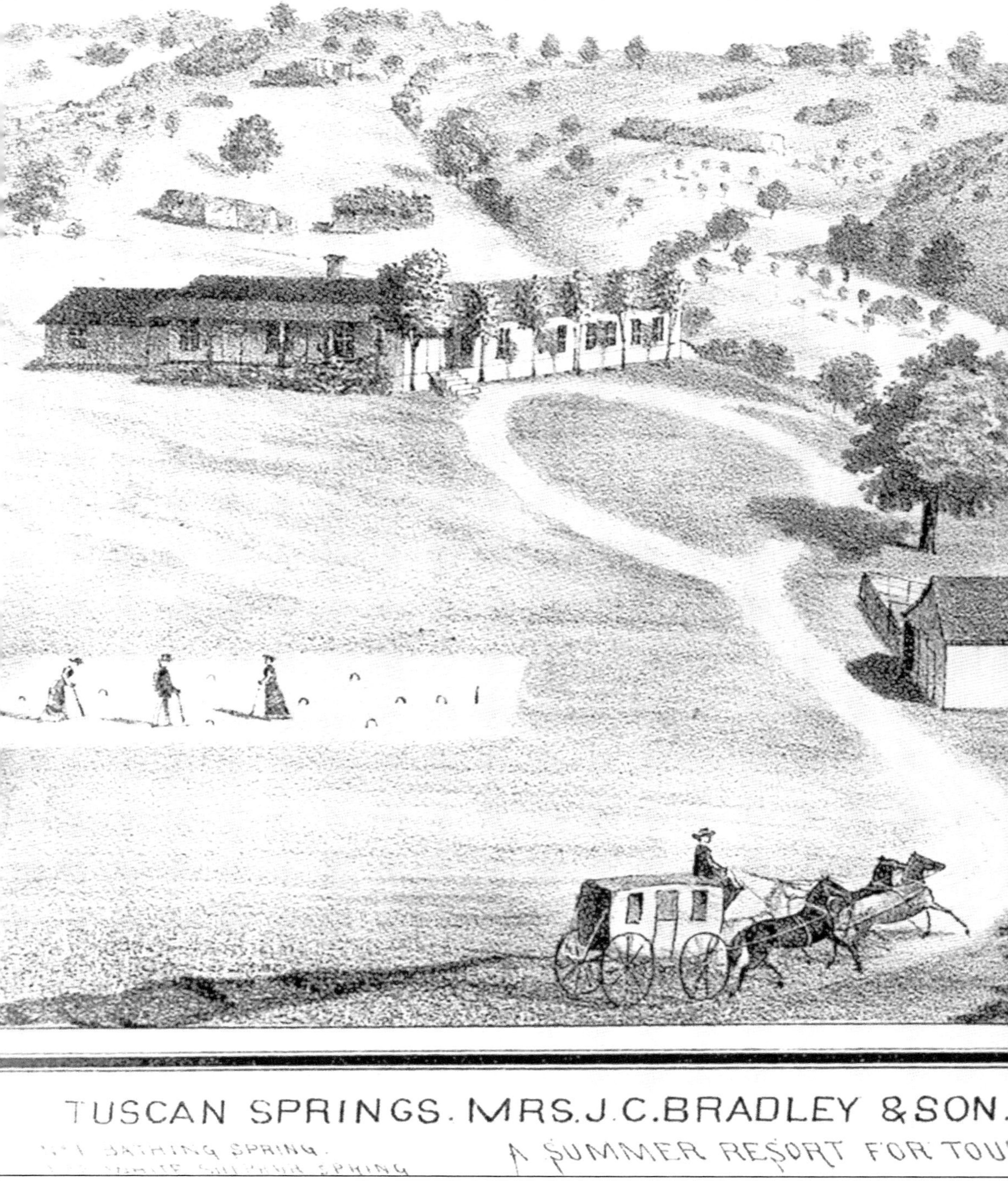

The only known representation that survives of Tuscan Springs during the ownership of Maj. Jefferson Calhoun and Mary Owens Bradley (1866–1887) is this romanticized depiction from *Illustrations of Tehama County With Historical Sketches*, published in 1880. Though the newspapers often mentioned numerous springs at the resort, this rendering indicates only three: a bathing

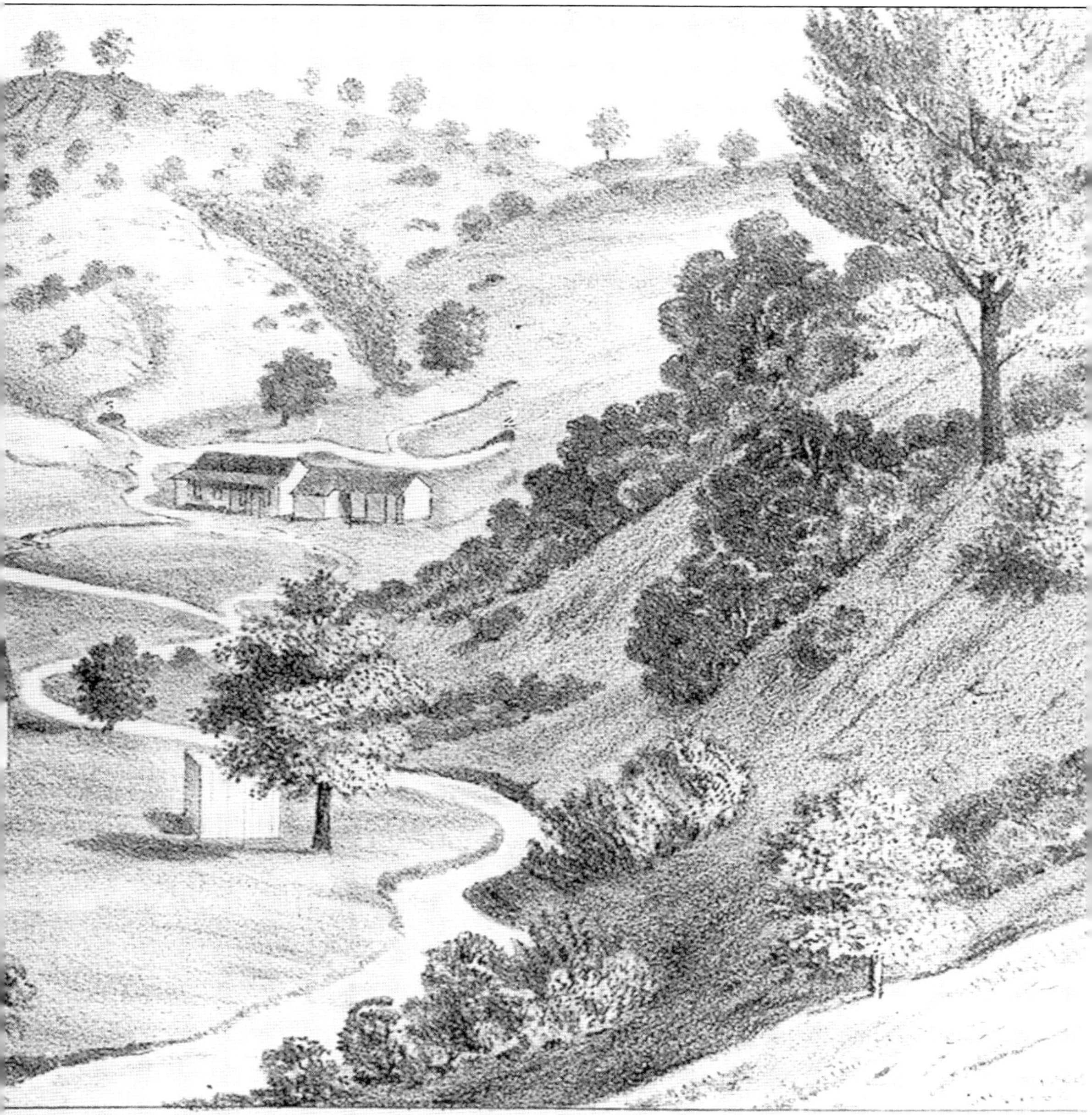

(red water?) spring, a white sulphur spring, and a black sulphur spring. Surprisingly, later analysis determined the bathing spring contained sulphuric, carbonic, and hydrochloric acids. The picture shows guests arriving by carriage as other visitors play a leisurely game of croquet along the path to the corral, cottages, bathhouse, and the permanent hotel that Bradley built.

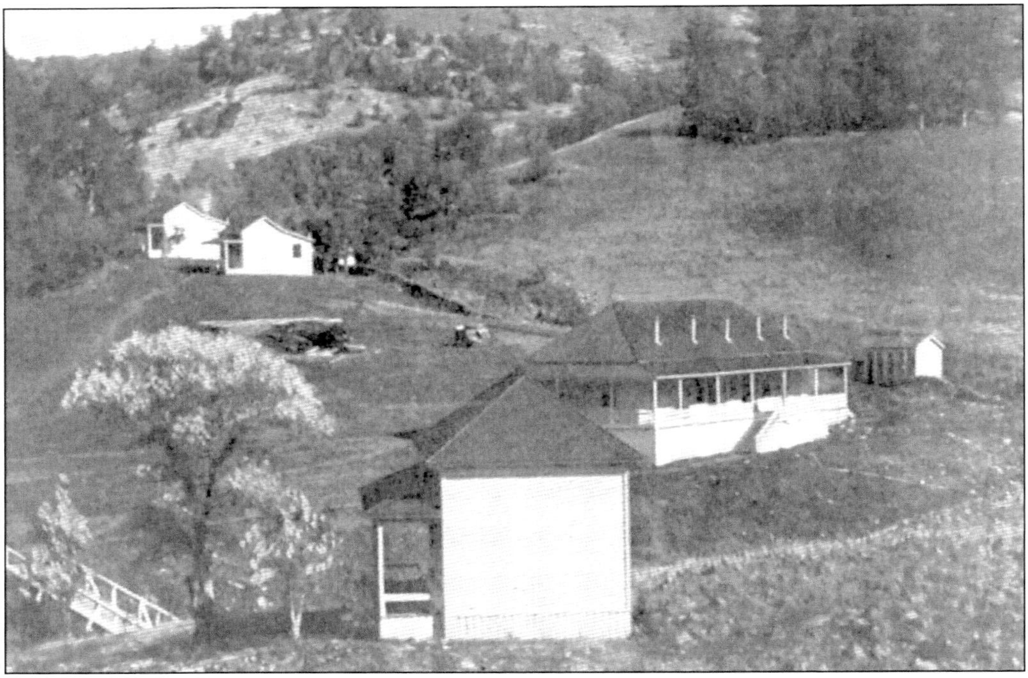

Though taken around 15 years after the Bradley era, the above photograph is a fair representation of the cottages that dotted Tuscan Springs from 1866 to 1887. Most were far enough from the large structures to be relatively safe during fires and were seldom renovated. By 1905, these same cottages were renting for between $2.50 and $5 a week. Not far from the hotel, a campground was also maintained where visitors could pitch tents free of charge. Below, hunting was allowed and encouraged at Tuscan Springs from the very beginning. Here, a hunter displays a buck he shot in the buttes around the hotel. (Both, author.)

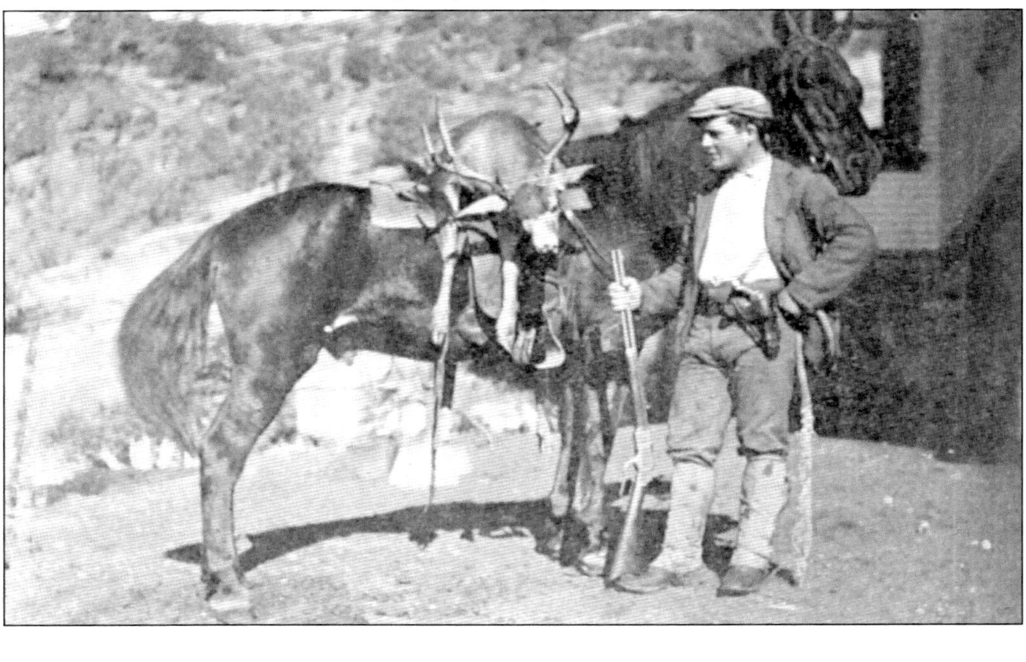

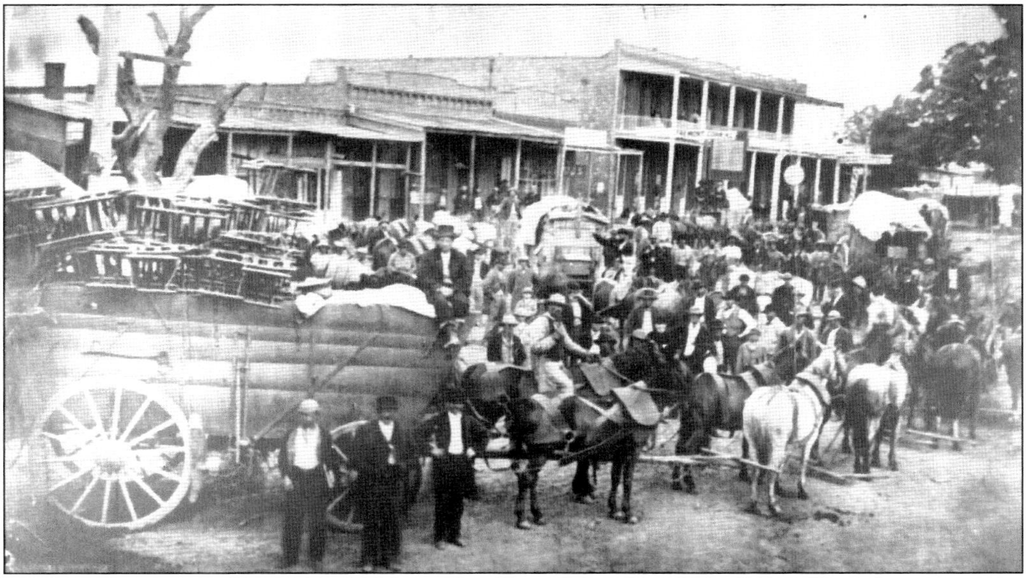

It was often chaotic in Red Bluff when the miners came to town for supplies, as seen in the image above from 1875—the same year that Tuscan Springs proprietor and former Tehama County coroner Maj. Jefferson C. Bradley was reportedly shot and killed. The photograph below shows a more serene moment from the same era. Main Street was unusually wide—100 feet from walkway to walkway—to allow for major traffic on days the miners visited and to accommodate the annual cattle drive down the street, when ranchers herded their cows and steers through town to get them to market.

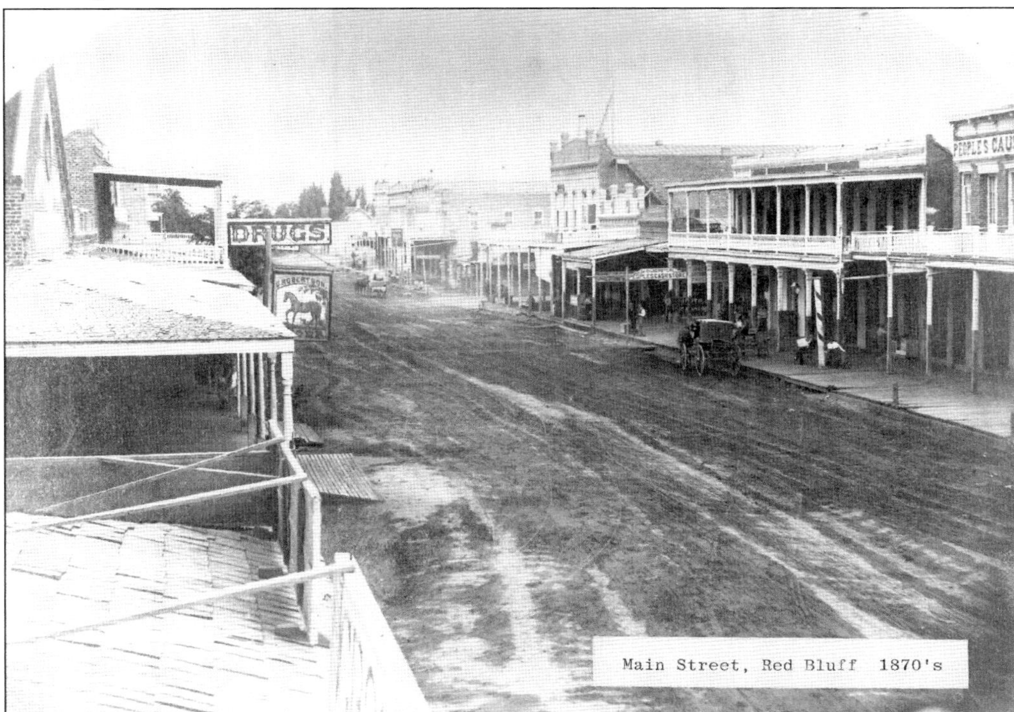

Main Street, Red Bluff 1870's

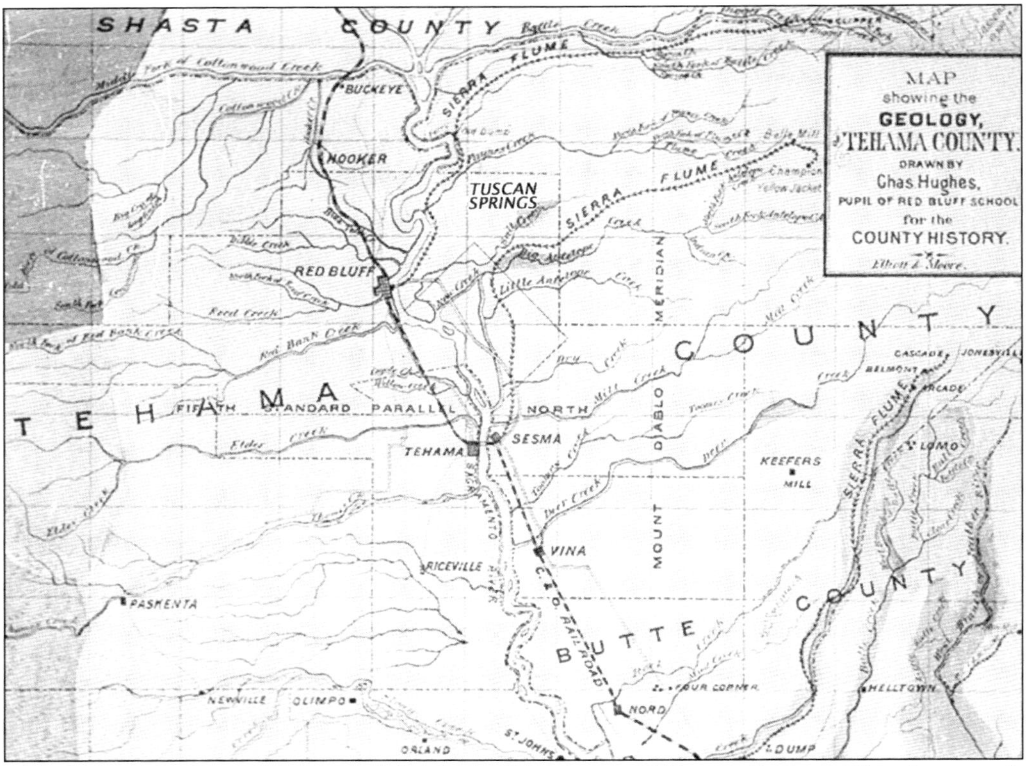

The above map shows the route of the Sierra Flume around Tuscan Springs. The photograph below shows its construction in 1872. The flume was originally completed by the Empire Lumber Company in 1873 at a cost of $5,000 per mile, but it was later sold to the Sierra Flume & Lumber Company. The first V flume west of the Sierras, it was designed by Charles F. Ellsworth, a woodsman from Maine. It was commonly referred to as "Ellsworth's Folly," either because most thought it would never work or because, during final construction, Ellsworth fell to his death from the top of the flume. (Below, TCM.)

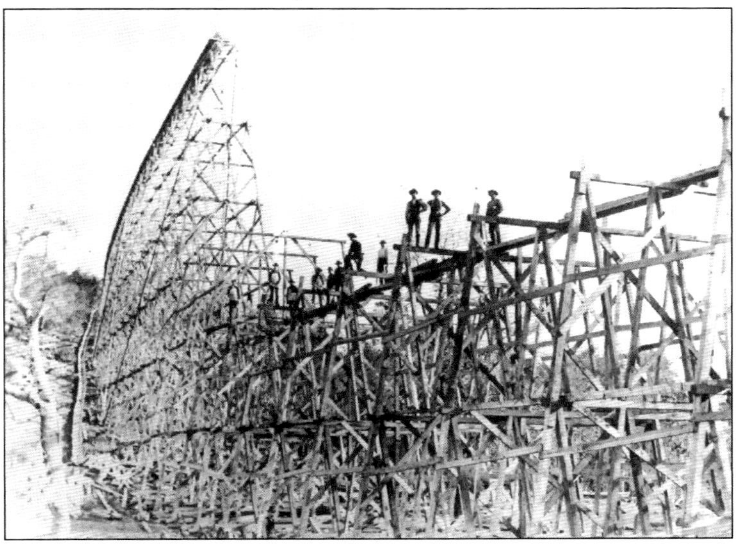

As depicted at right, tenders on narrow catwalks would ensure the lumber flowed smoothly along the flume route, monitor for major leaks, grease the flume as needed, and untangle any snags as they occurred. Dangerous work, it was not a job for those with vertigo as the flumes reached heights of 150 feet. Below, the flume snakes its way through Salt Creek Canyon and the Tuscan Buttes around Tuscan Springs, passing within three miles of the resort. When running smoothly, the flume could transport 8,500 feet of lumber an hour to the Sierra Mill in Red Bluff.

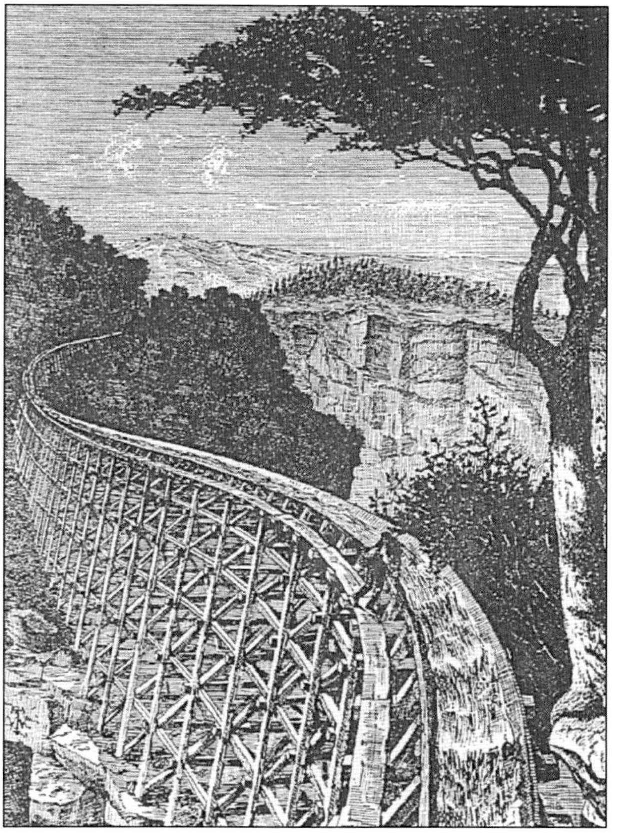

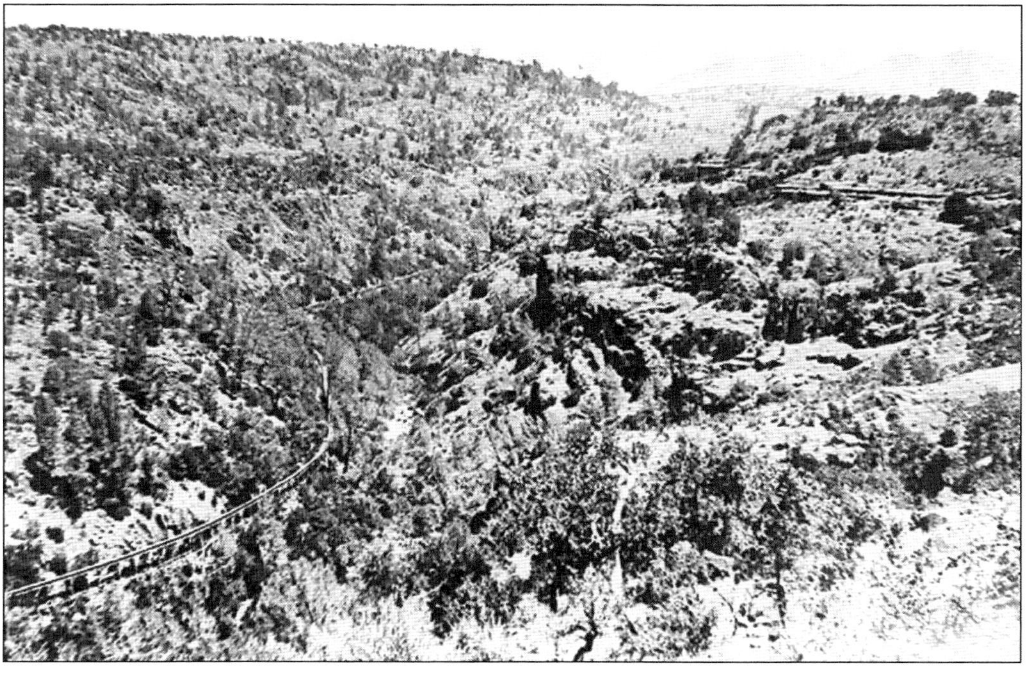

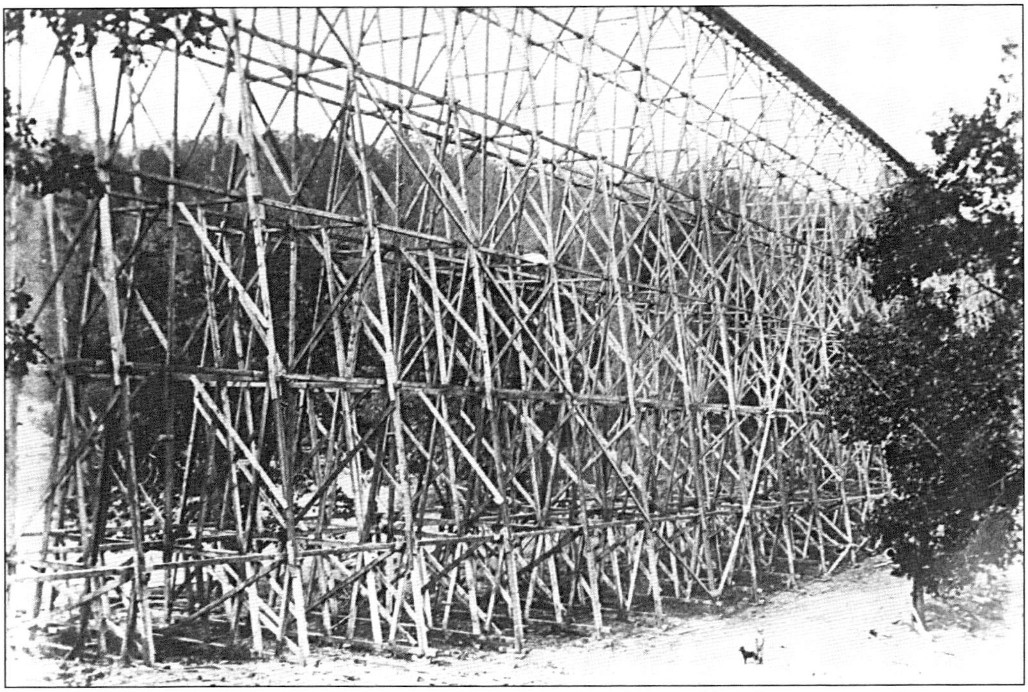

The image above shows the massive scale of the flume as a boy and his dog examine the awesome structure, which straddled trees and mountains on an ever-declining slope. Water had to be kept in the flume at all times to weigh it down because strong winds could actually blow it over. The flume could also double as a pleasant setting for a picnic, as seen in the image below of several youngsters enjoying a leisurely Sunday afternoon near Lyonsville. The man on the extreme right, with bow tie, is Andy Shaeffer, once Tehama County supervisor. The others are unidentified. (Above, KGHM.)

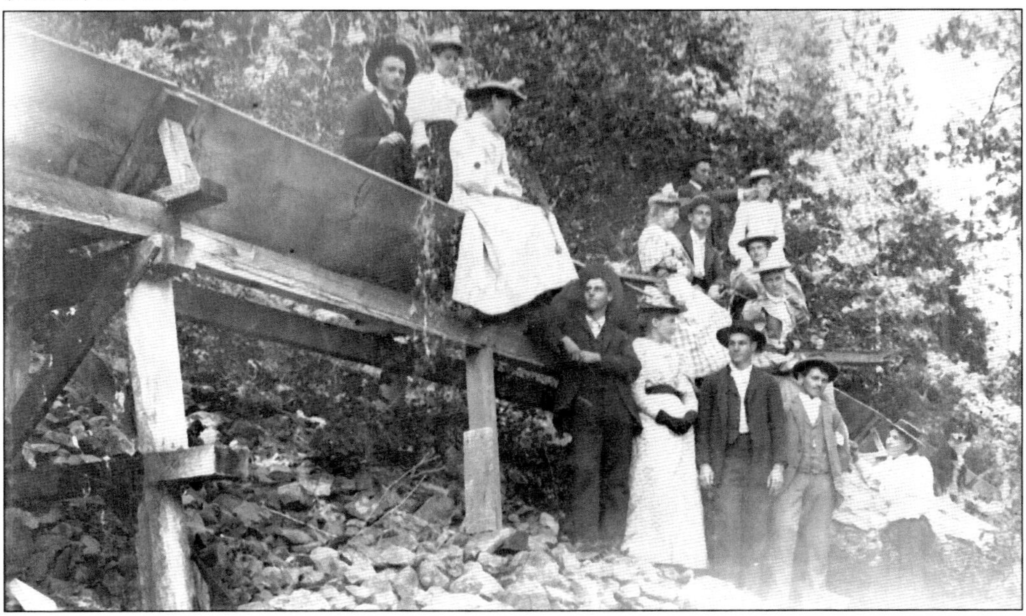

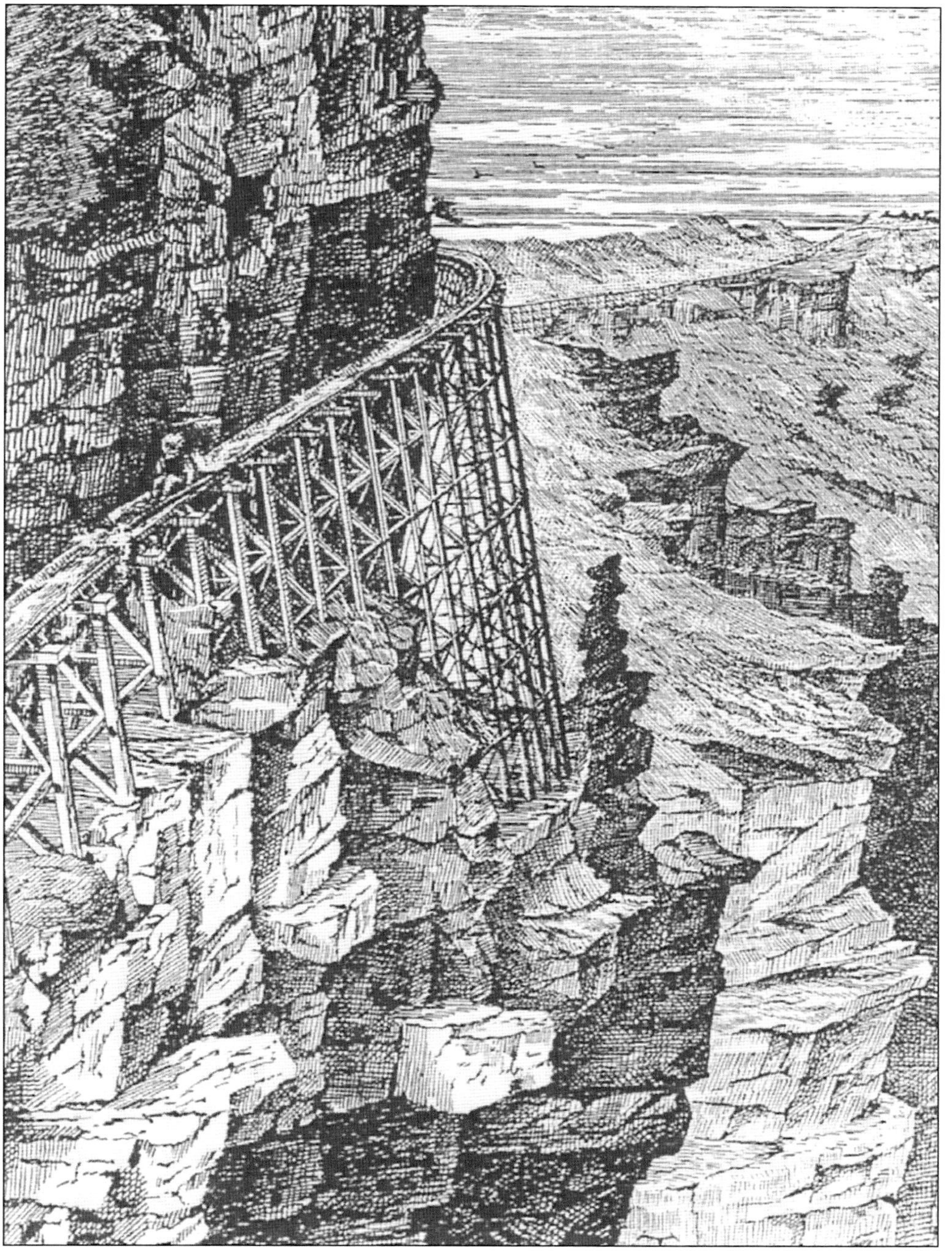

Though strongly discouraged, workers (and sometimes others) would occasionally straddle a log to "ride the flume" for fun, as depicted in this illustration from 1877. How passengers would stop their rides is unknown, especially at top speeds of more than 50 miles per hour. Generally, these trips would take place at the end of the day, after all the lumber had been transported. Other public uses of the flume included secretly siphoning its water for homes and gardens, and many cabins sprouted along its route. Late in his reign as proprietor, Edgerton Walbridge struck a deal with Sierra to tap its flume to supply fresh water to Tuscan Springs.

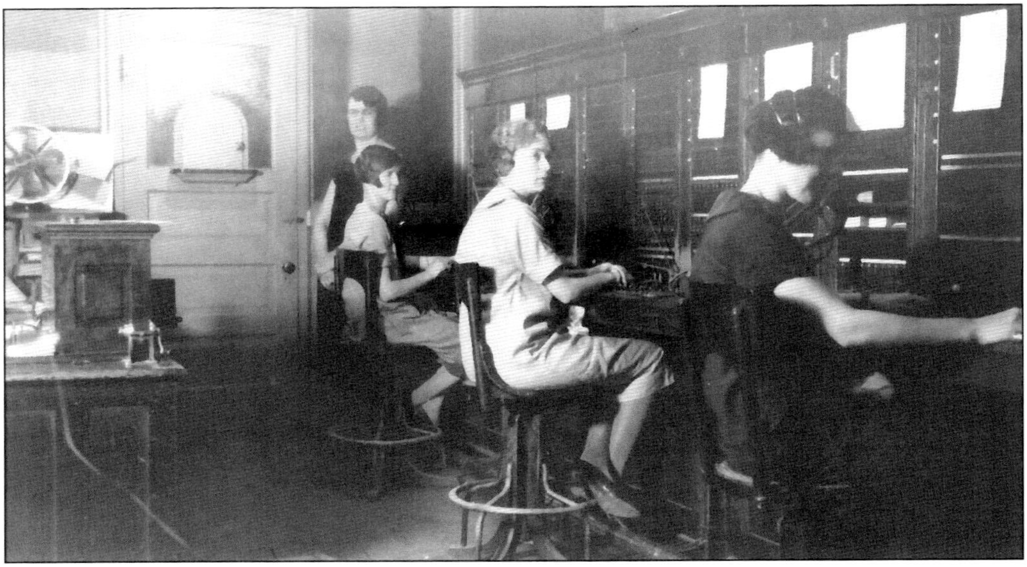

Telephone service connected Red Bluff to the Sacramento, Redding, and Portland systems in 1883, and local services were established by between 1892 and 1894. The above photograph was taken close to 1920, but the technology—and possibly even the staff—was roughly the same as it had been when service began. Callers rang the switchboard to request a destination, and operators connected the call by manually plugging and unplugging cables. Below, when electricity came to Tehama County in 1888, the dynamo on Antelope Creek was one of the earliest sources of power, supplying electricity to Tuscan Springs and other remote county areas.

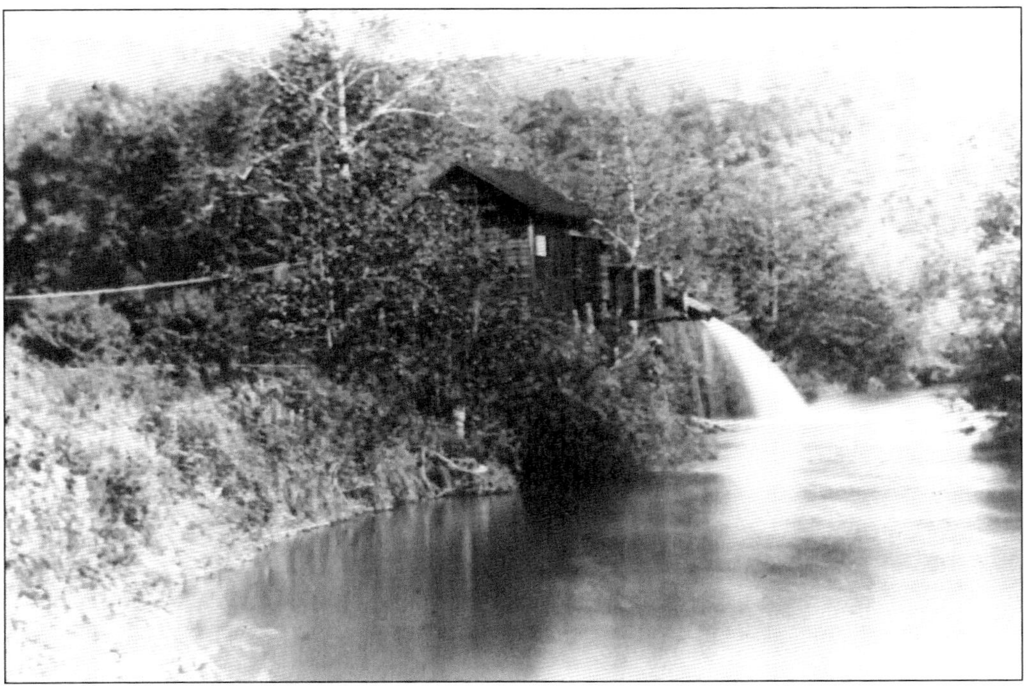

Four

The Best of Times

Born in Wisconsin in 1859, Edgerton Byron Walbridge was not even alive when Veatch discovered borax at Tuscan Springs. By age 14, Walbridge was a telegraph agent in Hancock County, Iowa. Moving to California, he was employed as a telegraph operator in Chico for a year before landing in Red Bluff in 1877 at the age of 18. He set up a downtown fruit stand next to Stoll's Sadlery, the profits of which soon enabled him to settle into a real storefront on the Tremont block.

A great socializer, Walbridge joined the Elks, Vespers, Shriners, Masons, and Templars. Described as "wide awake, enterprising and progressive," he was a hardy, barrel-chested man who loved a strong drink and a fat cigar and who was well liked in his community. Nonetheless, he faced more than his share of business obstacles, such as when a fire claimed some of the most popular businesses in Red Bluff, including his shop, in 1882. Then—after he had purchased the Union Hotel on Main Street—at around 1:30 a.m. on August 30, 1885, an alarm sounded in downtown Red Bluff. A fire had been spotted at a Johnson Street home, and as the city's new steamer battled the last of the flames, another cry of "Fire!" directed firemen to a blaze at the Union Hotel. The building was totaled. The cause, the *Weekly Sentinel* supposed, was a candle left burning when a Union guest left his room to observe the first fire.

Now out of business again, Walbridge purchased Tuscan Springs from the widowed Mary Bradley for an undisclosed price on July 22, 1887. At first, he ran the enterprise conservatively as Bradley had, but in March 1895, the *Daily News* reported piles of lumber were suddenly appearing on the resort grounds. A grand new Victorian hotel quickly materialized; two stories tall, with a single corner tower, it contained 108 rooms and could accommodate up to 125 guests.

The new resort became the talk of California, and fortunes were indeed about to change.

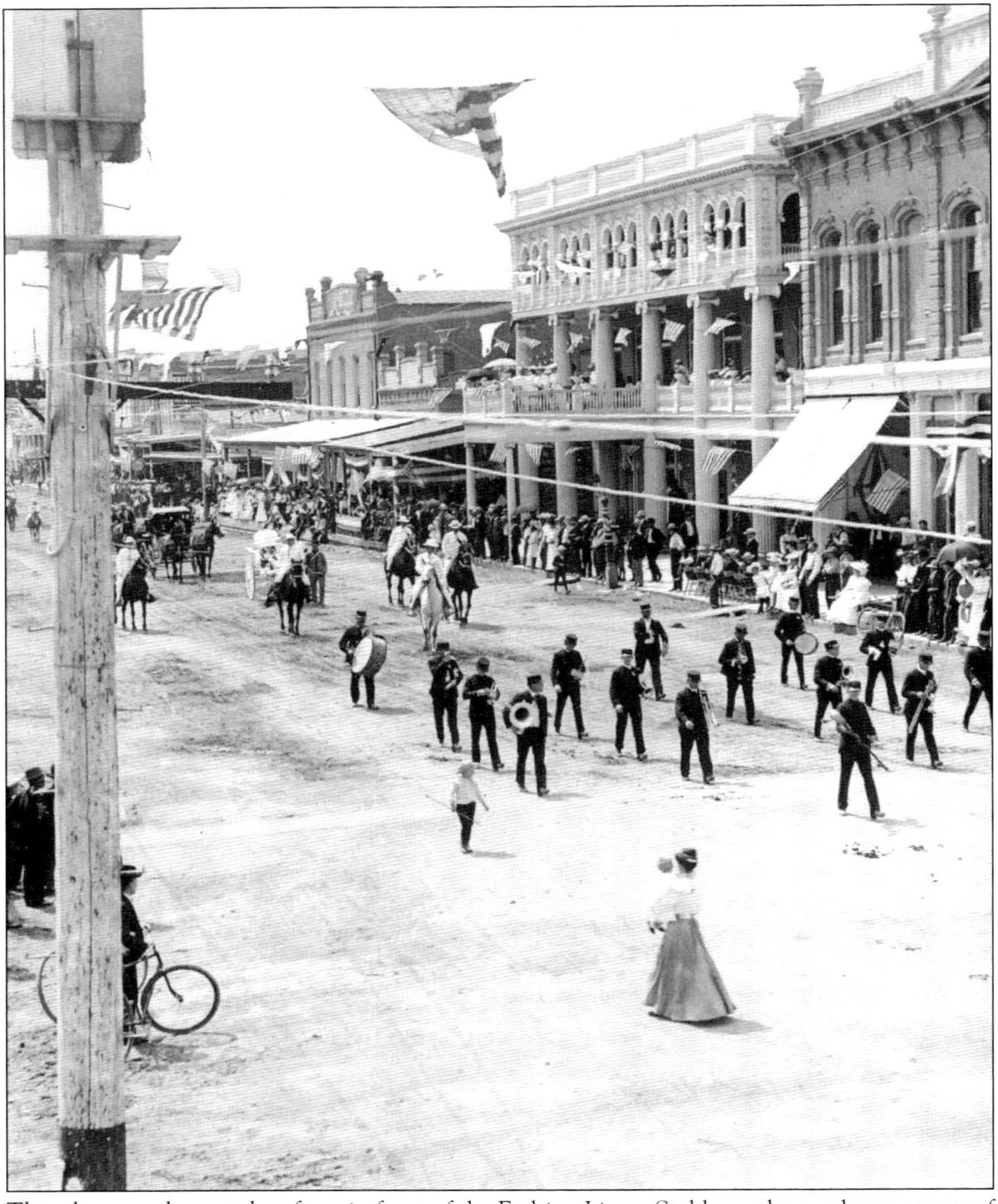

This photograph was taken from in front of the Fashion Livery Stable on the southeast corner of Main and Walnut Streets in 1900. It shows a mother and her child watching the Fourth of July parade in downtown Red Bluff. Across the street, people are waving from the third-story balcony of the popular Tremont Hotel, the same block that had been home to Walbridge's mercantile five years before. Though the streets of the city would not be paved for another 15 years, phone lines and power wires had just begun to crisscross the avenues of small-town 20th-century America. The annual Independence Day parade in Red Bluff (alternating with the city of Redding) was a very popular tradition in Tehama County for years and drew many out-of-town visitors.

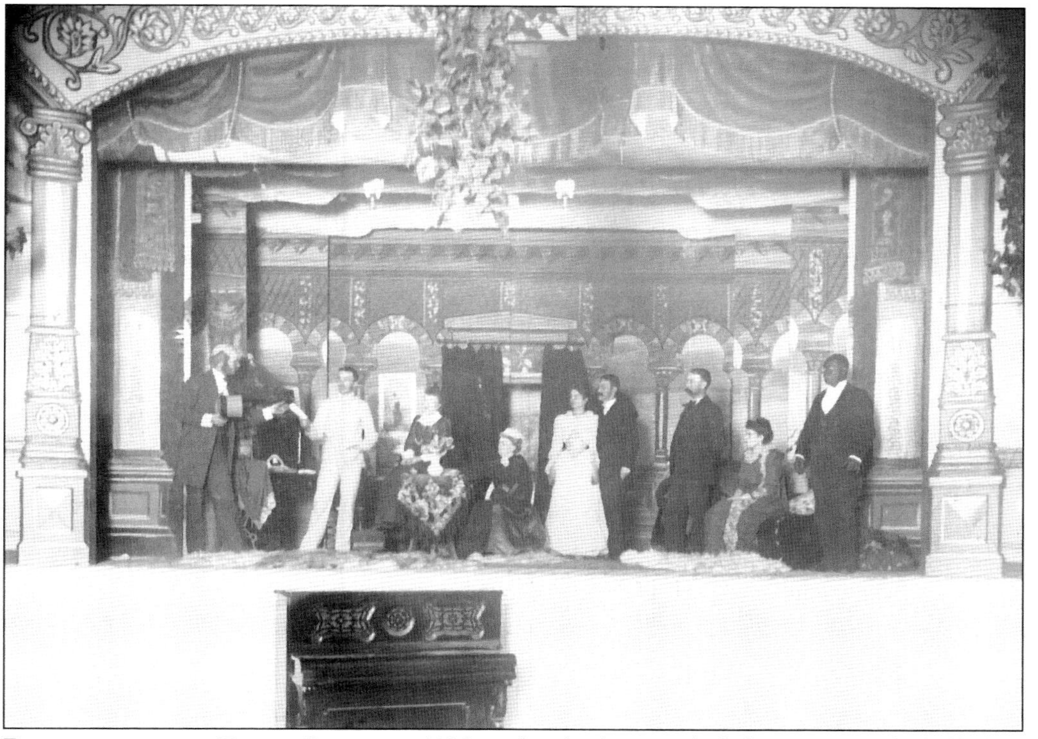

For many, a visit to Tuscan Springs in 1900 might also have included a stop at Red Bluff's first playhouse (above), where visitors could enjoy an evening's entertainment. Different plays were staged each week by the Jessie Shirley Stock Company and had admission prices of 10¢, 20¢, and 30¢. Or, visitors might have preferred to simply stroll around and look at the handsome homes (below), as they still do today. In this image of a typical Red Bluff residential street at the turn of the century are, from left to right, the homes of the Wiggets, the Campbells, and the Gooches.

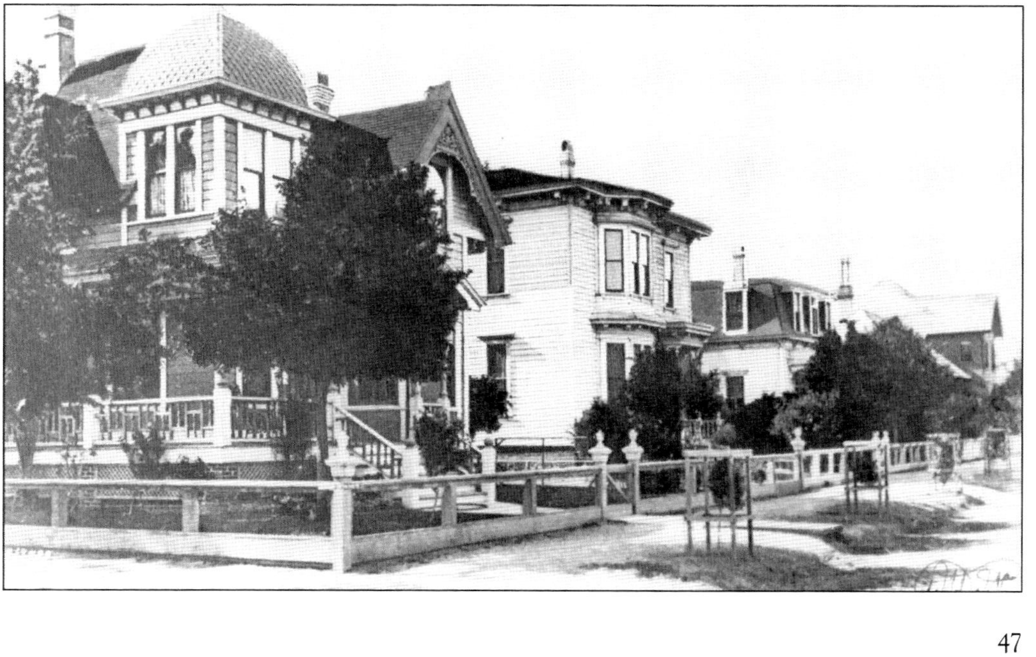

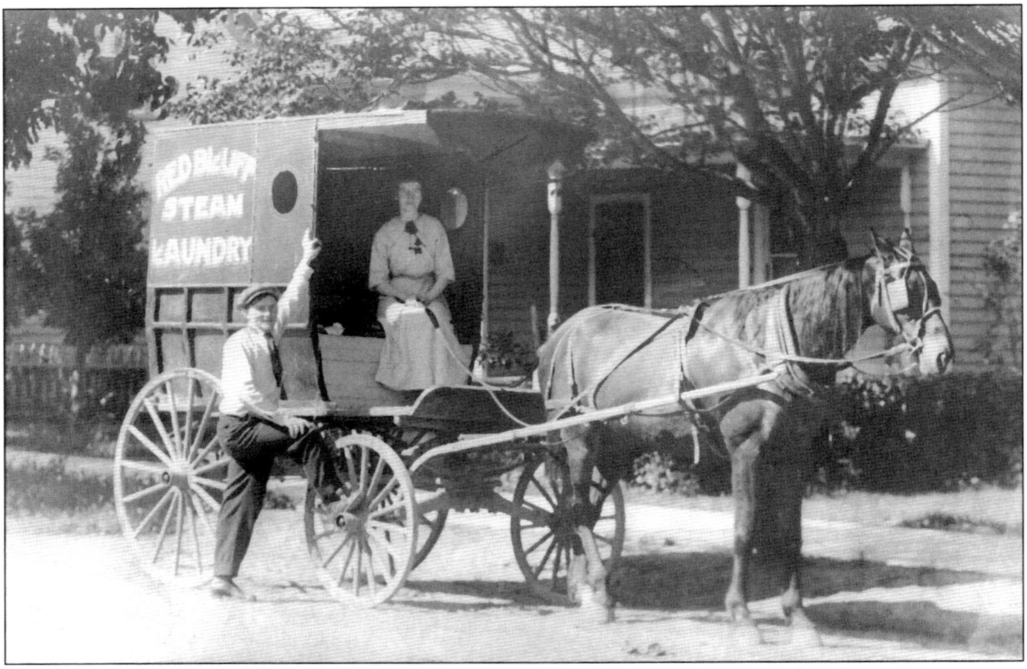

With a large hotel, cottages, steam baths, kitchens, and dining rooms, the cleaning needs of Tuscan Springs were significant, and much of the work—especially the dry cleaning—was handled by the Red Bluff Steam Laundry, which offered its own pickup and delivery services. Pictured above are laundry owner Sam Stragg and his wife in 1910. Below, the Garrett & Lyon Hardware Store supplied many of the practical items needed at Tuscan Spring throughout the Walbridge years, such as stoves, kitchenware, cutlery, gardening equipment, and tools. This business was in operation for nearly 100 years before closing in 1982.

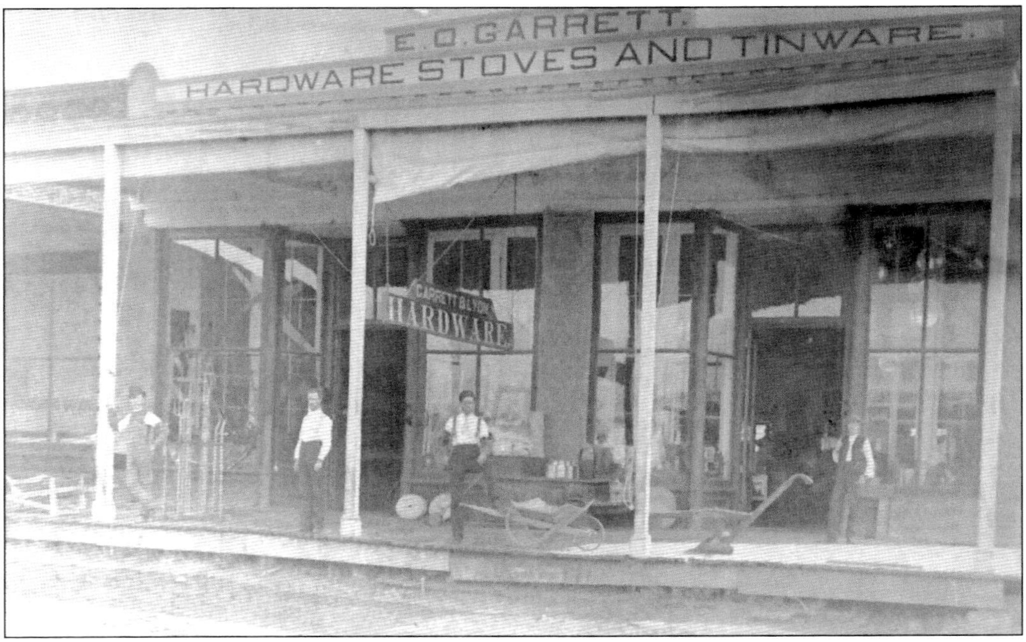

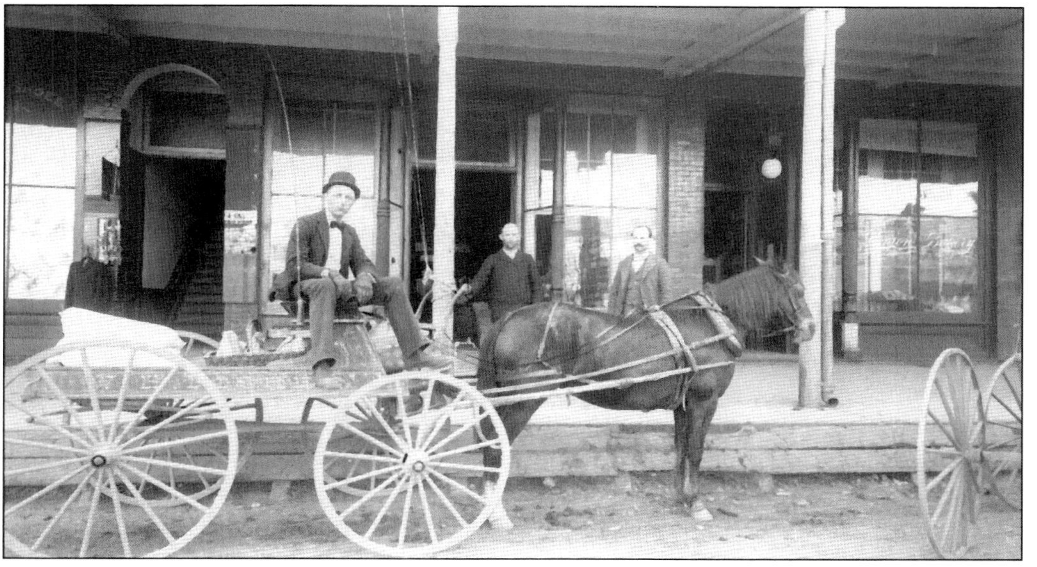

Many of the various groceries and supplies needed daily at Tuscan Springs, including such things as food, spices, pens, ink, and lamp wicks, came directly from W.H. Fisher's Groceries & Provisions, a very popular mercantile shop on Main Street in Red Bluff. Taken before 1890, the above photograph shows T.J. Brady (seated in the wagon), A.B. Fuller (center), and W.H. Fisher, the store owner. The photograph below shows the interior of the grocery shop. Pictured are, from left to right, A.B. Fuller, B.B. Robinson, owner W.H. Fisher, and T.J. Brady.

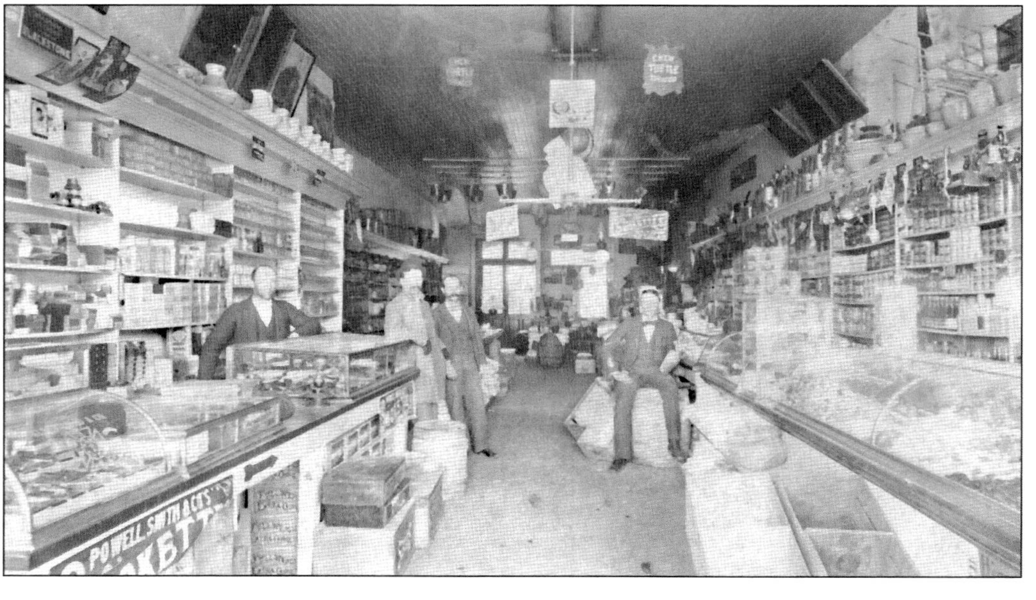

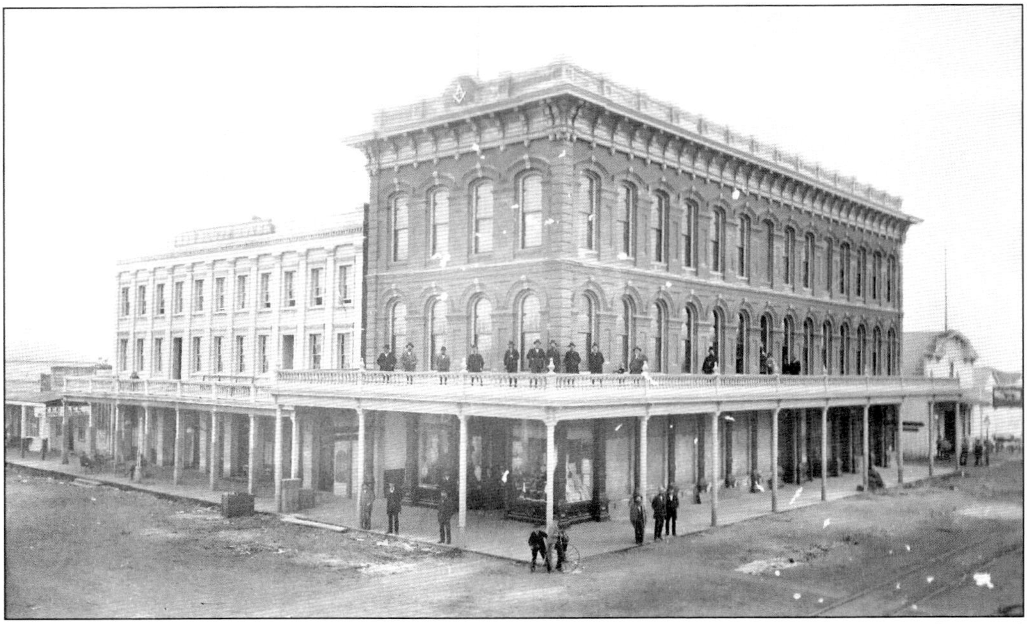

Pictured above around 1881, the Red Bluff Masonic Lodge was home to one of the many fraternal organizations of which Edgerton Walbridge was a practicing member. Located on the southwest corner of Main and Oak Streets, this building stood for only two years before burning down. Next to it was the Red Bluff Hotel; next to that was the Yee Lee Laundry, and behind it, Brady's Stables. Below, in a photograph from the following year, is the main hall of the lodge, where Walbridge and his fraternal brothers would hold their regular Masonic meetings and special events.

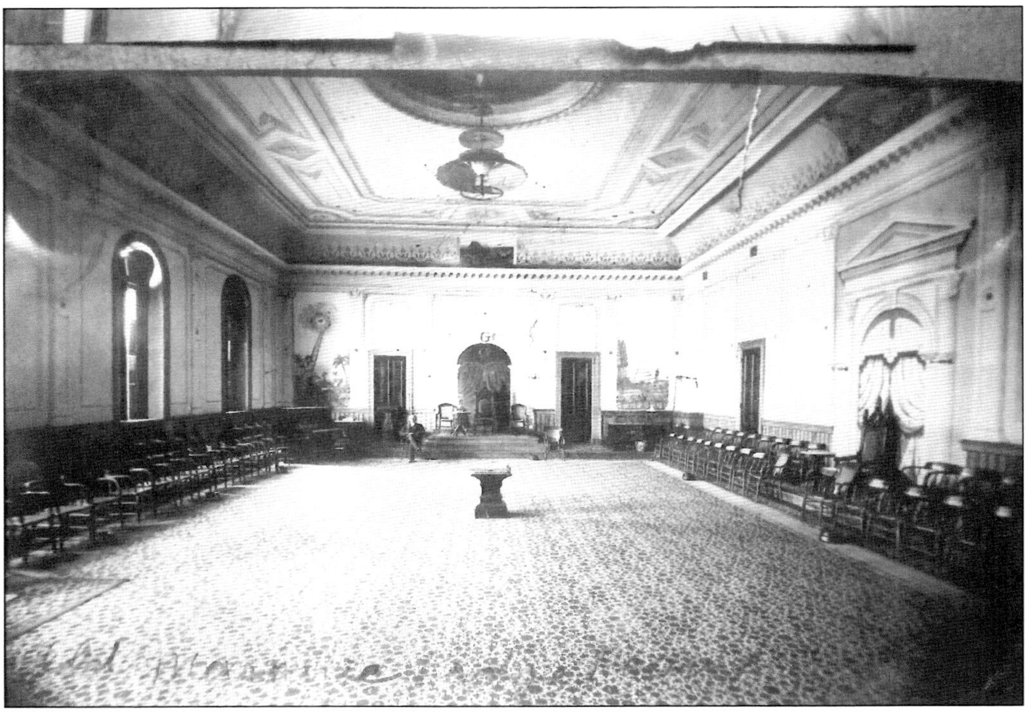

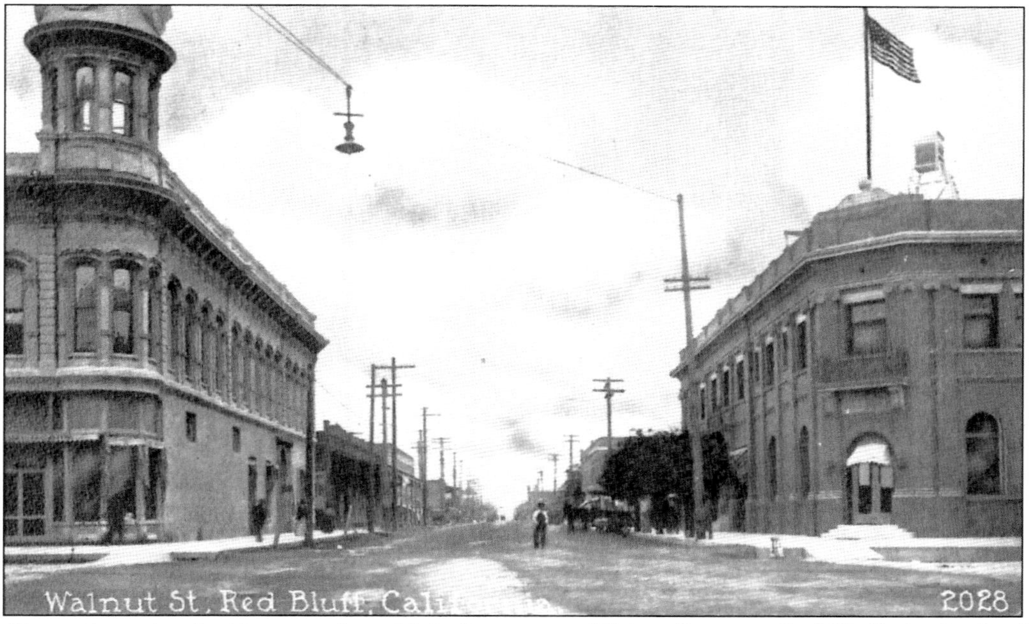

Above, in a view looking west from Main Street onto Walnut Street in Red Bluff, the Bank of Tehama County can be seen on the right. The first bank in the county, it was the institution where the accounts of Tuscan Springs were kept. Directly behind the bank, to the north (out of frame to the right), was where the Tuscan Springs Livery Stables was built and later, in 1911, the site of the Walbridge Garage. Below is an interior view of the bank from around 1900, a year after it moved into this building. Pictured are, from left to right, E.D. Gardener, Erle Gans, Will Caboone, and Charles Brown.

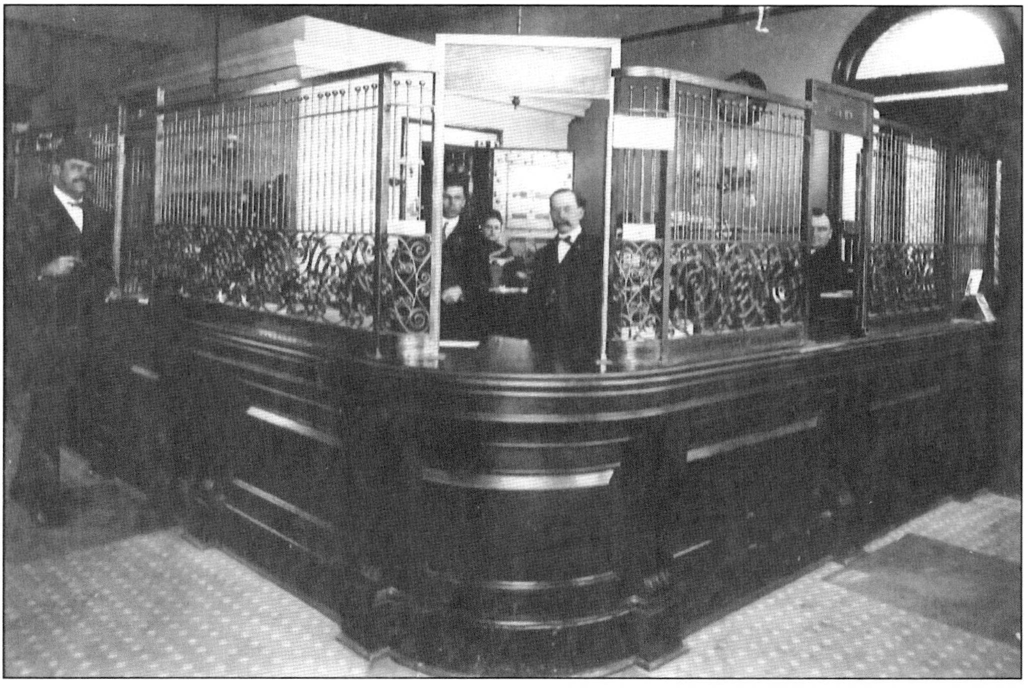

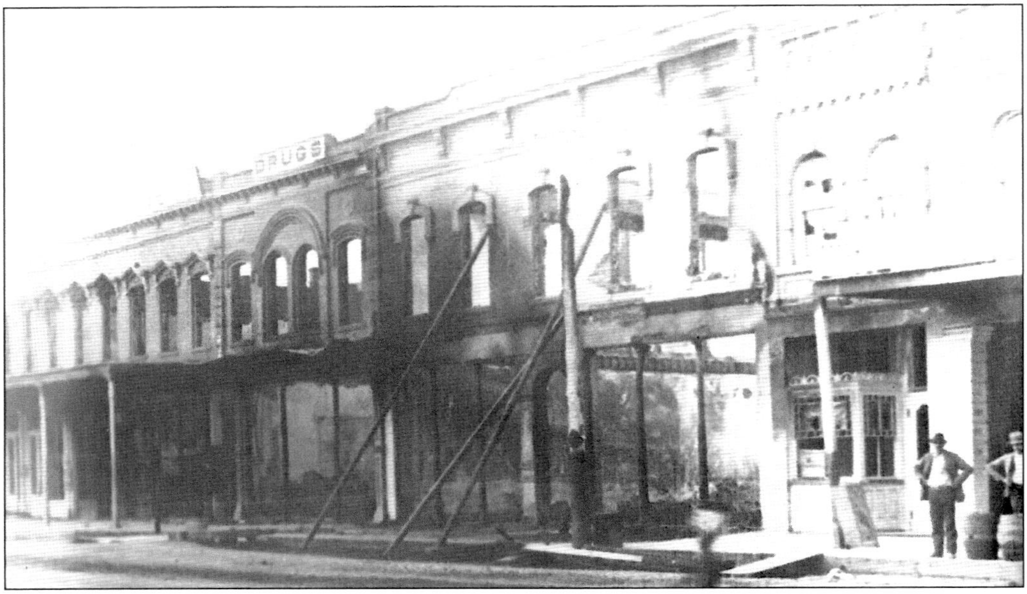

These two photographs show what was left standing after the downtown Red Bluff fire of 1882. The blaze consumed most of the businesses within two blocks on the west side of Main Street before jumping Oak Street and incinerating the livelihoods of more merchants. Destroyed were the Bank of Tehama County, the Red Bluff Hotel, the Masonic Lodge (pictured earlier), the post office, and the Walbridge's mercantile, among other businesses. The fire started in a cigar store on August 16 and quickly spread throughout the business district; it was the largest blaze in Red Bluff up to that time.

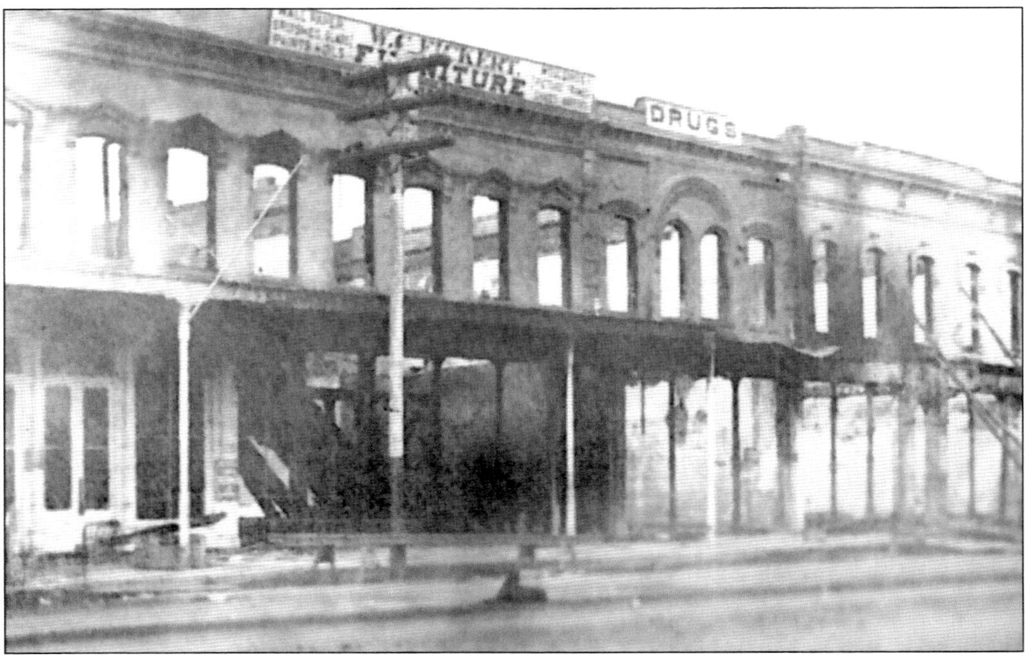

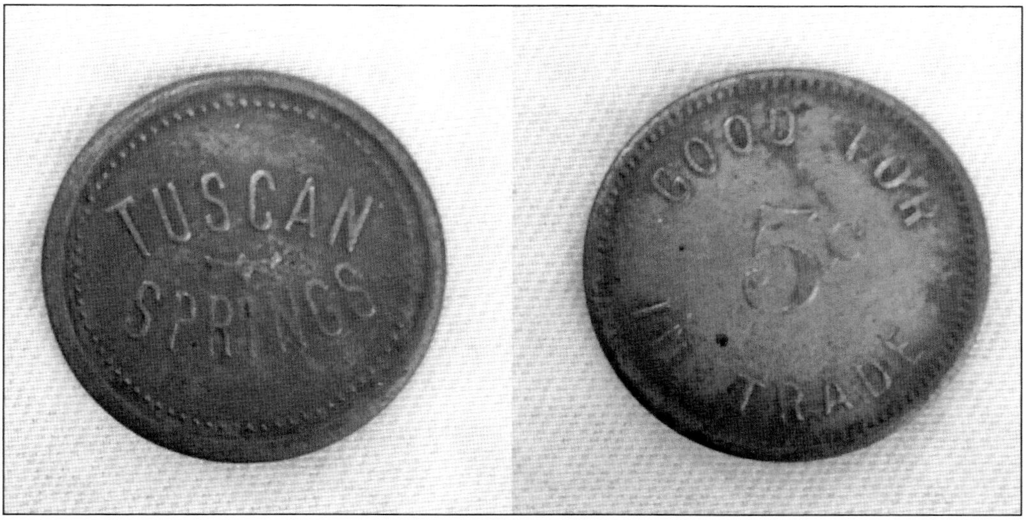

Above is a rare token (front and back) from Tuscan Springs, which guests might have traded for such things as a mug of beer, a fancy cigar, or a portion of a hotel bill. Legend has it that Walbridge always carried a pocketful of these coins and would give one away upon meeting anyone for the first time. In the photograph below, by Rufus Cook, Walbridge (far right) is seen networking with prominent out-of-town businessmen near one of his springs in September 1907. Among them are Louie Lubratich of the Peerlees Coffee Company (third from left) and Mike ? of Oakland's Acme Grill (fifth from left). (Both, author.)

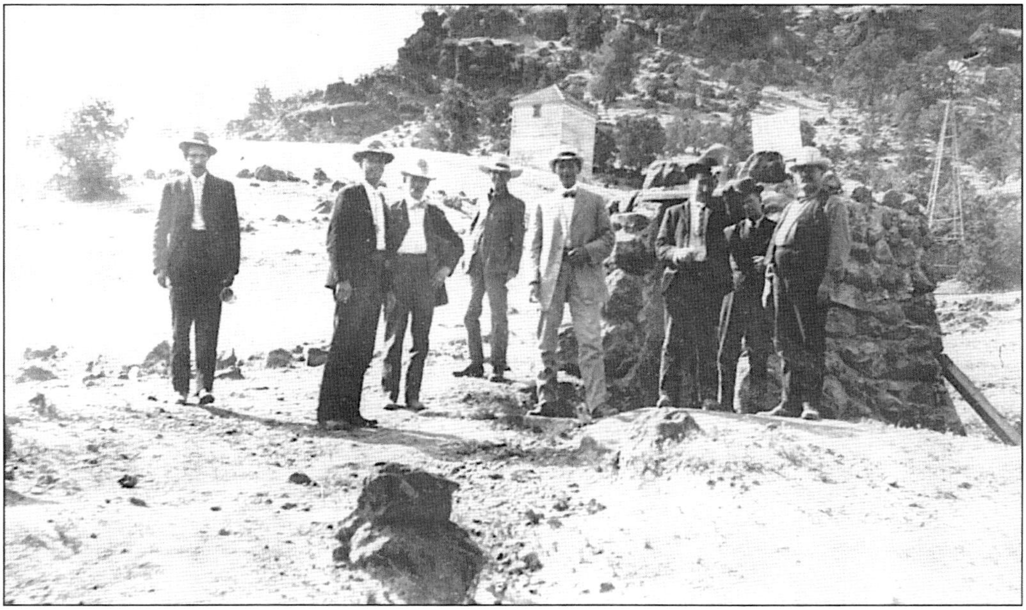

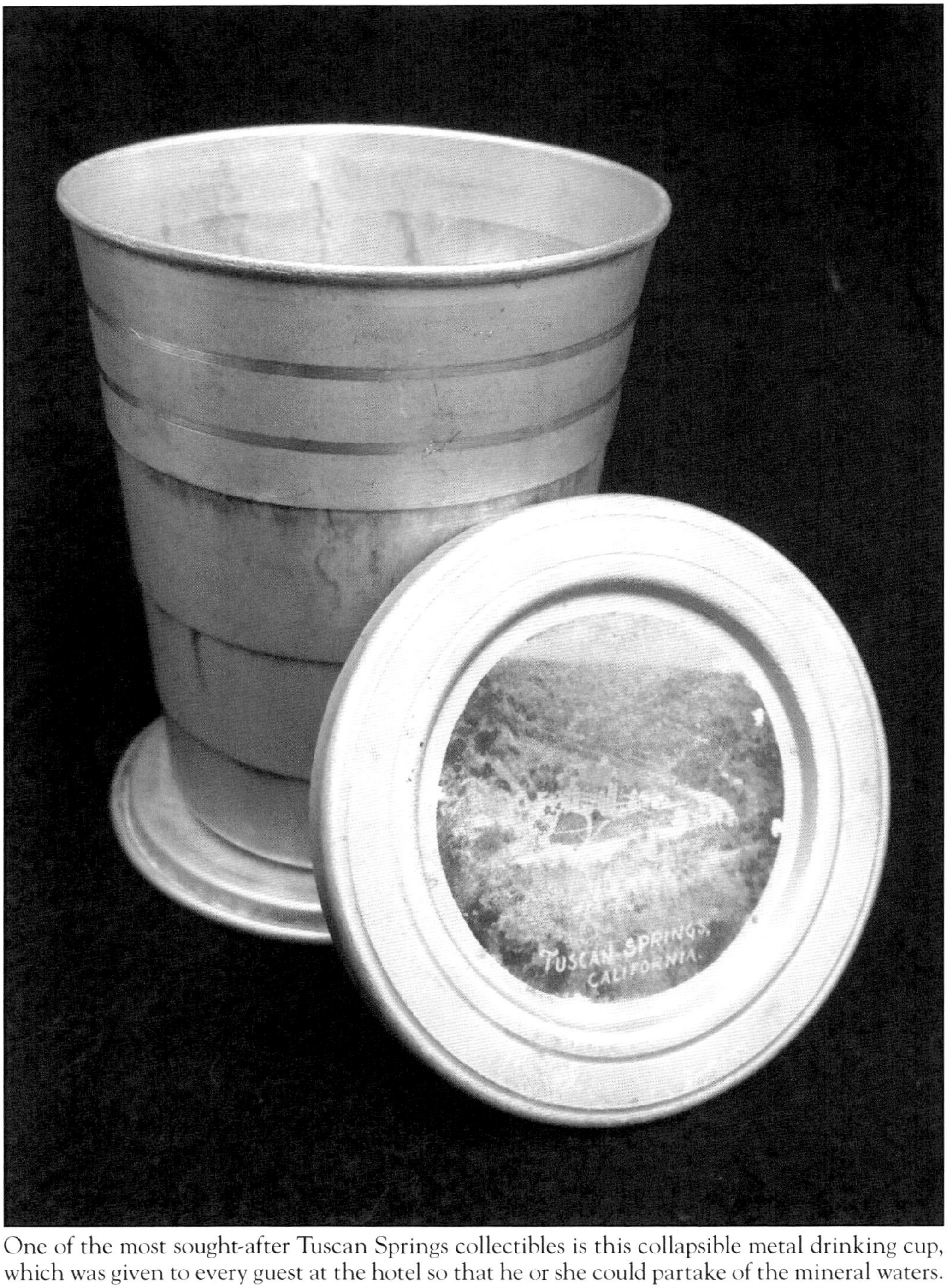

One of the most sought-after Tuscan Springs collectibles is this collapsible metal drinking cup, which was given to every guest at the hotel so that he or she could partake of the mineral waters. The lid bears an image of the resort and the words "Tuscan Springs, California." Early on, visitors would drink from a common tin cup hanging from a rope at each spring, but it may have eventually been determined that sharing a cup with ill people could be very counterproductive, and the resort began providing these take-home souvenirs just after the turn of the century. (Author.)

Five

THE WORST OF TIMES

Walbridge's grand new hotel boasted gas lighting, a telephone, hot and cold running water, two dining rooms and kitchens, a bar, and a post office.

In 1898, spring No. 8 was found to help ease catarrh (a sinus swelling), and Walbridge began dehydrating and bottling its salts. Soon, he was also producing silver polish, cleaning compounds, and stomach and kidney salts, and a lucrative mail-order business had begun.

In 1899, he installed an artificial 12-acre lake and stocked it with fish, ducks, and sailboats. More additions to the hotel had also begun when tragedy struck.

Around 1:00 a.m. on Monday, August 14, 1899, chambermaid Isabelle McKenzie was awakened by the smell of smoke inside the hotel. A roaring sound was heard from the kitchen, an alarm was sounded, and approximately 80 guests were rushed from the building. J.R. Howell, the contractor hired to paint the additions, was blocked from leaving his room by flames. He threw his clothing out his window and jumped, saved from serious injury only by the limbs of a tree. Badly bruised and blistered, he was "compelled to foresake [*sic*] his clothes" in the branches of the burning tree, despite the fact that he was wearing only an undershirt. He was, however, according to the *Daily News*, "able to limp around." A fellow worker, 70-year-old Charles Honeywell, escaped the fire by sliding down some scaffolding with the heat blistering his hands and head. After clearing all the guests, McKenzie returned to her room to gather her belongings, was cut off by a wall of flames, and burned to death. The glow from the inferno could be seen all the way to Red Bluff, and within half an hour, the four-year-old hotel was gone. The blaze was blamed on everything from a defective flue to a leaking gas pipe to a discarded cigarette.

Only the bathhouse, gashouse, a storage building, and four cottages were spared. Overall losses were estimated at $35,000, and the insurance coverage was insufficient. Nonetheless, Walbridge immediately announced his plans to rebuild.

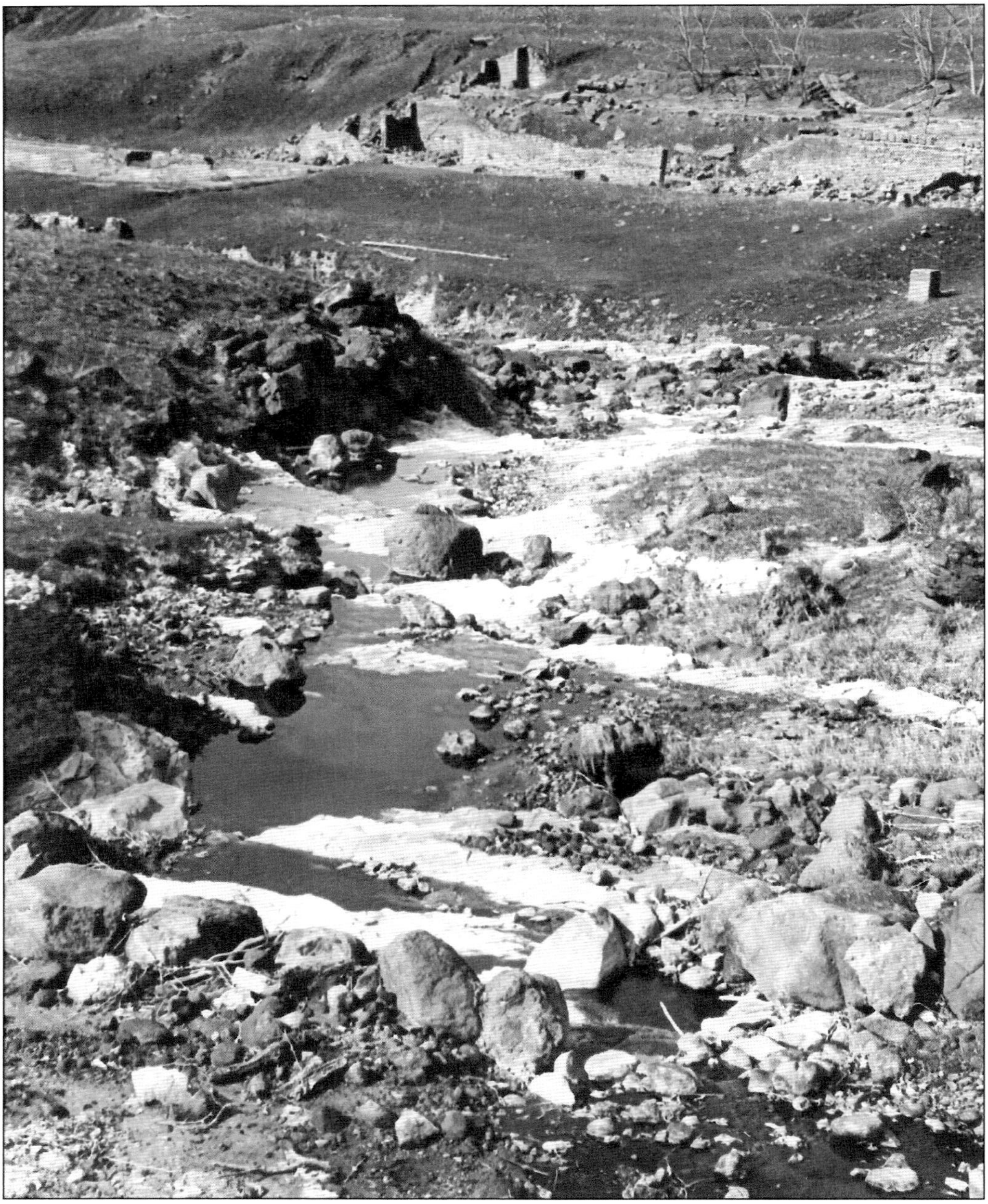

The aptly named Little Salt Creek is seen here running though the Tuscan Springs property. Though it did provide the pleasant background ambience of a babbling brook, the water was so full of salt and bitter minerals that it was unusable for drinking, cooking, or bathing. Providing fresh water to visitors at the resort was a problem from the very beginning, though rain-collection tanks helped to a degree. As patronage continued to increase, the dilemma became so bothersome that Walbridge spent nearly all of 1901 digging for drinkable water on the property. Finally, after boring eight potential wells over as many months, he announced he had hit upon a source in October and set to work blasting and cementing a 10,000-gallon cistern in the nearby rocky buttes with which to contain it. (Bayles.)

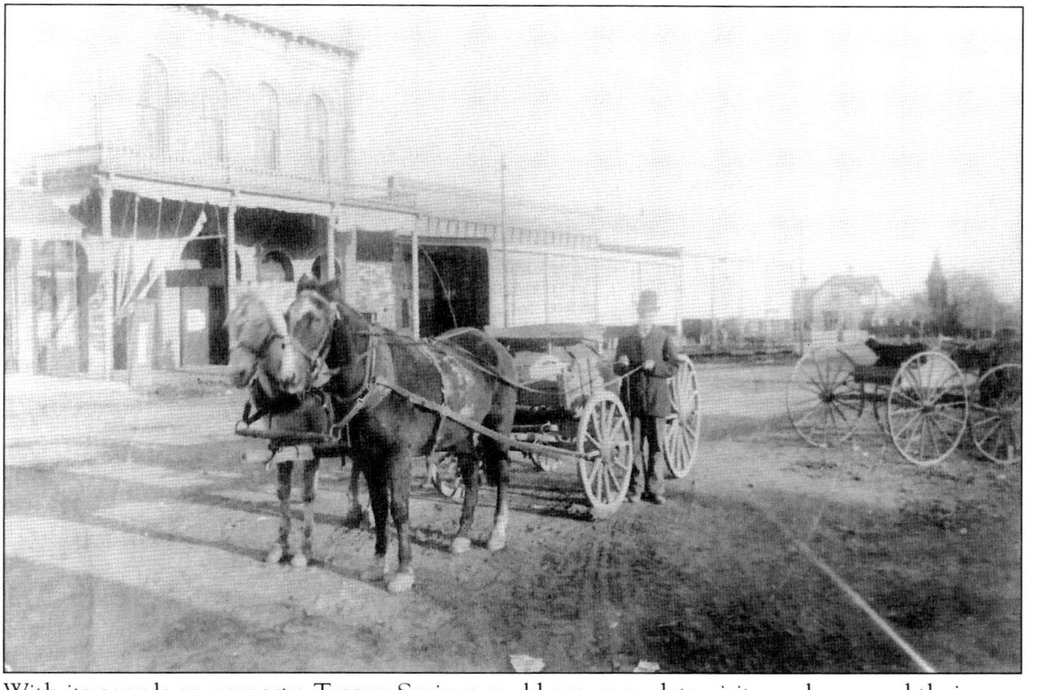

With its corrals on property, Tuscan Springs could accommodate visitors who owned their own horses or carriages (above), still the most popular form of transportation around 1900. But the resort also provided transport by stage, through Freeman's Fashion Stables and, later, Walbridge's own downtown stables. When affordable automobiles were finally in mass production, Walbridge purchased the first autostage to be used in Tehama County. In the photograph below, travelers wait for the Tuscan Springs autostage—which was scheduled to depart daily at 1:00 p.m.—in the park behind the Red Bluff Southern Pacific train depot. (Both, author.)

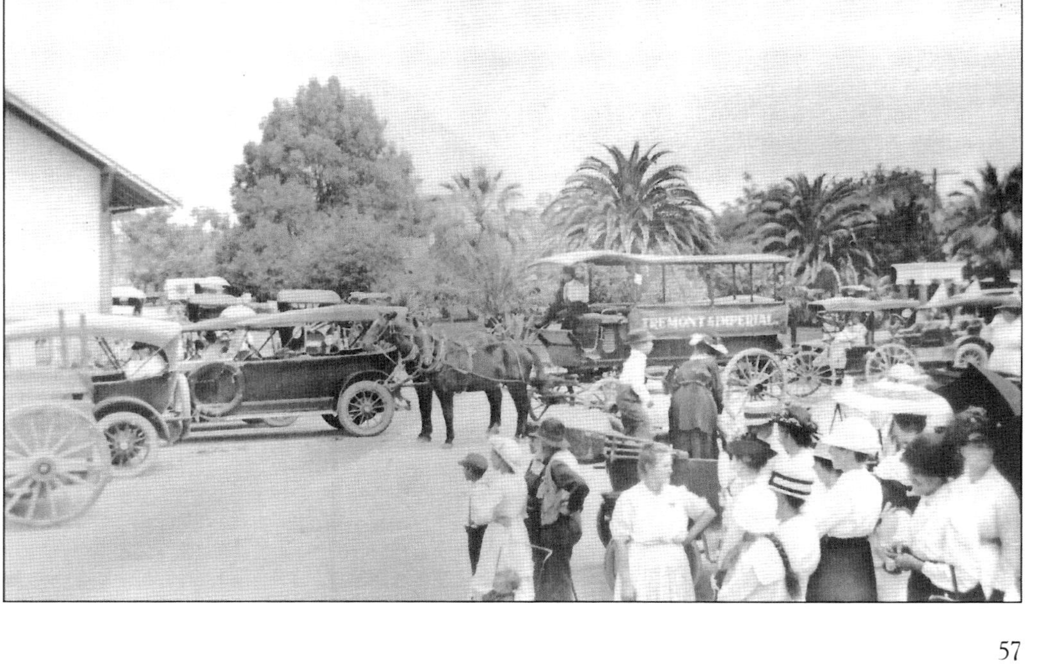

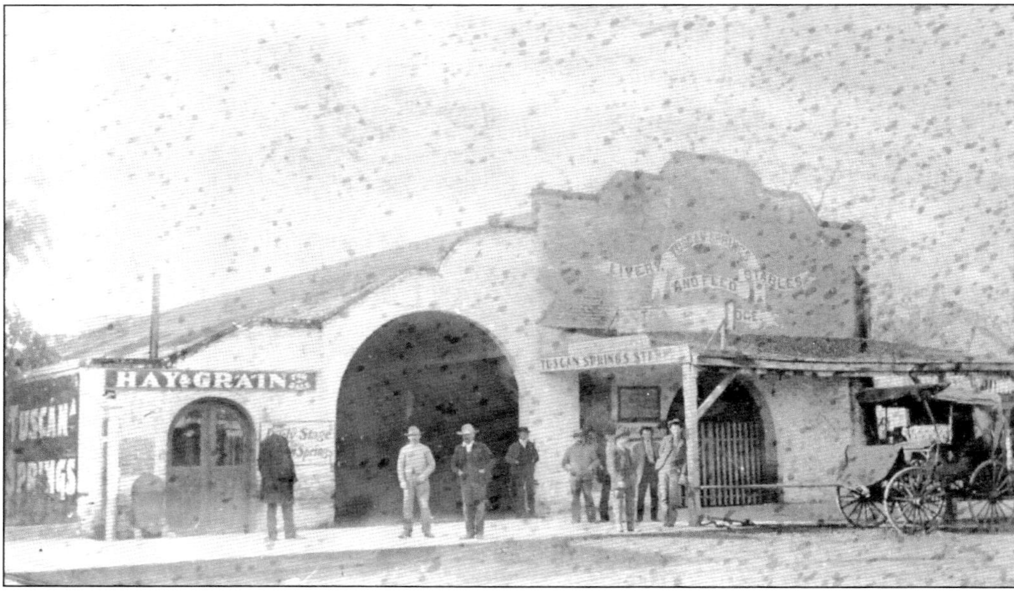

So lucrative was the transportation business that Walbridge finally built the Tuscan Springs Stables on Main Street behind the Bank of Tehama County in Red Bluff. A trip in either direction by horse-drawn stage took nearly three hours; the same trip by later autostage took about one hour. Either method cost only $1 at first. But, when the horse-drawn stages were discontinued, the price of the autostage increased to $6, whether it was carrying only one person or four. Handheld luggage and small bags were free, but larger bags or trunks cost 50¢. (Both, author.)

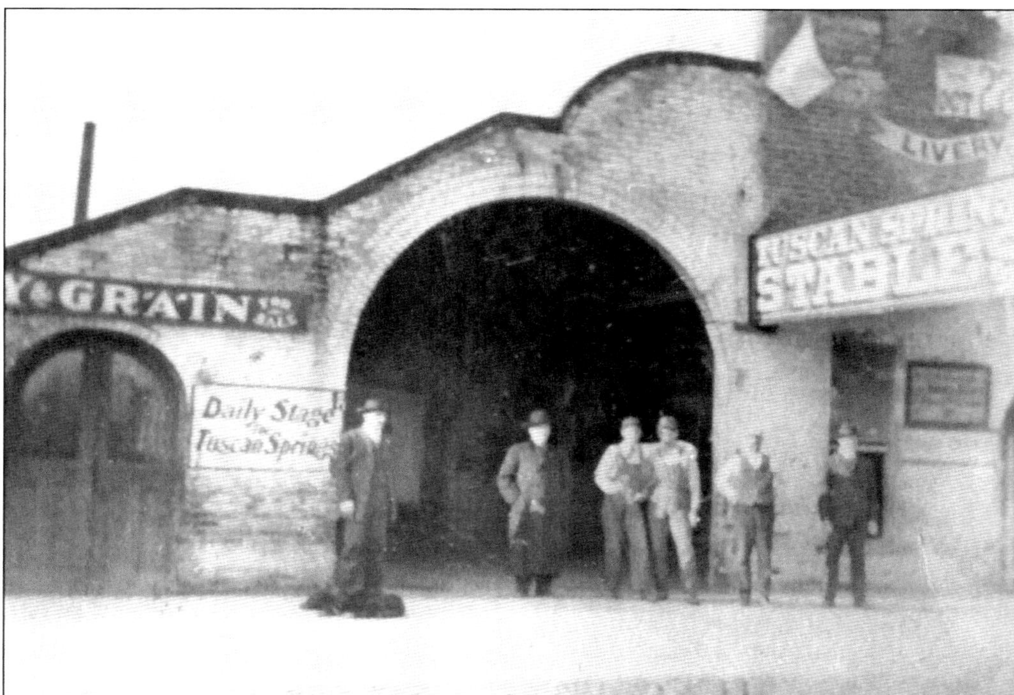

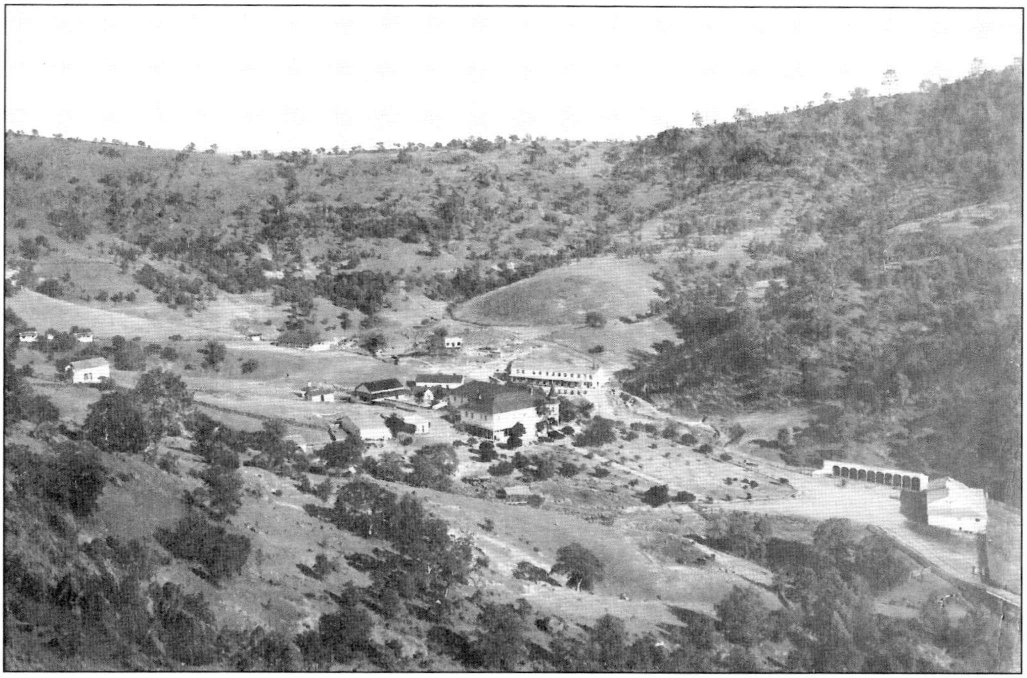

These views from the buttes surrounding the Tuscan Springs property show the layout of the resort. This arrangement of buildings would stay relatively unchanged throughout its history. The L-shaped hotel, built in 1895, was based on Major Bradley's original version. However, it was larger and could accommodate twice as many guests in two stories; it also featured a single cylindrical corner tower. Around the property can be seen the cottages, corral, bathhouse, saloon, and other buildings. The same year it was constructed, the resort was granted a US charter for a post office on the property. (Both, author.)

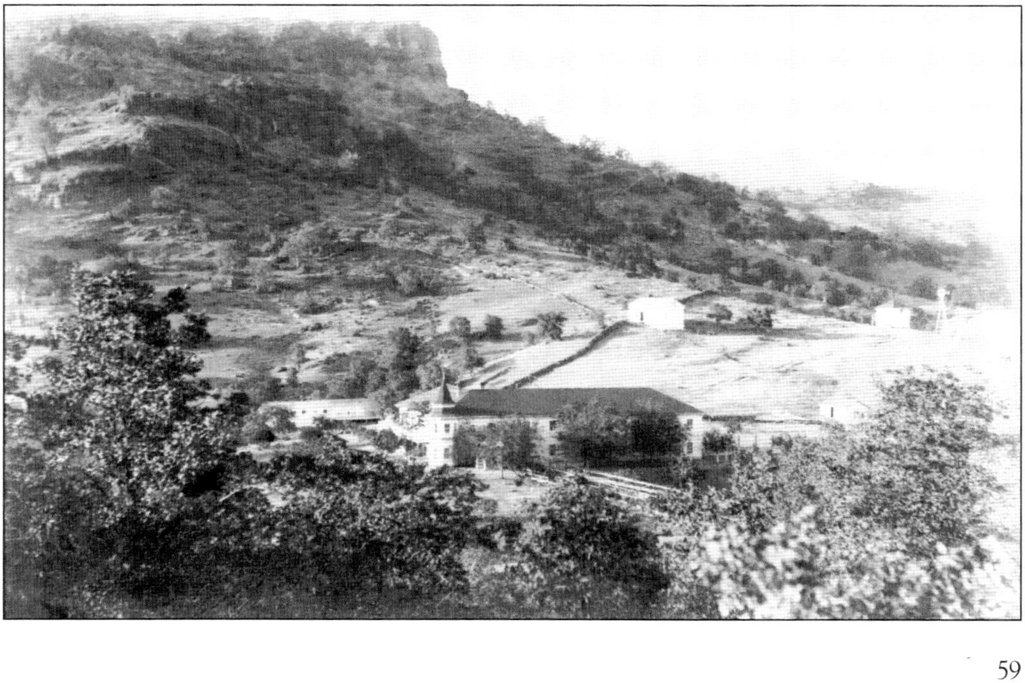

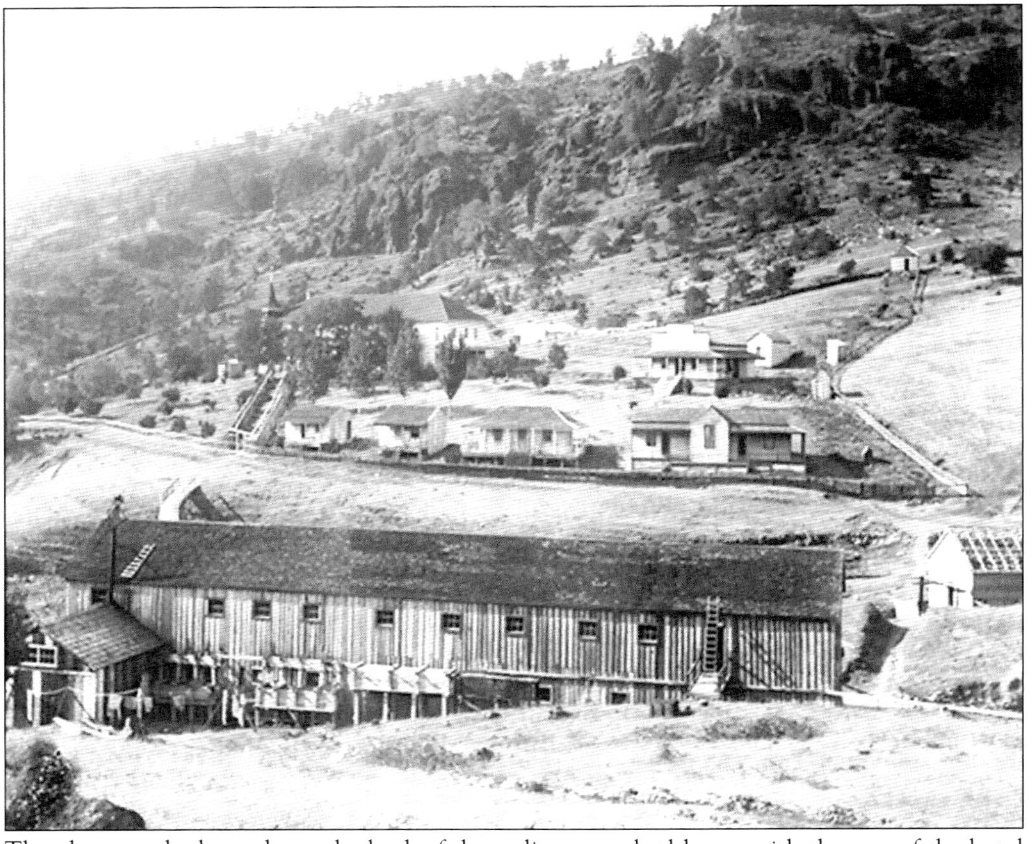

The photograph above shows the back of the rudimentary bathhouse with the rear of the hotel in the distance. Beside the bathhouse could usually be seen large piles of wood, used to fuel the cottage stoves and to help heat the steam baths. The building with the white, rectangular front behind the hotel is the saloon and billiards room. This bathhouse burned down in 1904. The photograph below shows a climber on the rocky buttes that surrounded the resort. Aside from hunting, croquet, bowling, gambling, and bathing, climbing the nearby hills and exploring their caves was a popular pastime among visitors. (Both, author.)

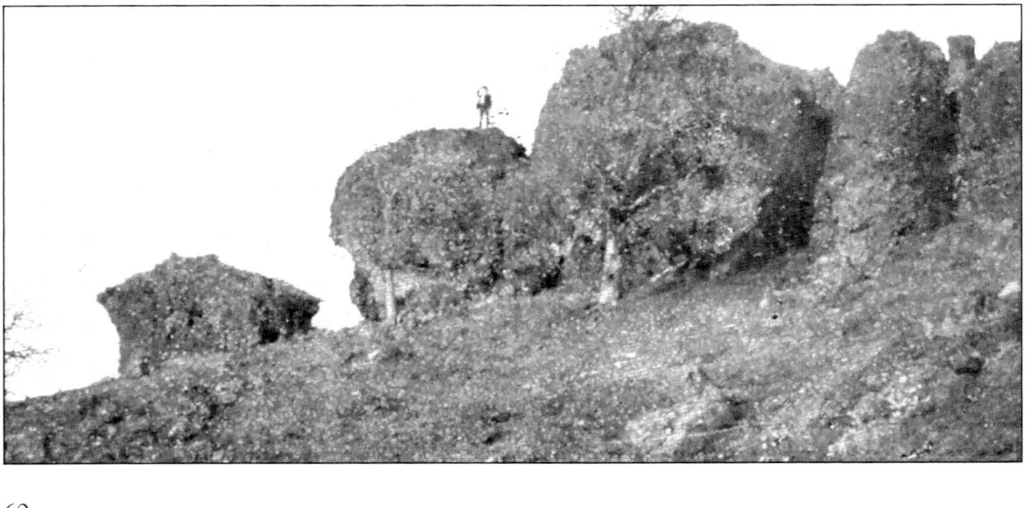

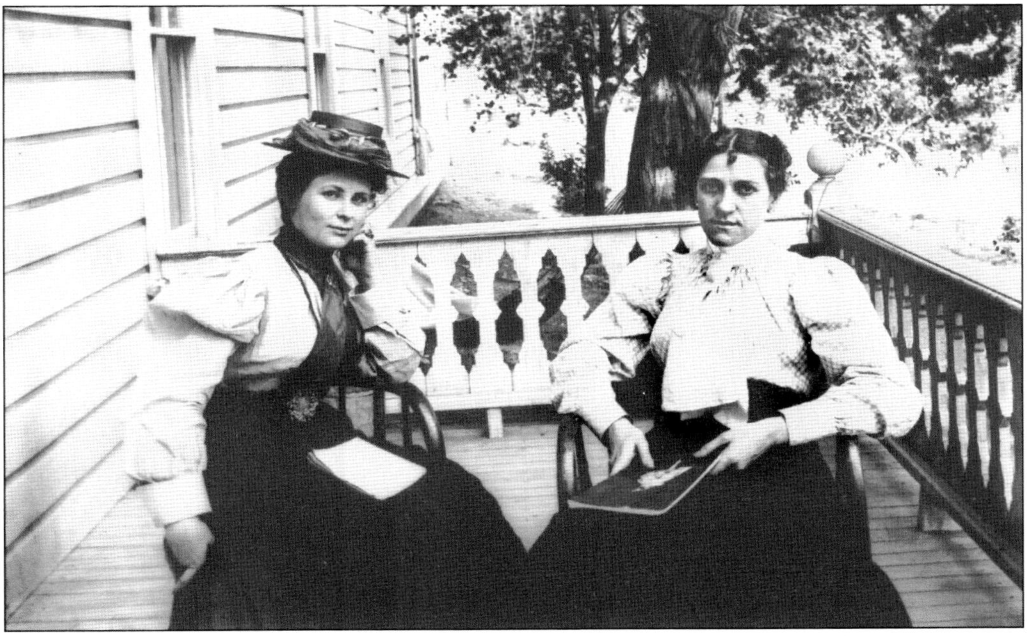

Here, a Miss Foster (left) and a Mrs. Waldron enjoy some morning reading and conversation on a shaded patio of the hotel. This glass-plate photograph was taken by James F. Morehead on June 20, 1898. (CSUC.)

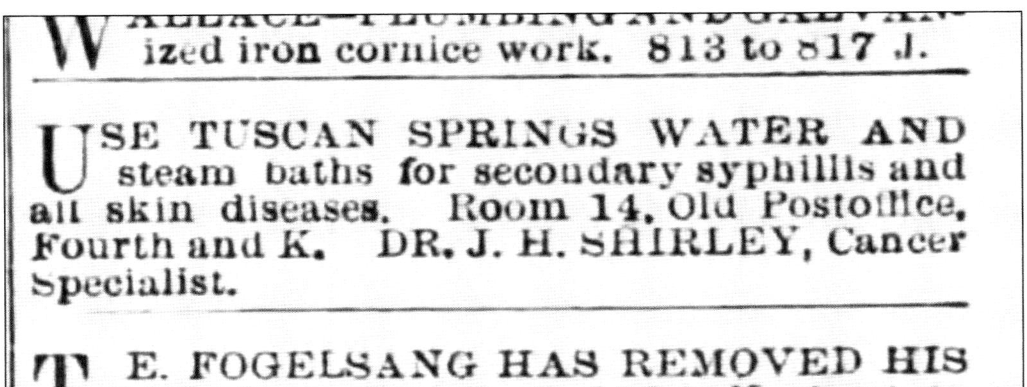

W ized iron cornice work. 813 to 817 J.

USE TUSCAN SPRINGS WATER AND steam baths for secondary syphilis and all skin diseases. Room 14, Old Postoffice, Fourth and K. DR. J. H. SHIRLEY, Cancer Specialist.

T E. FOGELSANG HAS REMOVED HIS

This newspaper advertisement printed in the *Sacramento Record Union* on June 10, 1895, promises the mineral waters of Tuscan Springs will cure even advanced syphilis "and all skin diseases." So-called working women from Sacramento, San Francisco, and other faraway urban areas were widely known to take the steamboat to Red Bluff specifically to visit Tuscan Springs in the hopes that they could remedy their various "professional afflictions" in the waters of its springs. (Author.)

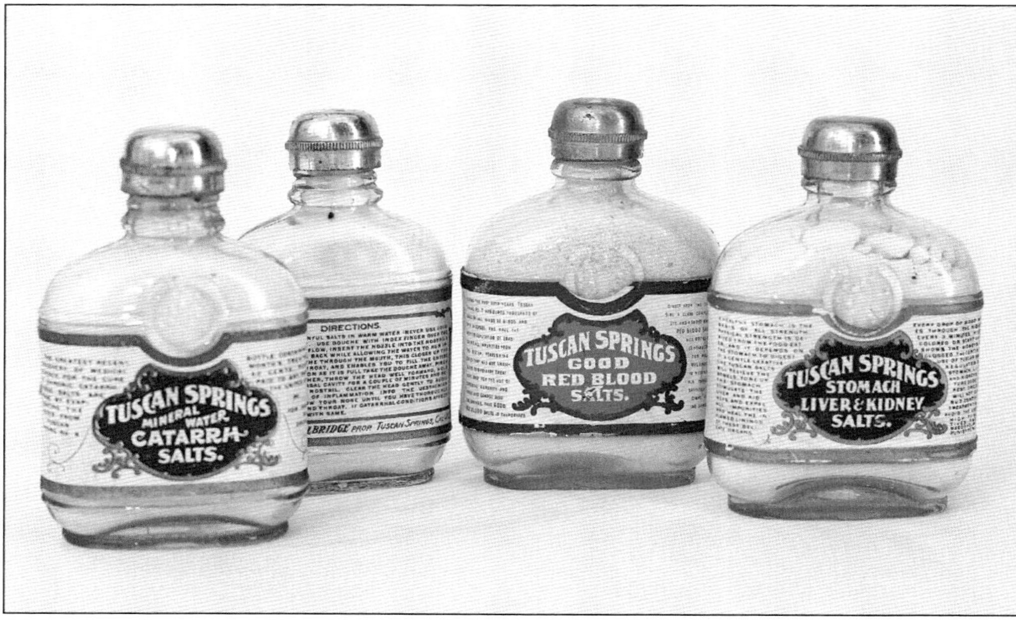

In 1898, spring No. 8 was found to help with catarrh, a sinus swelling, and Walbridge began selling its evaporated salts pictured above. This brought in an additional $5,000 profit the first year (five months of hotel proceeds equal to $138,000 today)—so he started selling other products, even offering bottled water straight from the springs, launching a very successful mail-order business. The bottle label below instructs users to consume one teaspoon of the stomach, liver, and kidney salts in hot water four times a day, one before each meal, and one at bedtime. "Nature needs help," the label reads, "not punishment." (Both, author.)

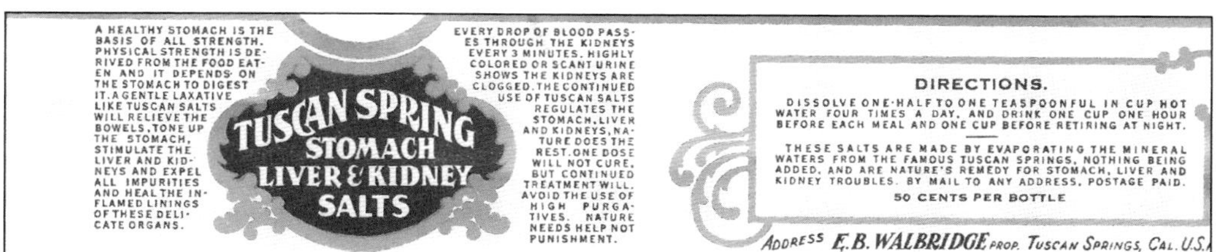

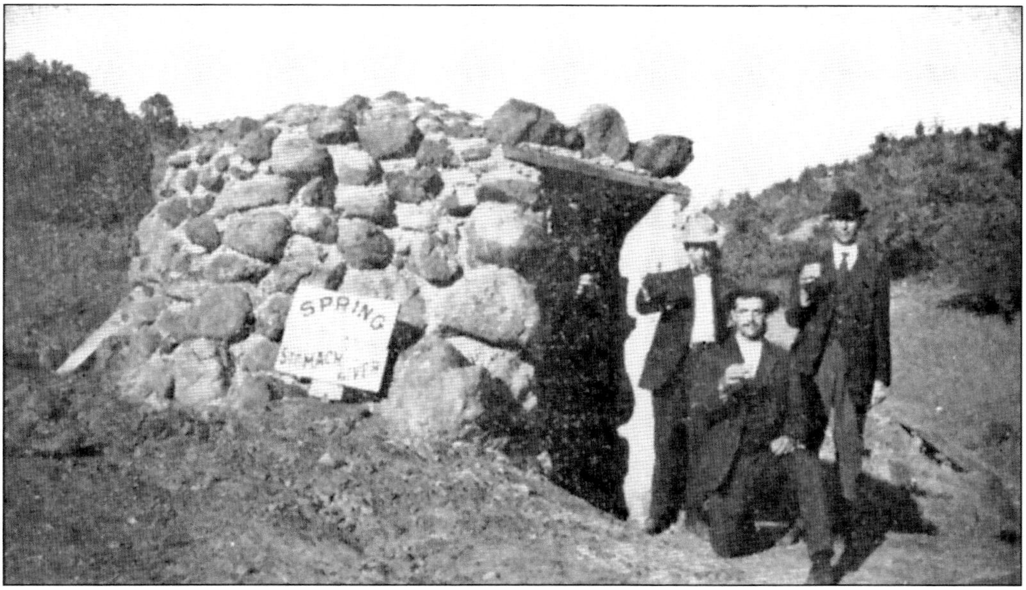

Above, three unidentified men gather for a publicity photograph near spring No. 27, the "stomach and liver" spring, around 1910. Below, the same three men pose at spring No. 25, the "stomach affections" spring. In both images, the men are seen toasting with the collapsible metal drinking cups that were provided by the tavern. These photographs are used in Walbridge's *Let Others Tell The Story* mailer pamphlet from around 1911, which was available through the post for free by sending a request to simply "E.B. Walbridge—Tuscan Springs, California." (Both, author.)

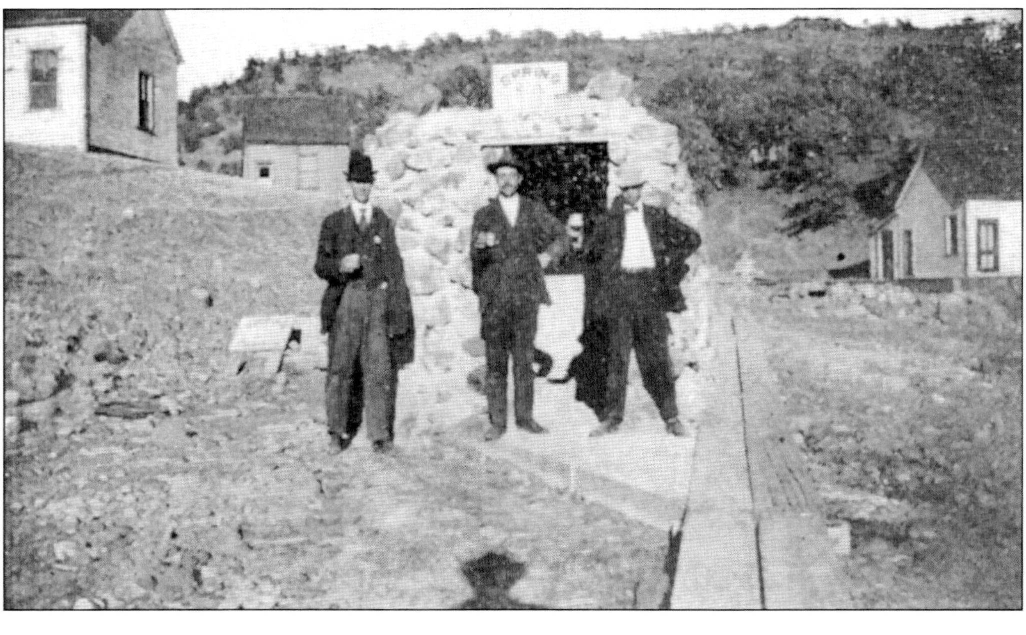

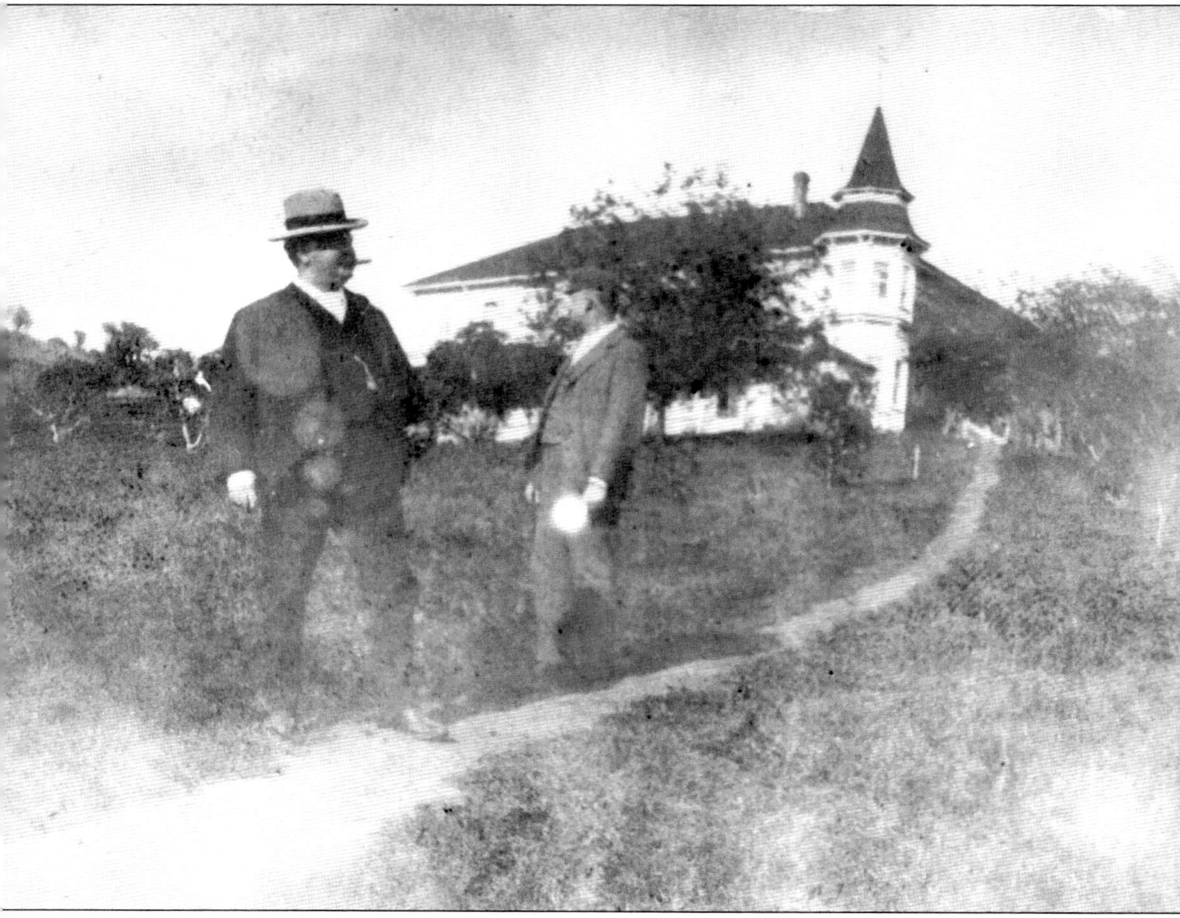

This is one of only three photographs known to exist of Edgerton Walbridge. Taken between 1896 and 1899, it shows the proprietor enjoying a cigar as he surveys his estate. A handwritten note on the back of the photograph claims that his companion is a "midget bodyguard who was a crack shot with either hand." The glint in his left hand is reportedly his pistol. The problems with raids by Native Americans near the resort (which had plagued former owner Meredith Meador until he sold the property) had gradually disappeared with the relocation and elimination of the area's tribes, but catering to the ill, desperate, and sometimes disgruntled could require protection, especially considering that a previous owner, Major Bradley, had been the victim of a fatal gunshot. (Author.)

Six

Defying Fortune's Spite

Walbridge declared in October 1899 that he had received the blueprints for the new hotel, and construction began by the end of the year while guests were accommodated in the bathhouse. During this time, the Southern Pacific Railroad, eying huge potential profit, offered Walbridge $100,000 for the property. Considering the recent increases in income, he held out for $125,000, but the railroad declined, and construction continued through completion in November at a cost of $60,000.

The new centerpiece of the resort was a true monument to Mark Twain's *Gilded Age*. Using half a million feet of lumber, the new three-story tavern featured two distinctly mismatched corner towers and included between 126 and 130 rooms (holding up to 200 guests). Any room could be used as a single or combined into a suite, and all opened onto large verandas. Additionally, the structure featured a reception area and dining room, each 2,500 square feet, as well as a parlor, card rooms, reading rooms, a ballroom, and ample fire escapes.

Providing fresh water to the isolated location was an obstacle from the earliest days as every drop within miles was tainted with minerals. In 1900, Walbridge had 16,000 pounds of iron pipe shipped by steamboat and delivered to the resort for the specific purpose of piping water. Through most of 1901, he was digging well after well on his property searching for said water, and finally, in October, he reported he had found it. He spent the following month arranging to have a 10,000-gallon cistern blasted from a hill 200 feet above the hotel. Water would be piped into the cistern and, from there, run to the hotel, stables, and grounds using an engine powered by natural gas.

In 1902, Walbridge was digging well after well in search of more natural gas. Doubtless tired from all the excavation, fires, and frustrations, he finally decided, after 16 years, that it might be best to just get out of the hotel business altogether. At the beginning of 1903, he listed the land for sale.

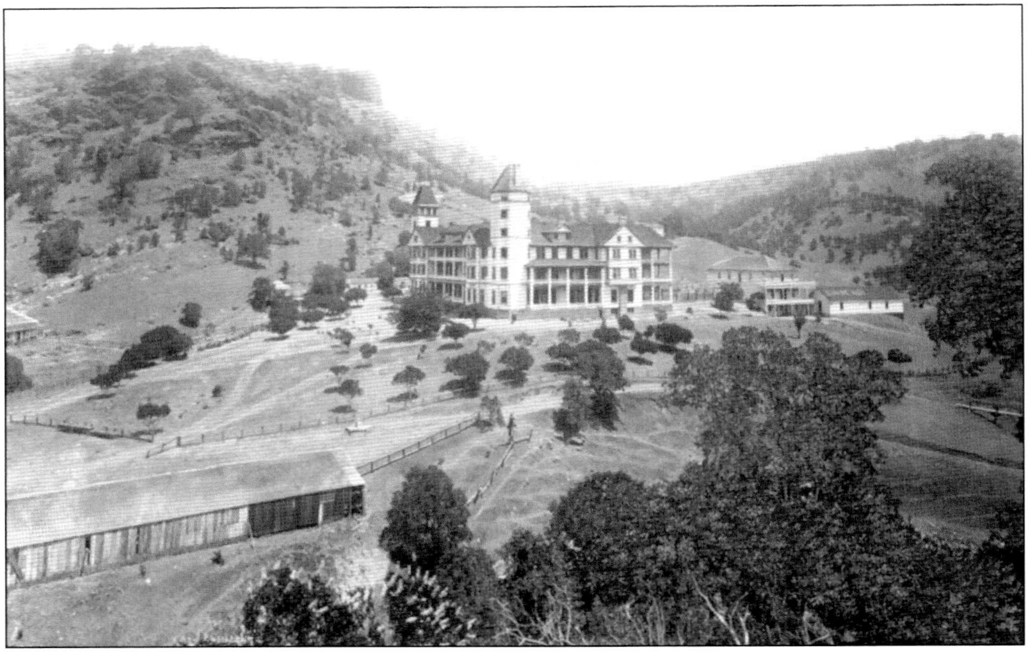

Walbridge's new tavern, built after the fire of August 14, 1899, was even bigger and more elaborate than the last. At 260 feet wide by 120 feet deep and three stories tall, with two uniquely mismatched corner towers, it had rooms for up to 200 guests. Completed in November 1900 at a cost of about $60,000 (nearly $2 million today), it also included a reception area and dining room, both 2,500 square feet, a large kitchen, reading rooms, a ladies' parlor, a card room, and a post office. In 1901, rooms were renting for $10 and up per week, including meals. (Both, author.)

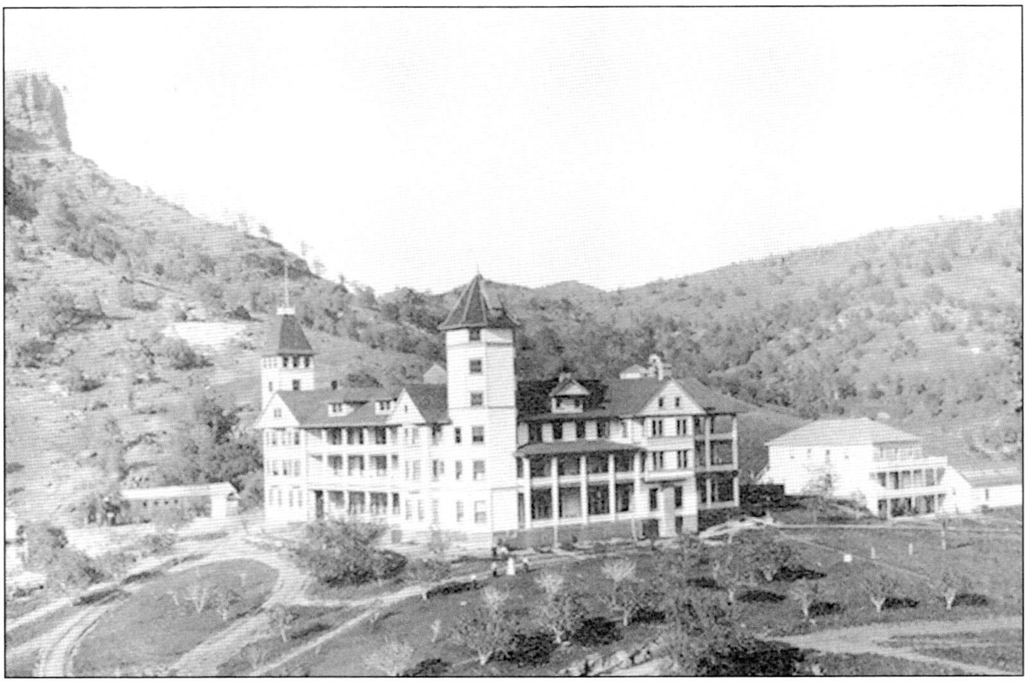

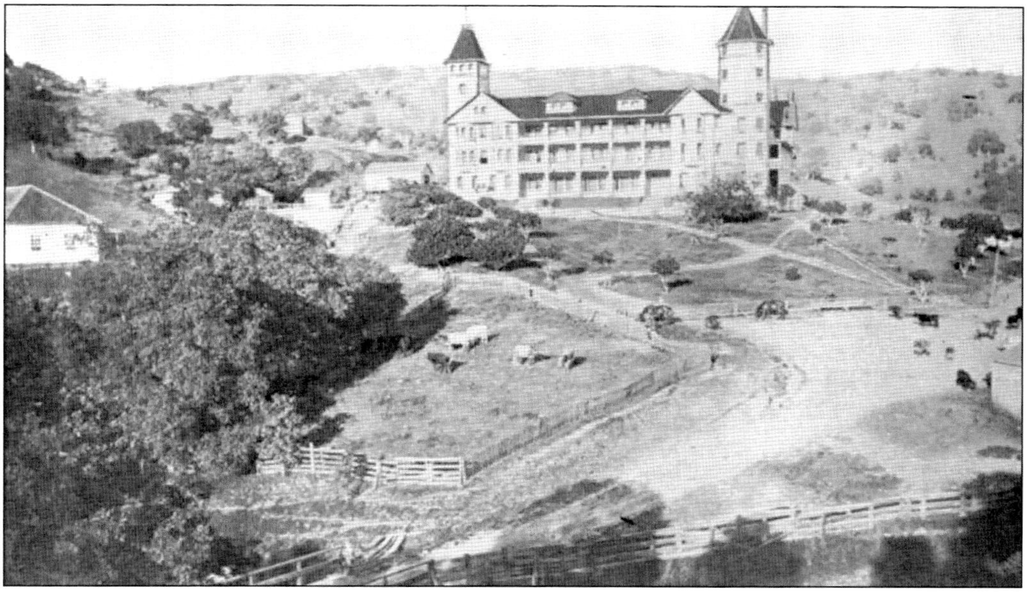

Cows, pigs, chickens, goats, and sheep were allowed free range in the fenced areas of the property, including the front yard of the tavern, and even wandered inside from time to time if not watched carefully. They provided much of the meat, milk, and eggs enjoyed at the resort. The back of the tavern (seldom seen in photographs) featured numerous fire escape ramps that ran from the upper stories to the ground on each side of the building. By 1899, Walbridge had lost two businesses to fires, which continued to destroy buildings in Tehama County almost annually. Below, workers collect the morning milk from the Tuscan cows. (Both, author.)

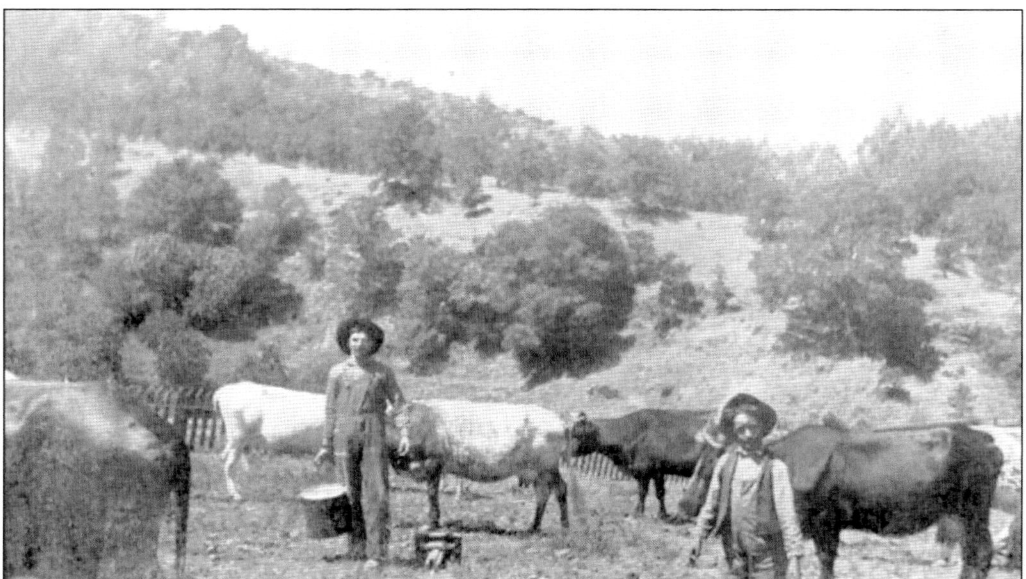

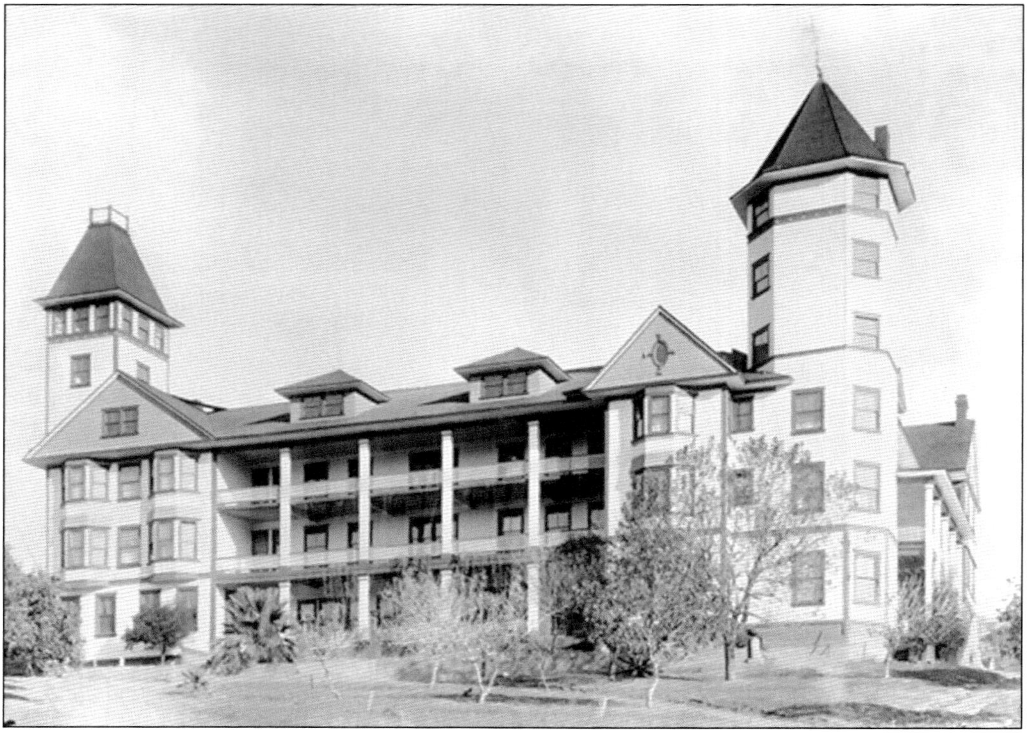

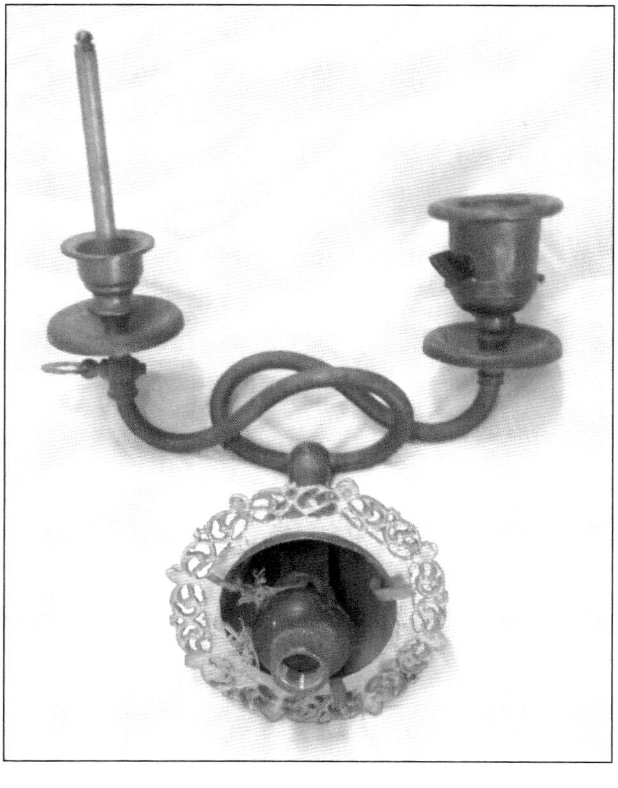

Natural gas had been used at Tuscan Springs as early as 1859, when the *Sacramento Union* noted the resort was the first it had seen to pipe natural gas from the springs to heat the water used for vapor and steam baths. However, Walbridge's new tavern also offered electrical lighting, which had only been introduced in Tehama County two years before construction. Oddly, both gas and electricity were fed through the same sconces (seen from the wall side in the photograph left), which seems a potentially volatile combination; however, the pairing was never reported as the cause of any fires. (Above, author; left, NCT.)

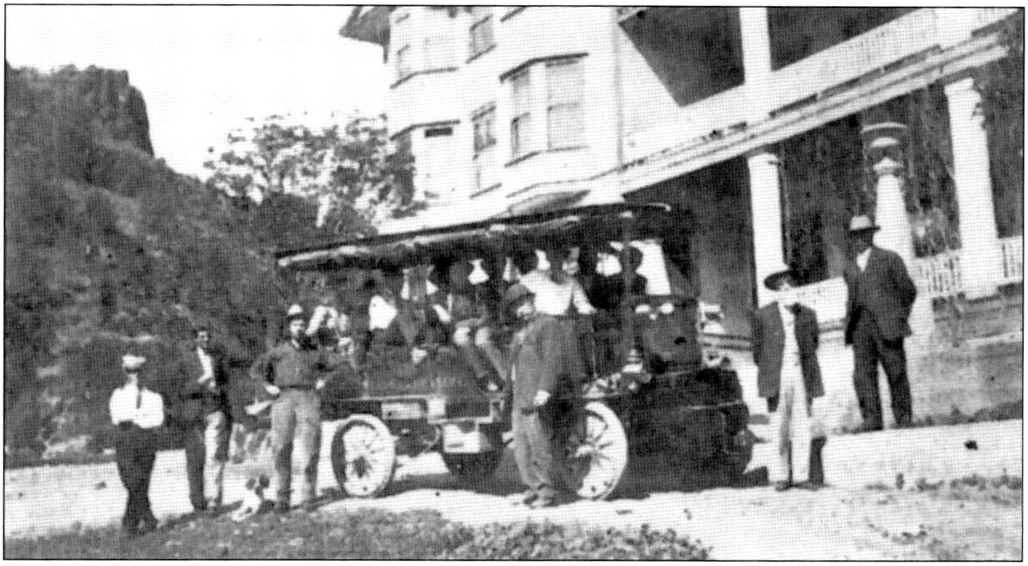

Unidentified men are seen here in front of the tavern with the Tuscan Springs autocoach (possibly a Knox Transport) around 1910. The hand-cranked coach, which could carry four passengers and baggage comfortably, was the preferred method of transportation in summer as it made for shorter trips in the Tehama County sun, where temperatures could reach 120 degrees. The automobile was not as reliable on winter rural roads, however, so those months were reserved for horse stages. In 1900, the automobile was still "a rich man's toy," and there were only 8,000 in the United States; however, within 20 years, it had mostly replaced animal transportation. (Both, author.)

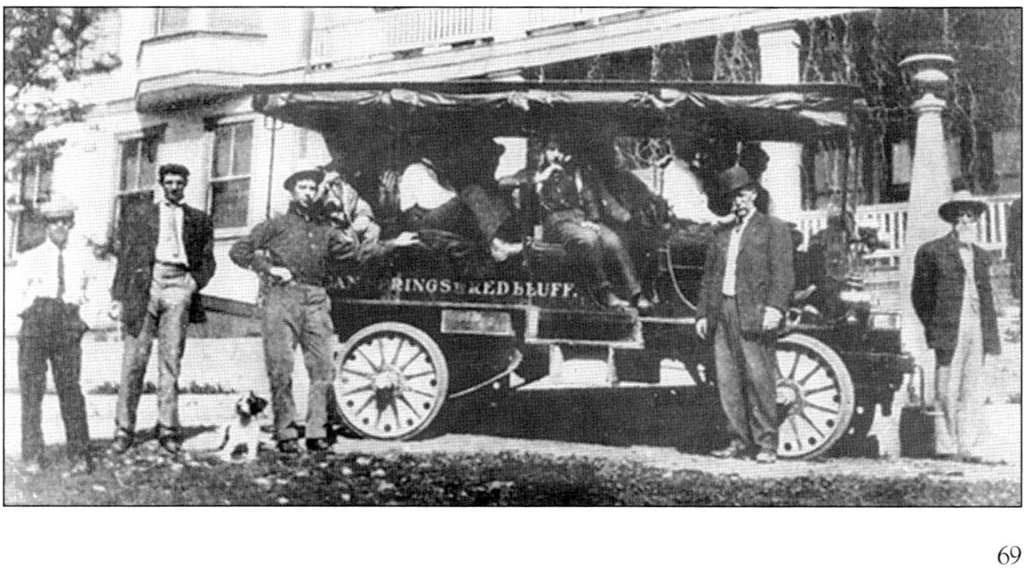

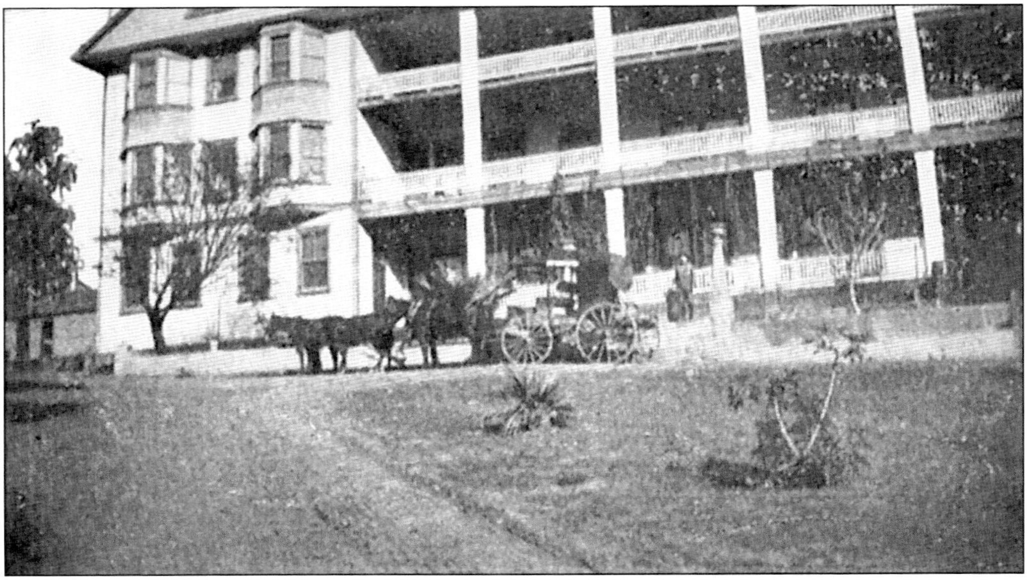

The old standby coach, above, awaits passengers at the tavern entrance. Though not as smooth or fast, it was infinitely better in bad weather and significantly less expensive, and no one ever risked breaking an arm from improperly cranking the horses. Below is the clubhouse of the resort (left), which offered billiards, poker, drinks, and haircuts for men. Behind it is the bowling alley, one of the later additions to the resort. The rules for American tenpin bowling were established in 1895, and it had become incredibly popular across the country, which may be the reason the building is so prominently labeled. (Both, author.)

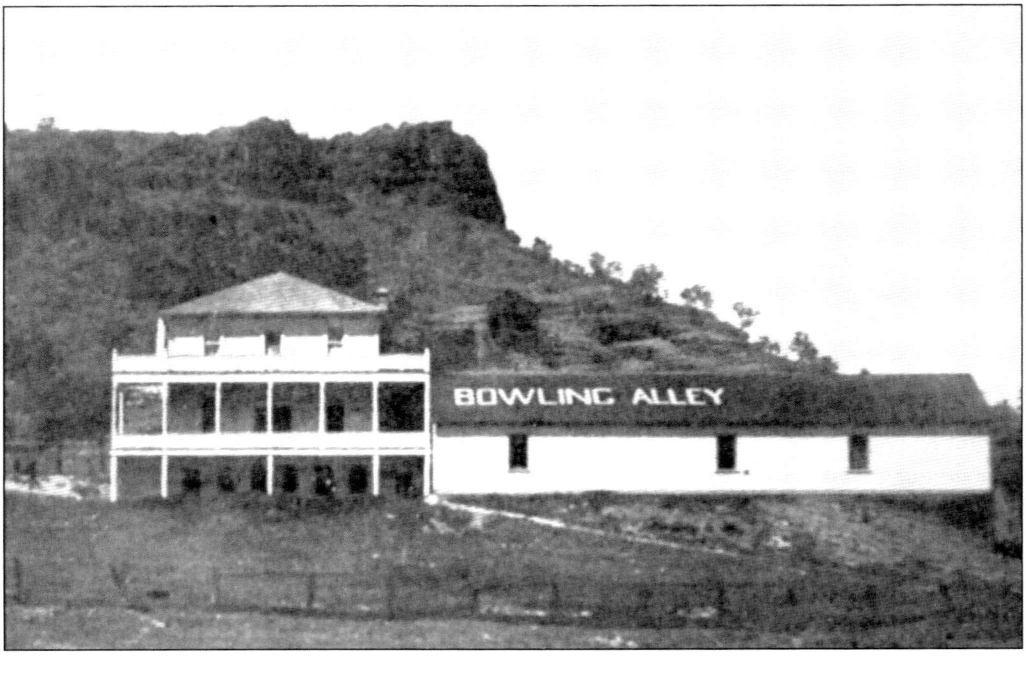

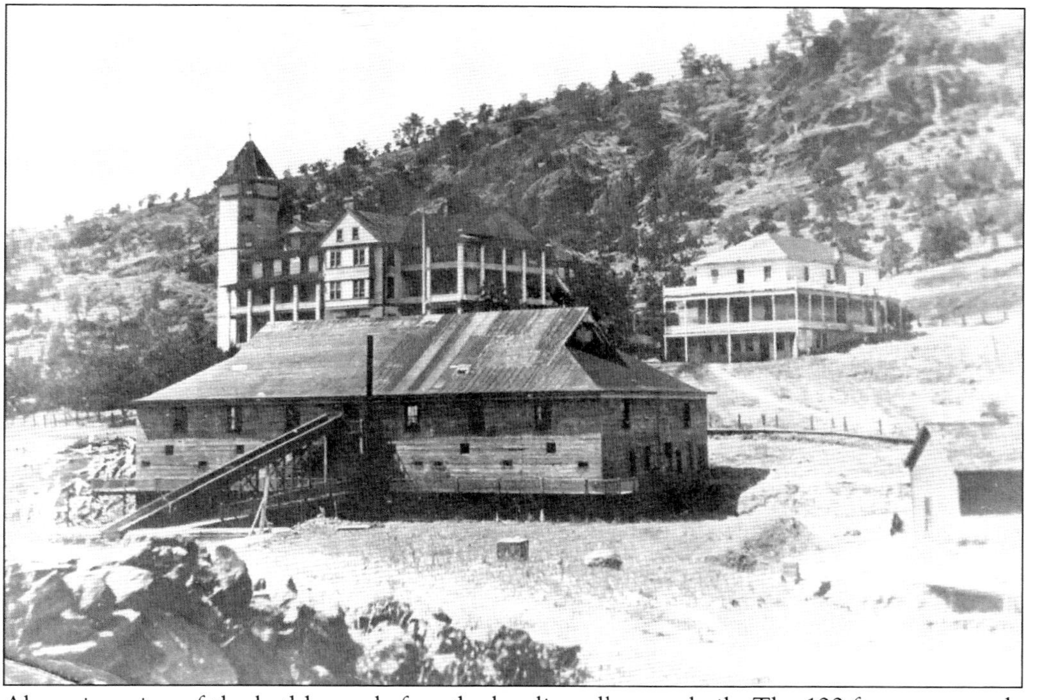

Above is a view of the bathhouse before the bowling alley was built. The 100-foot ramp made it convenient for guests to quickly alternate between the cold baths indoors and the hot plunge bath outside. This form of hydrotherapy was thought to boost circulation and stimulate the release of toxicity. The image below shows the same building after having been whitewashed a few years later. Though it does not look it in the photographs, the structure was actually three stories tall (the pool was higher than the building's ground floor) and measured 54 feet wide by 116 feet long. (Both, author.)

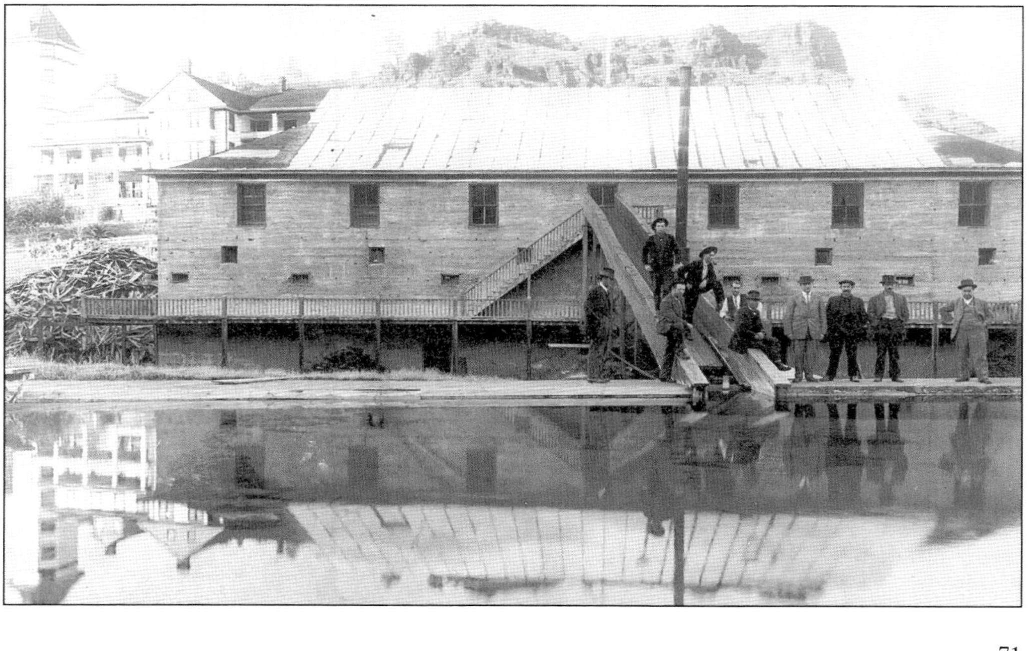

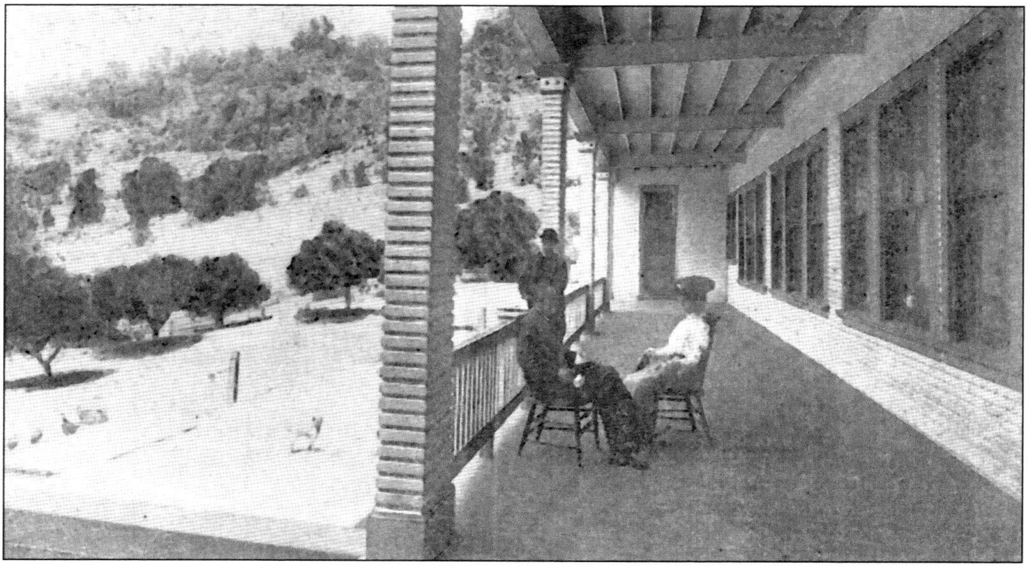

These photographs show three guests enjoying shelter from the noontime sun on the wraparound verandas at the rear of the tavern. Lazy hours could be pleasantly spent conversing there while watching the chickens peck the yard for food or watching patrons travel to and from the bathhouse (in the background of the image below). The ample and covered verandas were a marked improvement over the narrow patios of the previous hotel—where shade came mainly from nearby trees and only at certain times of the day—especially considering the heavy layering of Victorian-era clothing. (Both, author.)

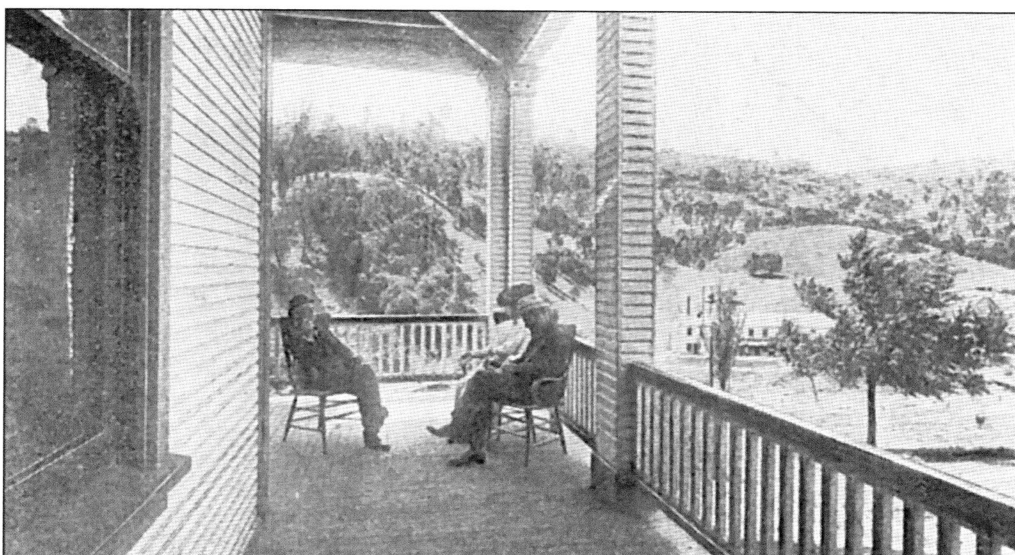

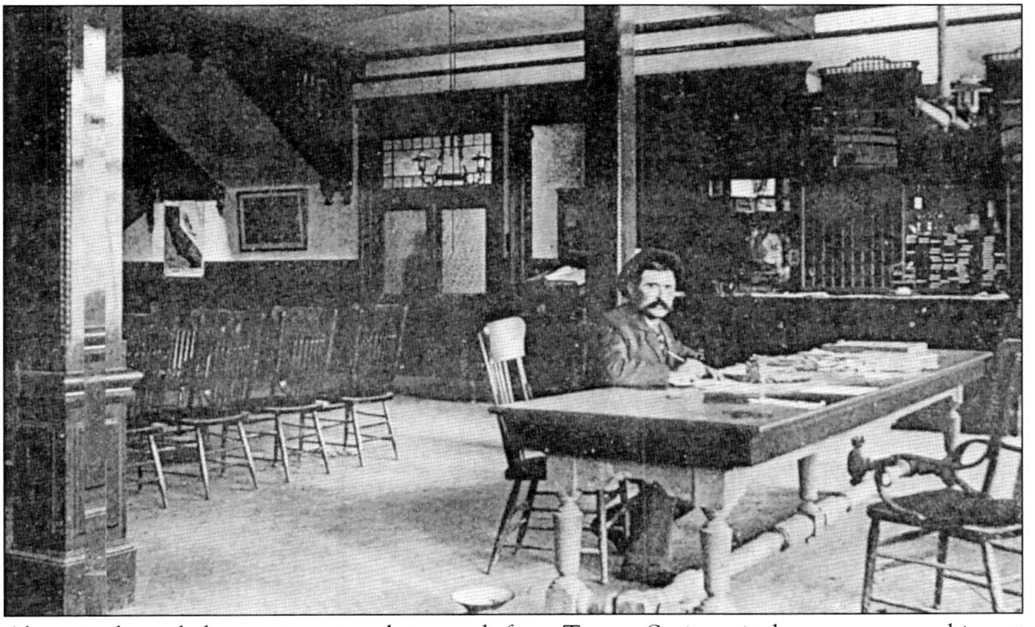

Above is the only known interior photograph from Tuscan Springs; it shows a man working at a desk in the tavern. He may be hotel clerk Frank Atkinson, the person on duty when the hotel burned a few years later, and the area to the right may be the tavern's front desk or post office. License to operate a post office was maintained until May 15, 1919, the year Walbridge's daughter was awarded half his estate. The extended licensing and the fact that Martha Walbridge had paid off her mortgage and regained title to the property in 1917 indicate that she hoped to reopen the resort. Below is a view looking north at the tavern. (Both, author.)

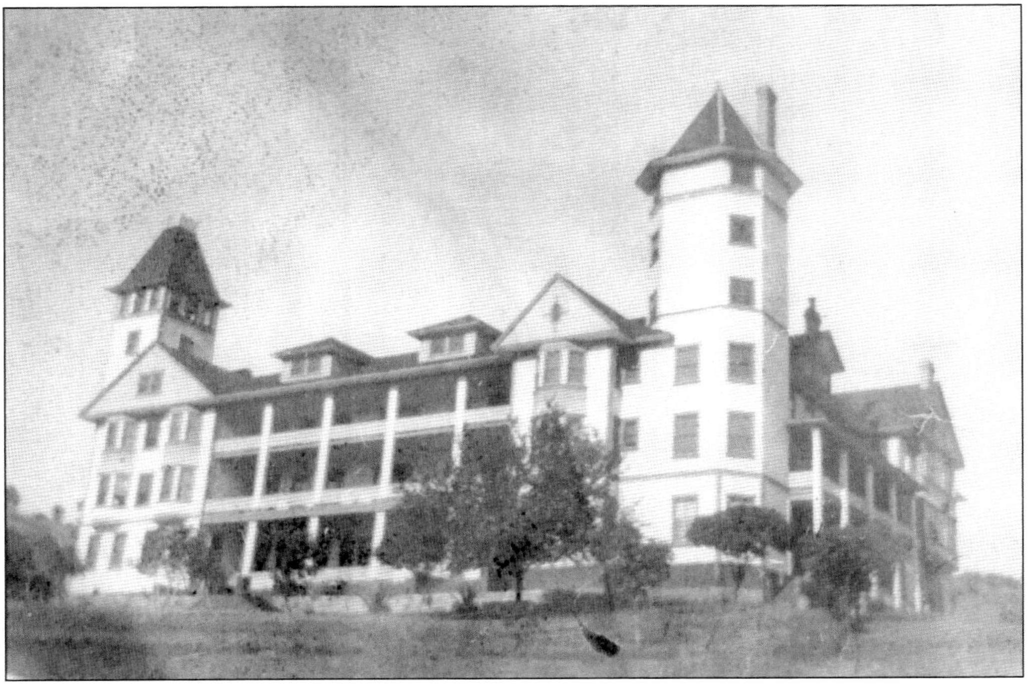

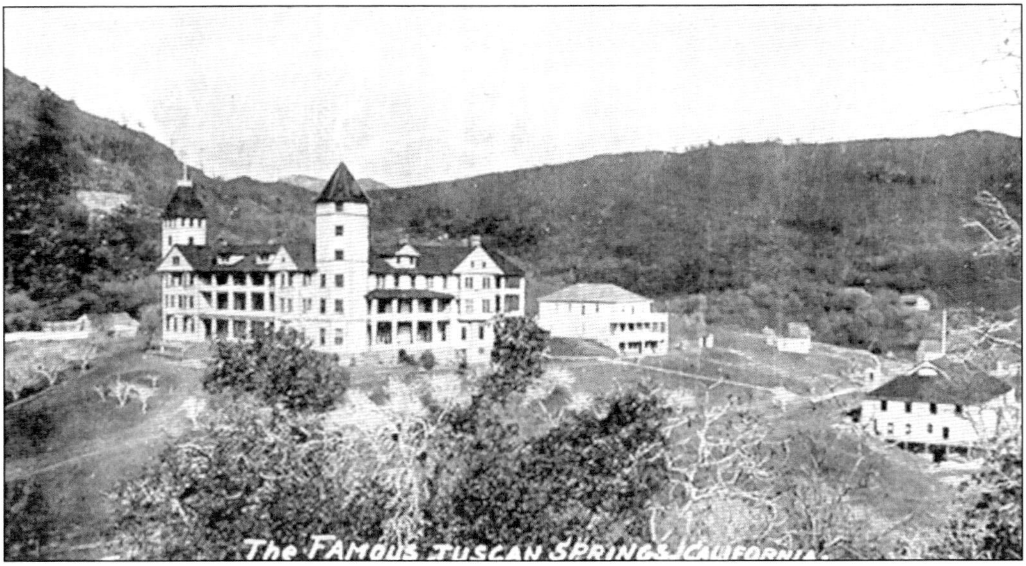

These photographs were taken just a couple of years apart. The above was for a magazine advertisement around 1903; the below, from around 1905, shows some minor landscaping changes and the addition of the bowling alley. The structure to the left of the tavern in each photograph is likely where the Walbridges lived, though a portion of the building may also have been the residence of other staff, including the resort physician. The salaried doctor was constantly on call and was present when guests arrived, to determine their afflictions and provide a diagnosis card instructing them which springs to drink from, which baths to use, and how often. (Both, author.)

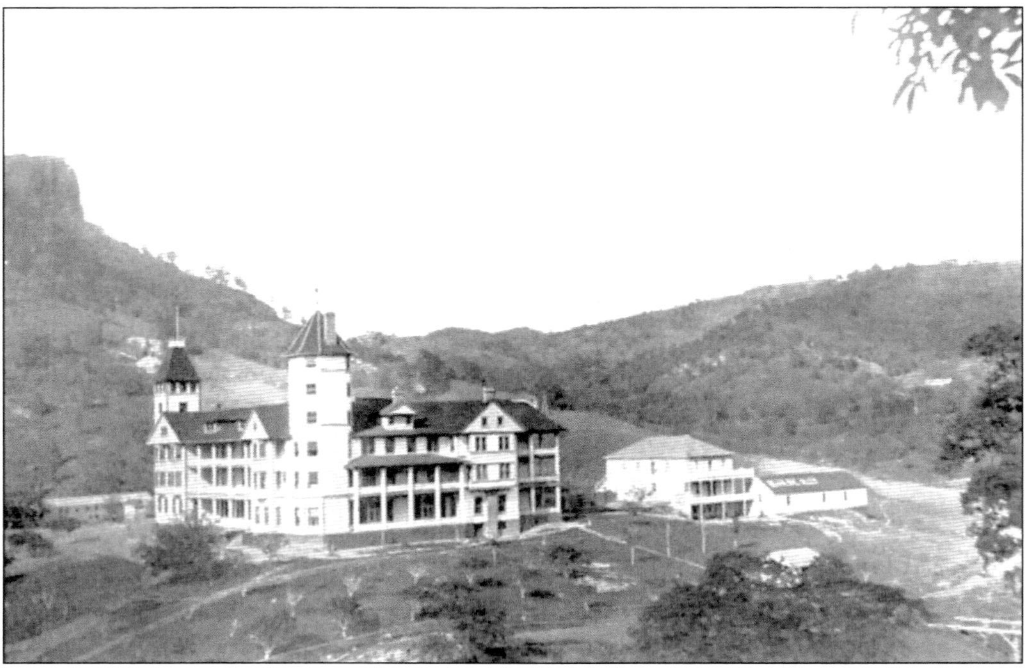

Seven

Of Mice and (Mad) Men

Having solved his fresh-water problem by arranging to pipe it from the Sierra Flume, Walbridge had no trouble finding interested buyers for his modern hotel.

On July 20, 1903, a lease-to-buy arrangement was made with the Tuscan Mineral Springs Corporation (TMSC), composed of Portland doctors, politicians, and businessmen, and organized by Frank J. Hellen, a retired spa regular. The corporation immediately announced major changes—including bathhouse renovations and plans for a trolley system from Red Bluff—and launched an unprecedented promotional campaign.

Then, quite suddenly, in September 1904, Hellen simply disappeared. By October, the TMSC was publicly searching for its levanting manager as debtors came calling for $6,500 in bills. On October 13, Hellen was tracked to a San Francisco hotel, where he was awaiting a boat to Honolulu. He told the *Daily News* he had left because of poor health and blamed Walbridge for all the "lies" being spread.

On November 11, the TMSC filed an unexpected $11,000 suit against Walbridge, claiming springs 5, 8, and 15 had not been fixed as agreed but only salted to appear active. Hellen also filed a $10,000 libel lawsuit against Walbridge, insisting all accusations about his "insolvency, lack of responsibility and flight from debts" were malicious.

However, when Hellen was found to be all of those things, both lawsuits were dropped.

Despite the grief, Walbridge had learned much from Hellen's use of print advertisements, pamphlets, and branding, and all promotional materials surviving today began with Hellen. Now reinvigorated, Walbridge determined to refrain from ever again leasing the resort. To ensure he would never lose his crucial bathhouse again, he built a concrete version in 1905.

By 1906, both national popularity of mineral waters and Walbridge's income were at all-time highs. By 1913, all obstacles were behind him, and the 54-year-old could finally begin to enjoy a little leisure time. That October, however, while visiting his Red Bluff garage, Walbridge suddenly became disoriented and backed out. He was rushed unconscious to the local Sisters' Hospital.

IMPORTANT ANNOUNCEMENT!

Change in the Ownership and Management
of

TUSCAN MINERAL SPRINGS

Located nine miles northeast of Red Bluff on the line of the Southern Pacific Railroad.

The undersigned begs to inform the public that it has succeeded to the ownership and management of these famous springs, and it is their purpose to conduct them in a manner that will insure such care and comfort to its patrons as will be thoroughly satisfactory. Particular attention will be given to the cuisine and dining room service. Furthermore, it is the intention of the new owners to extensively improve and beautify the property—which, added to the marvelous curative properties of the various springs in cases of Gout, Rheumatism, Catarrh of the Bladder, Gravel, Diabetes, Kidney Troubles of every variety, Urinary troubles, Skin Diseases, Dyspepsia, Cystitis and Blood Diseases of every description will place the "TUSCAN SPRINGS" in the front rank of the famous mineral springs of the world.

Cases of RHEUMATISM, GOUT AND ALL BLOOD DISEASES WILL BE ACCEPTED UNDER A GUARANTEE THAT THEY WILL BE CURED WITHIN A SPECIFIED TIME OR ALL EXPENSES, INCLUDING RAILWAY FARE, WILL BE REFUNDED.

These wonderful springs can be reached by the Southern Pacific Company's system of railways and its connections throughout the United States.

TUSCAN MINERAL SPRINGS CORPORATION.

Stage and automobile transfer service between Red Bluff and Tuscan Springs.

For rates of fare and routes of travel apply to any Southern Pacific Railroad Agent.

From the July 24, 1903, edition of the *San Francisco Chronicle*, this advertisement is the first to officially announce that Tuscan Springs was under new ownership. The Tuscan Mineral Springs Corporation, composed of wealthy Portland, Oregon, businessmen and politicians under the management of Frank J. Hellen, took over the resort about one week before this notice ran. Drawing attention to railroad discounts and services, it indicates a closer relationship with the Southern Pacific than had previously existed. It also emphasizes a planned improvement in the food and dining services at the resort and is the first resort advertisement ever to offer a money-back guarantee (even including railroad fare) if a guest is not cured as promised. In other advertisements, the corporation promised renovations of the resort grounds and an "electric road" trolley service to and from Red Bluff. (Author.)

This October 21, 1903, *Chronicle* advertisement (right), placed by Frank Hellen, claims not only that the springs can cure malaria but also that they have never failed to cure any illness and that there has never been a death at Tuscan Springs. Apparently, the new management forgot about C.V. Lewis of Oakland, who died at the springs seven months earlier, or J.J. Schmadeka of Angels Camp, who expired there just two months before the advertisement. The notice below, a rare photograph advertisement from a 1904 *Sunset Magazine*, promotes discounted round-trip fares through Southern Pacific. (Both, author.)

TUSCAN

MINERAL SPRINGS

OPEN THE YEAR ROUND

ALL CASES OF RHEUMATISM, GOUT AND BLOOD DISEASES TAKEN UNDER A GUARANTEE TO CURE IN FROM TWO TO THREE MONTHS' TIME, OR ALL EXPENSES, INCLUDING RAILROAD FARES BOTH WAYS, REFUNDED.

Kidney Troubles, Dropsy, Diabetes, Stone in the Kidney or Bladder, Catarrh of the Bladder, Cystitis, Diseases of the Urinary Organs, Delicate Women, Skin Diseases, Scrofula and General Debility are treated with pre-eminent success. Any case of Malaria cured in from 10 days to two weeks. Never a failure known.

Among the thousands of cases that have been treated here in the last 15 years there has never been a death.

Send 50c. for a bottle of Catarrh Salts and sample of Metal Polish, products of Tuscan Springs. Round-trip tickets at reduced rates. Inquire of any Southern Pacific Railroad agent.

TUSCAN MINERAL SPRINGS CORP., Tuscan Springs, Cal. FRANK J. HELLEN, Mgr.

Cases of Dyspepsia, Indigestion, Catarrh of Head and Stomach, Gout, Rheumatism and *all blood diseases* taken under a guarantee to be cured in a specified time, or all expenses including railroad fares both ways refunded

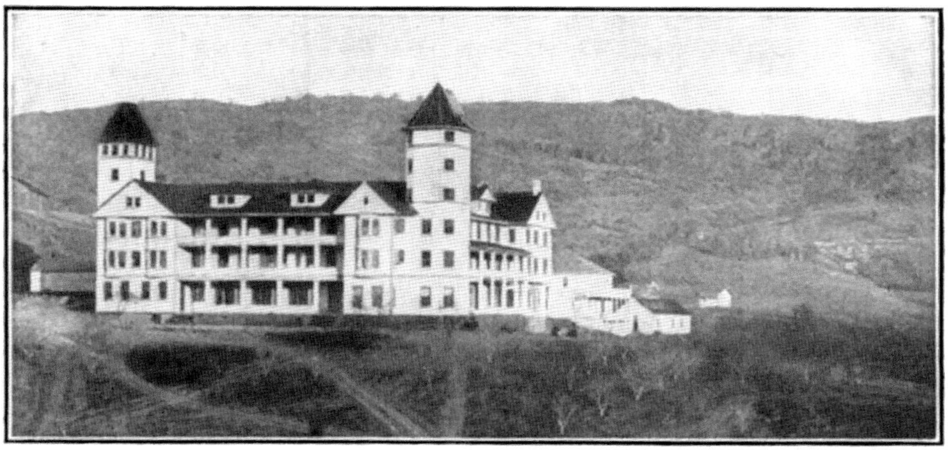

Send fifty cents, in stamps for bottle of STOMACH and CATARRH SALTS : : : :

For reduced round-trip rates address any Southern Pacific Railway Agent : : : : :

FRANK J. HELLEN, *Manager*

TUSCAN MINERAL SPRINGS CORPORATION

Tuscan Springs, - - - California

TUSCAN

MINERAL SPRINGS

OPEN EVERY DAY OF THE YEAR

DOUGLAS (A. T.), June 3, 1904.
Mr. F. J. Hellen, Mgr., Tuscan Springs, Cal.
Dear Sir and Friend: Arrived safely, fine and dandy. Stomach trouble all disappeared; getting as strong and husky as a jerry. Stomach trouble yields to Tuscan waters as the harvest does to the reaper's scythe.
Very truly, C. E. CRITES.
Care H. Clay Herrick.

We have hundreds of testimonials from others; send 50c in stamps for bottle of Stomach and Catarrh Salts. Round trip tickets at reduced rates—Southern Pacific.

TUSCAN MINERAL SPRINGS CORP.
Tuscan, Cal.

From the July 13, 1904 *Chronicle*—nearly a year into Hellen's proprietorship—the advertisement above represents the practice of running short testimonials allegedly reprinted from thank-you letters written by satisfied visitors to the resort. "Stomach trouble all disappeared," it reads, "getting as strong and husky as a jerry." The notice below from the June 20, 1906, *Chronicle* represents Walbridge's scaled-down approach to marketing: it is not as large, and it lacks the outrageous claims and money-back guarantees. In it, he simply announces the completion of the resort's new three-story fireproof bathhouse and offers a free pamphlet by mail. (Both, author.)

TUSCAN SPRINGS

We have just completed a new modern fire proof three story bathhouse, steam heated throughout and up-to-date. All kinds of baths given by competent attendants. Tuscan Springs mineral waters excel in the cure of human ailments. Send for booklet entitled "Let Others Tell the Story." Information at **PECK'S BUREAU**, 414 14th st., Oakland; or, address **ED. B. WALBRIDGE**, Tuscan, Cal.

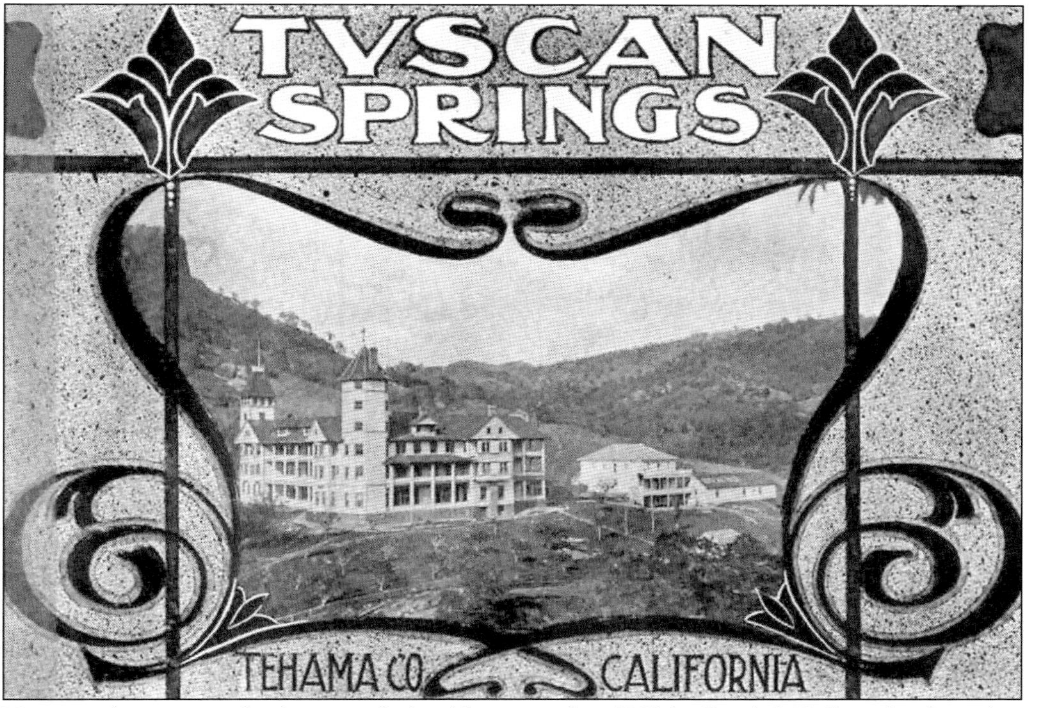

Here are the cover and title page of a booklet created in 1903 by Frank J. Hellen. At about five inches by seven inches, the 50-page black-and-white booklet recounts the history of the resort and painstakingly details the beneficial minerals in the waters and the symptoms and treatments for the many major diseases they are claimed to cure. It also includes many of the photographs that survive today, several of which are reprinted in this book. The booklet, which was available free of charge to anyone who requested it, represents the first use of direct-mail advertising for the resort. (Both, author.)

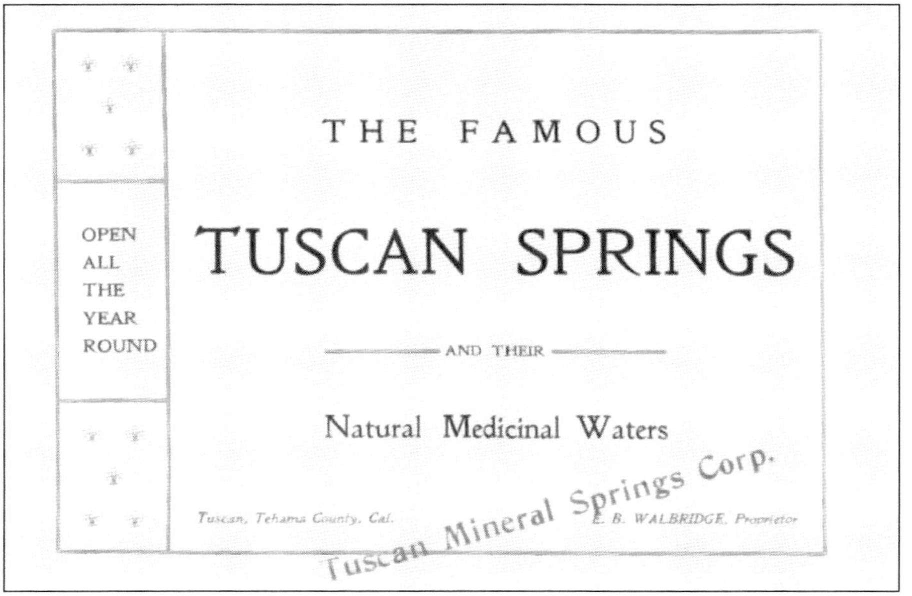

OPEN ALL THE YEAR ROUND

THE FAMOUS

TUSCAN SPRINGS

AND THEIR

Natural Medicinal Waters

Tuscan, Tehama County, Cal.

E. B. WALBRIDGE, Proprietor

Tuscan Mineral Springs Corp.

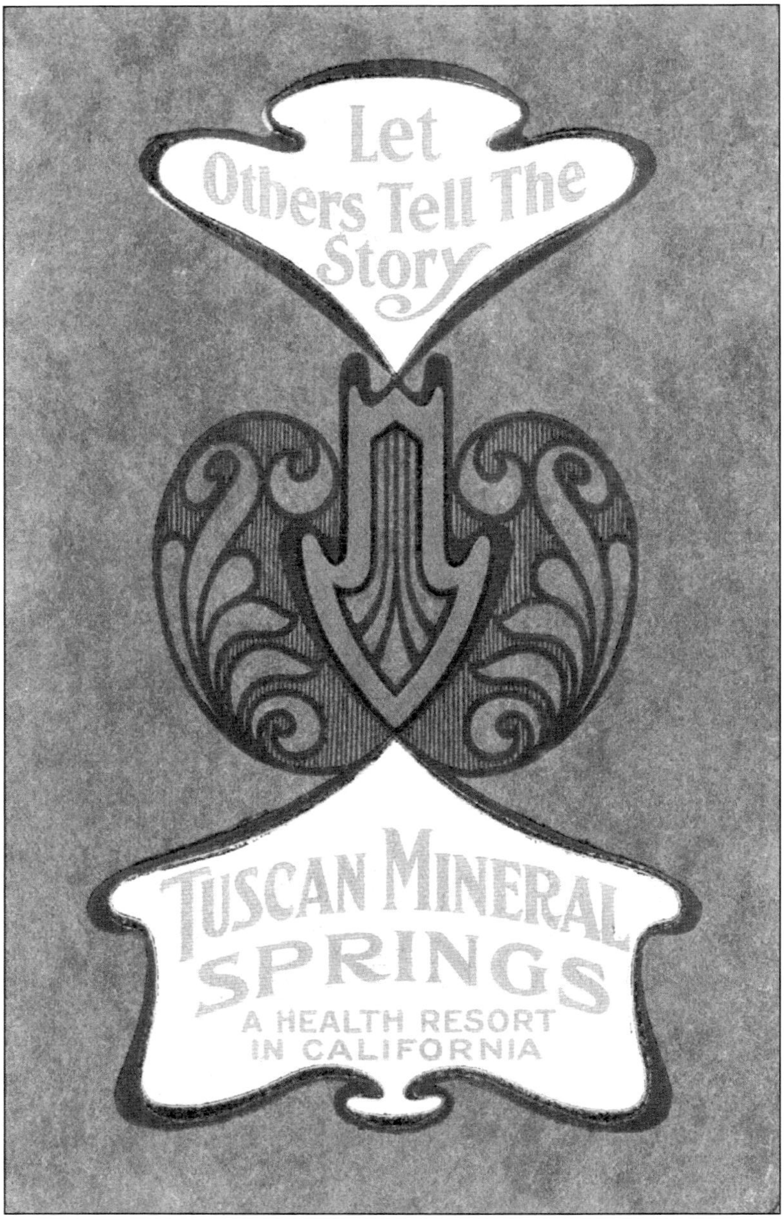

Walbridge's more conservative version of the direct-mail booklet, *Let Others Tell The Story*, was printed around 1911 (though there may have been other variations published before this version). It measures less than half the size of Hellen's publication and includes only 32 pages. Far less technical and dry, it focuses more on the attractive features of the resort and the appeal of Red Bluff and Tehama County; it also includes letters by doctors and chemists extolling the virtues of the Tuscan Springs mineral waters. Additionally, it provides numerous photographs, though several were recycled from Hellen's brochure. This later version demonstrates that Walbridge recognized the value of the marketing approach but, like the best businessmen, realized that the same results could be achieved at far less expense. The cover of the pamphlet, seen here, was printed on colored card stock. (Author.)

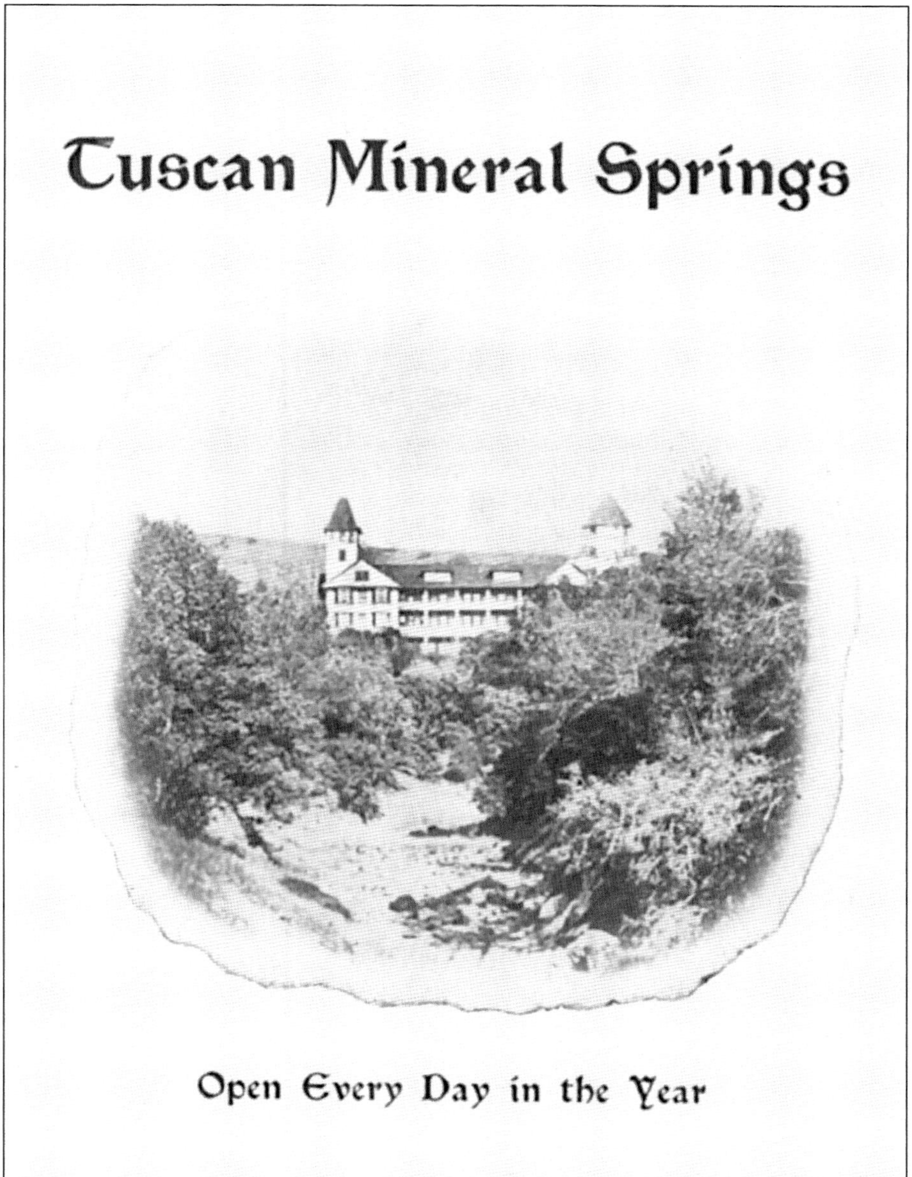
Tuscan Mineral Springs

Open Every Day in the Year

The title page of *Let Others Tell The Story* reminds readers that the resort is open not just in summers but throughout the year. Summers were far and away the busiest season of the year at Tuscan Springs from the very beginning. This was partially because out-of-towners assumed that June through August would offer the most pleasant weather. Often, however, just the opposite was true: the summer temperatures in Tehama County could be extremely unpleasant (especially with the surrounding buttes trapping the heat), and the winters in the area were unusually mild. Snow was almost never seen, and the area was sheltered from harsh winds and rains by the 400-foot buttes surrounding it. To combat the slow winter months, proprietors tried at every opportunity to distribute patronage (and income) more evenly throughout the year. (Author.)

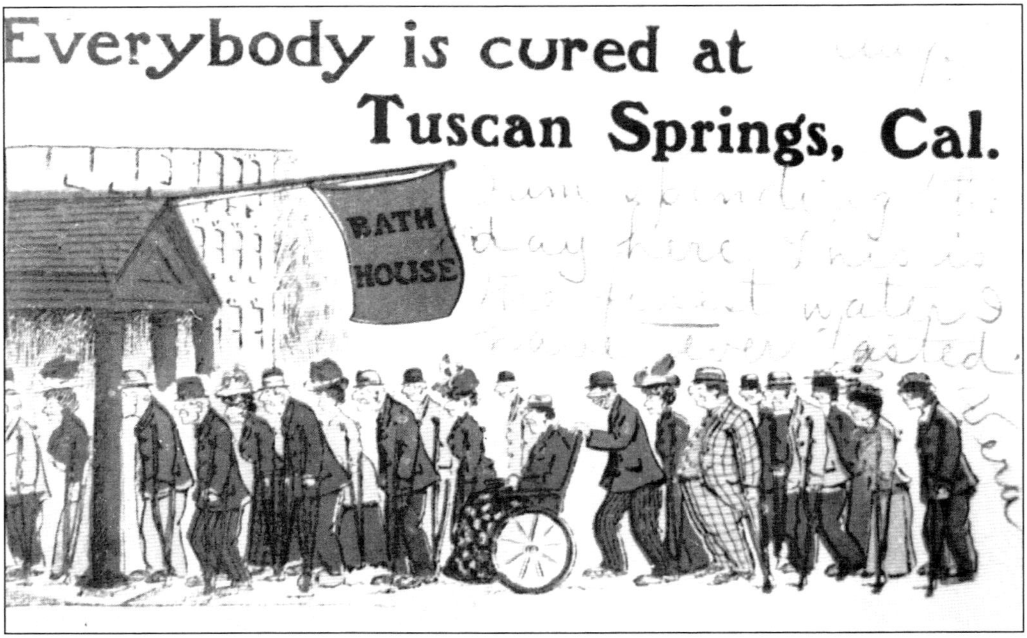

As the Edwardian era began, an even greater appreciation for keepsakes and novelties developed, and postcards became extremely popular throughout the world. This Twitter of yesteryear allowed people to dash off a fast sentiment of one or two sentences for just 1¢. The US Post Office Department approved nongovernment postcards in 1901, but any message had to be written on the picture side. These two Tuscan Springs postcards are from that era. Interestingly, 75 percent of all postcards sold in America then were created by European publishers, especially those in Germany. (Both, author.)

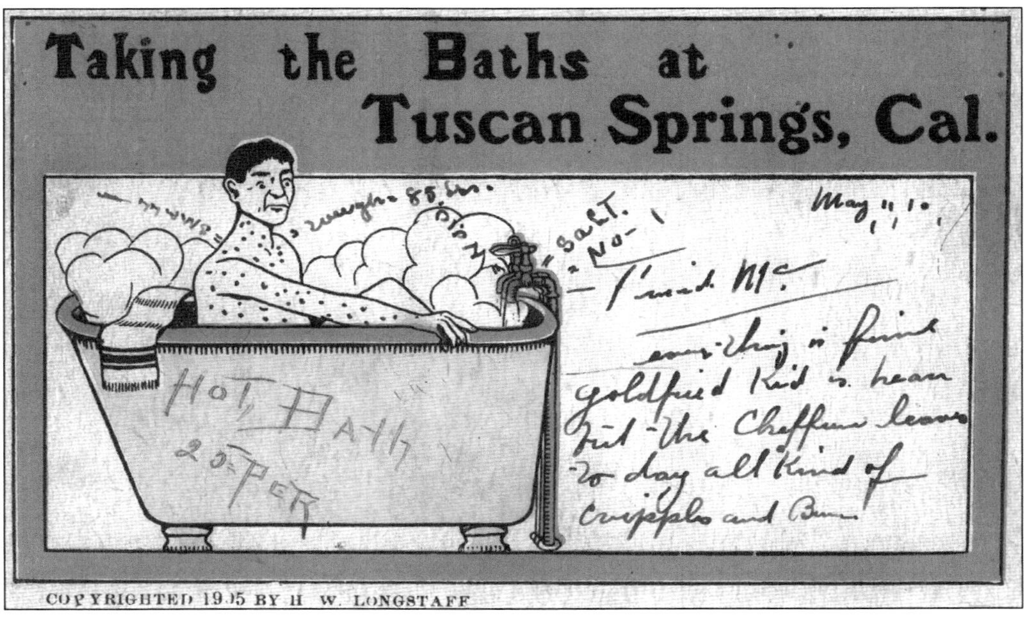

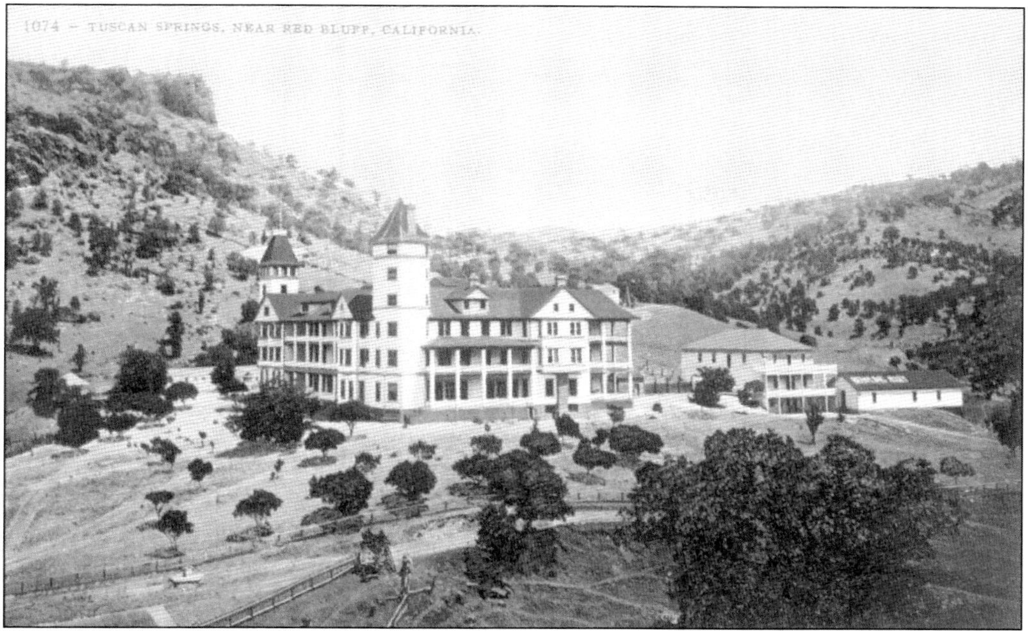

The postcard above, a hand-painted lithograph, was published around 1908, a year after the postal regulations changed to allow messages on the reverse of picture cards. Though printers were capable of rendering realistic color images, the popular taste was for augmented reality with over-saturated colors that made faraway places seem even more enticing and exotic. This popular image was reprinted many times on postcards by numerous lithographers. The photograph below is of an ashtray that may have been a souvenir giveaway item like the drinking cup. The image on the tray is from 1905–1916. (Above, author; below, TCM.)

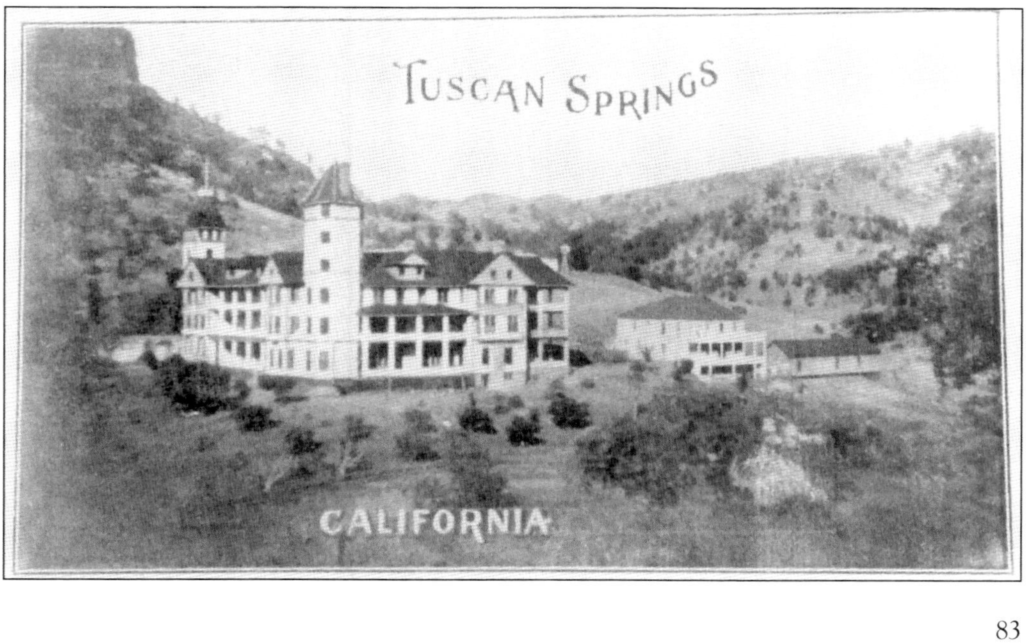

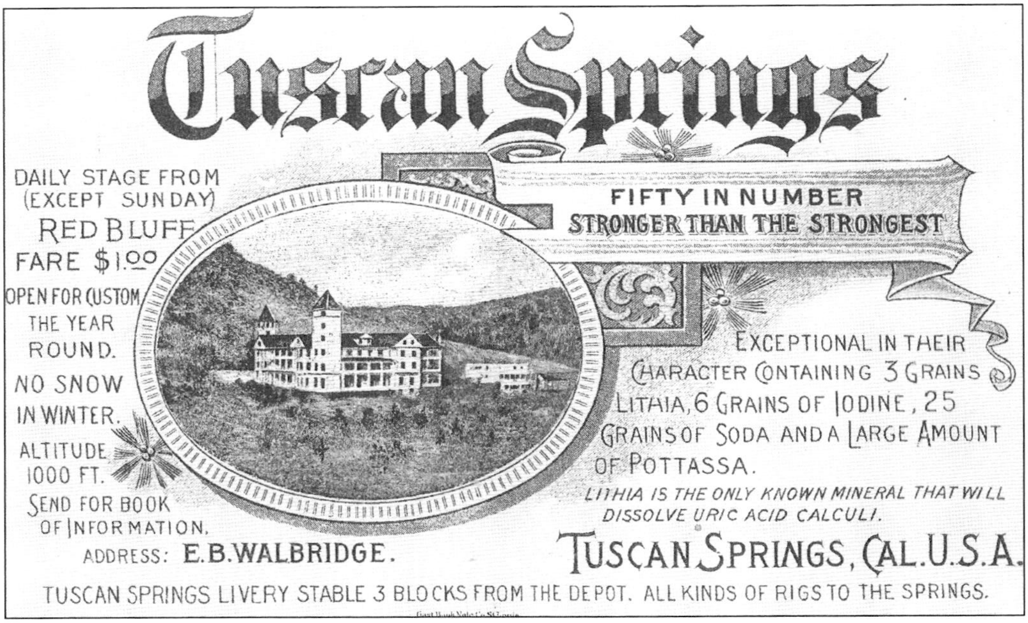

These images show the front and back of what was once known as a calling card. About the size of a playing card, these were central to a complicated upper- and middle-class Victorian tradition of calling upon acquaintances. Subtle messages could be conveyed by, for example, folding or tearing the top left corner to indicate a social call, the top right for congratulations or good news, the bottom left if the sender were leaving town, and the lower right for condolences. This card would have been printed near the end of the first decade of the 20th century and before 1911, which was when the Tuscan Springs Livery Stable mentioned was torn down. (Both, author.)

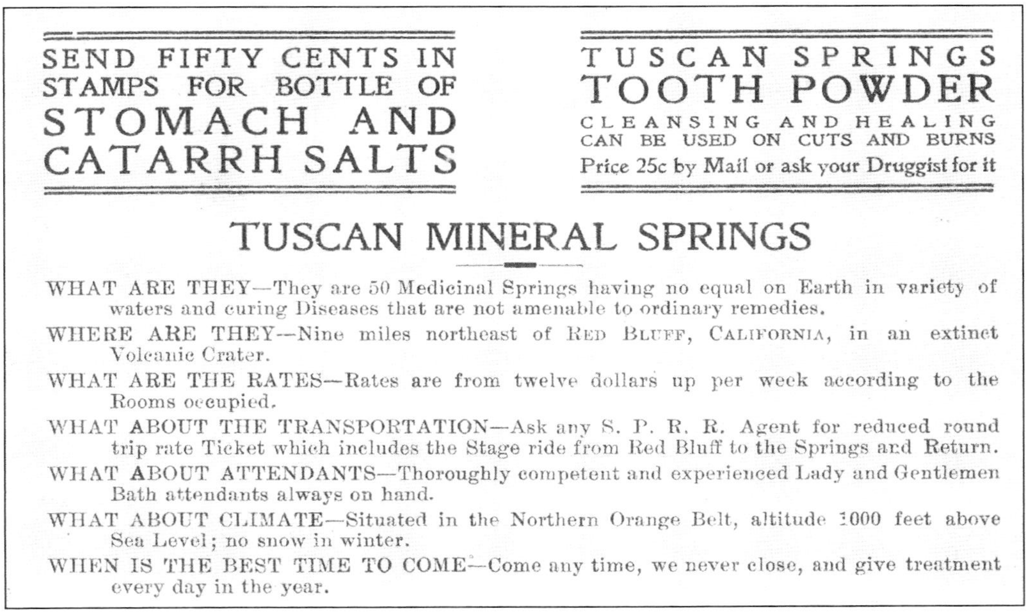

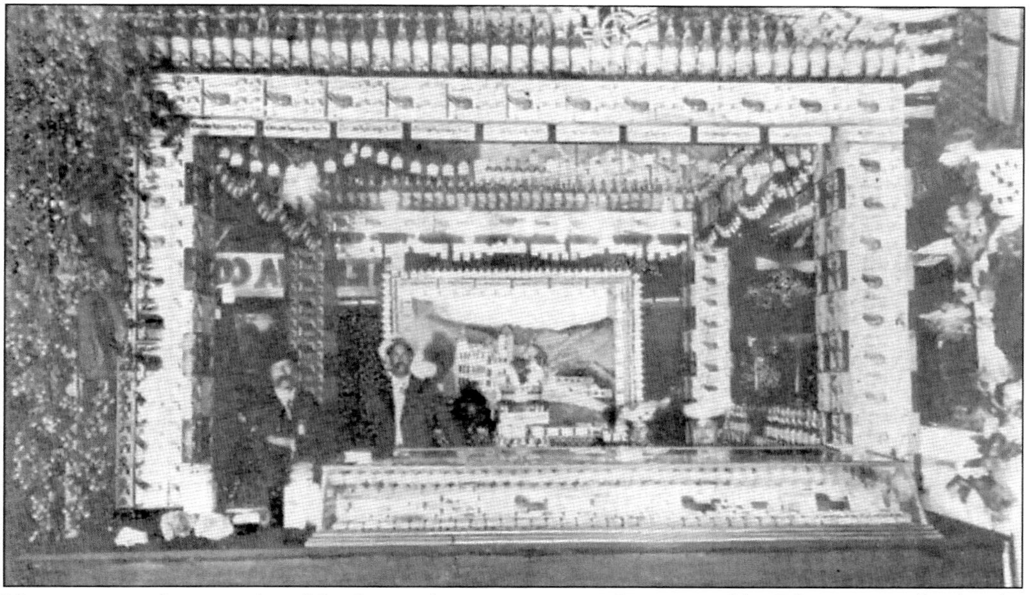

Here are two photographs of displays either commissioned or created by Edgerton Walbridge for the annual California State Fair in Sacramento. The above photograph shows his mineral waters display, lined top and bottom with cases and bottles of the Tuscan Springs mineral waters (also available for purchase) and with examples of various resort rocks and minerals presented for viewing. In the background is a large painting of the tavern Walbridge had commissioned. The piece later hung in the Walbridge Garage for years. Below is seen the Tehama County display, which also features large stacks of Tuscan Springs products. (Both, author.)

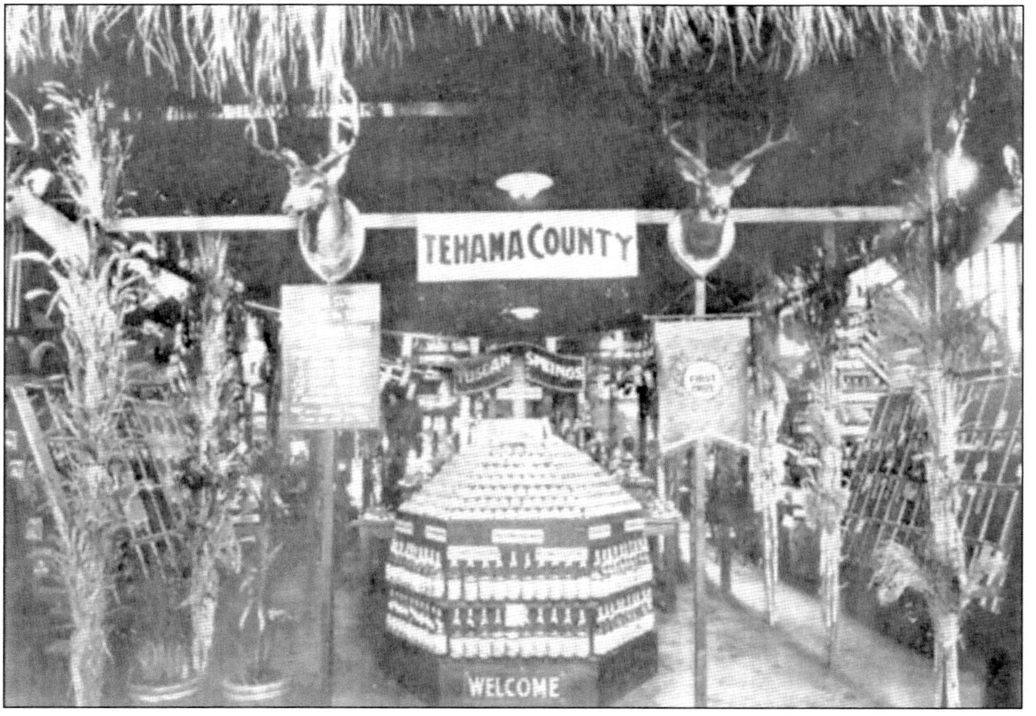

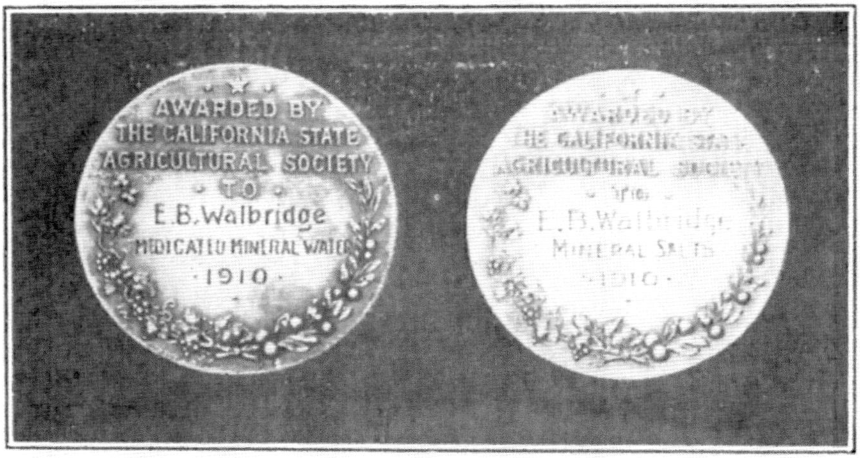

MEDALS OF AWARD

Given us at the California State Fair for Exhibits of Mineral Water and Medicated Mineral Salts

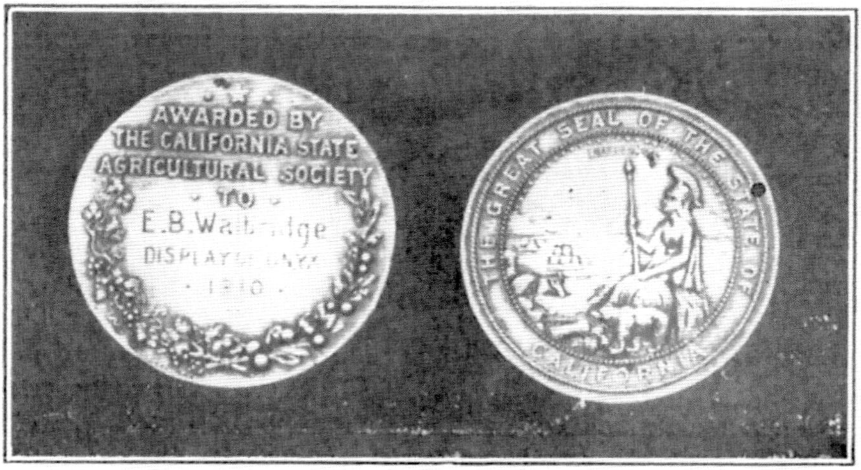

We have always taken home the Bacon wherever we exhibit

This photograph, from the *Let Others Tell the Story* pamphlet, shows the three medals Walbridge won for his displays at the California State Fair in 1910. The medals, awarded by the California State Agricultural Society, were for his mineral salts, medicated mineral waters, and onyx displays. He had also won similar awards at the state fair in 1908. The large annual event was a very effective way to reach potential new customers both from Sacramento and from other cities in California and bordering states. One Red Bluff old-timer reported that he was later walking down the streets of Sacramento with Walbridge and that the latter was stopped every few feet to have his hand enthusiastically and appreciatively shaken by city residents who had visited Tuscan Springs, many of whom first learned about the resort at the state fair. (Author.)

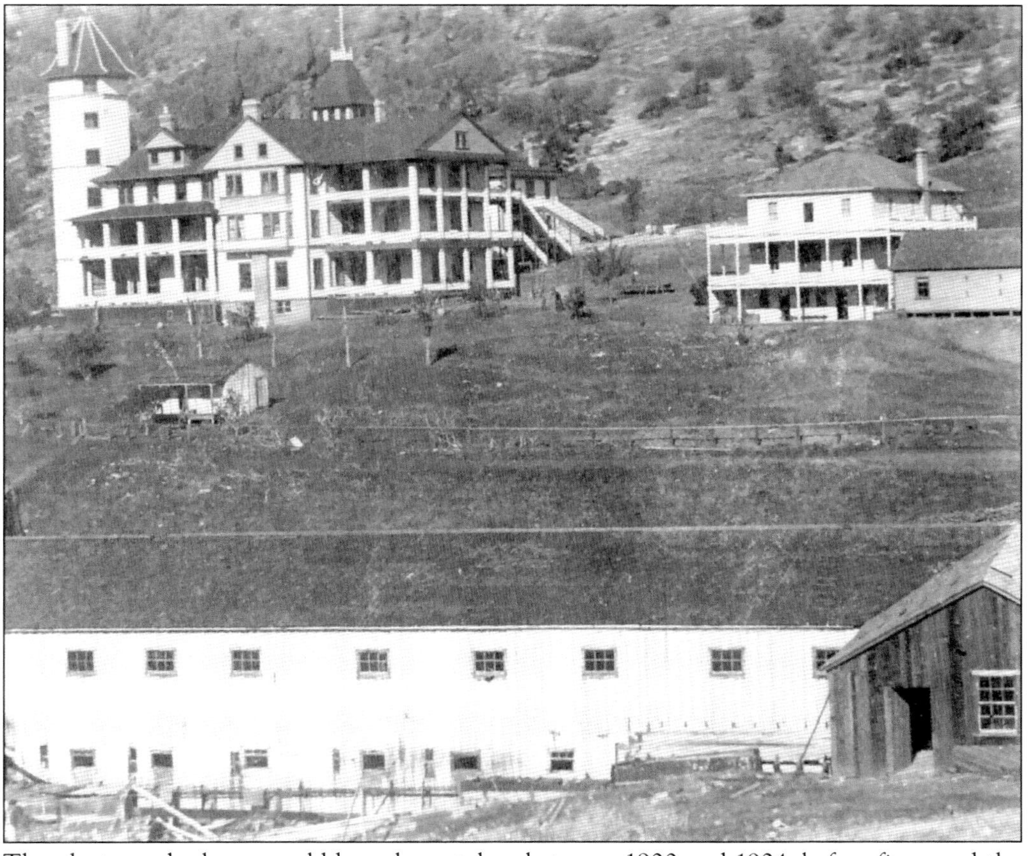

The photograph above would have been taken between 1900 and 1904, before fire razed the wooden bathhouse. The photograph below was taken after 1905, when the new three-story concrete bathhouse was built at a cost of about $25,000 ($650,000 today). In it, the ramp and plunge bath have been installed, and the bowling alley next to the clubhouse is no longer present. In both photographs, the fire escape ramps at the rear of the hotel can be seen leading down from the upper stories. (Both, author.)

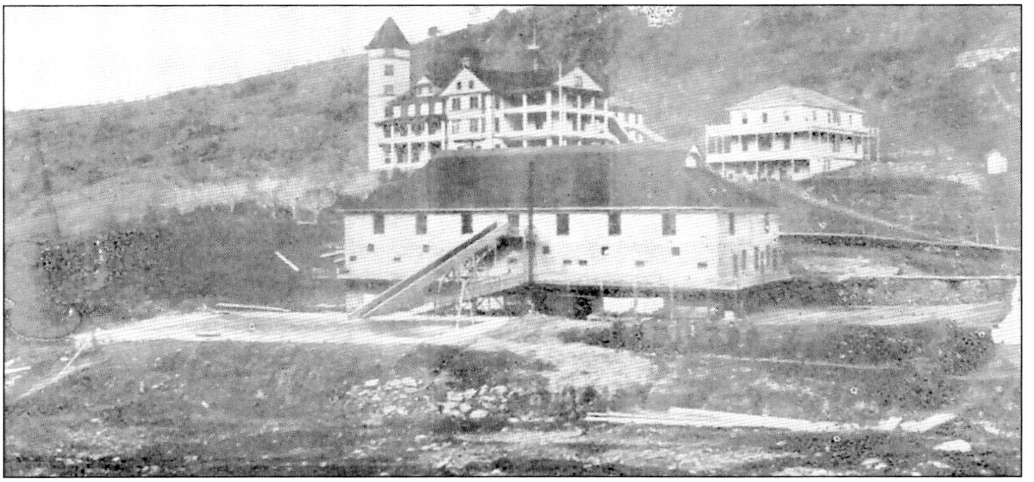

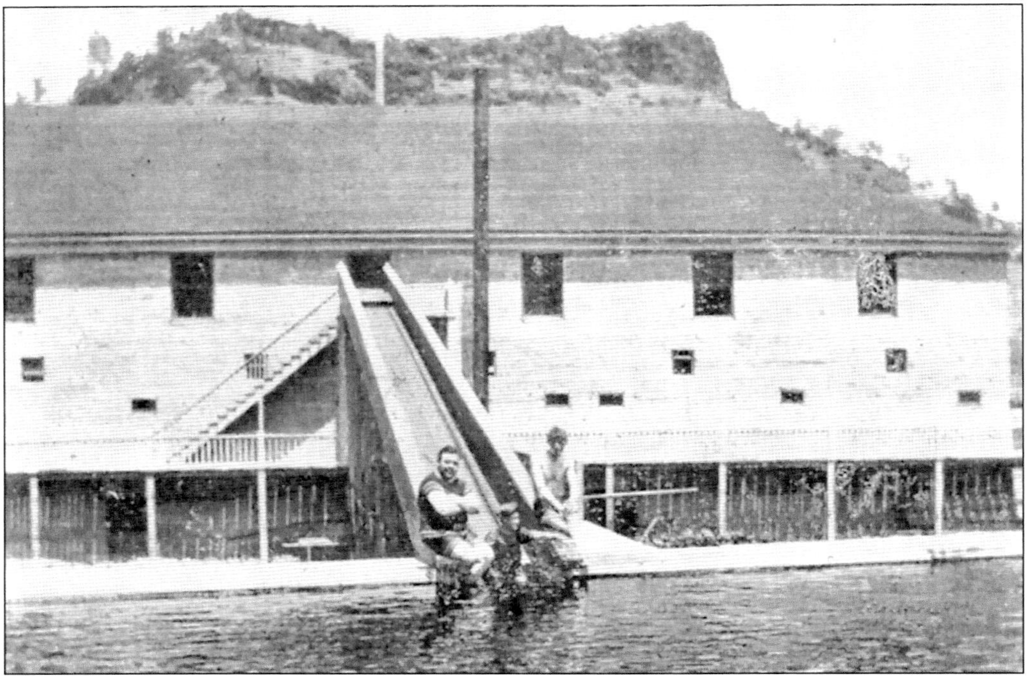

The first floor of the final bathhouse contained the boiler rooms, laundry, mud baths, and hot and cold showers. The second floor housed separate men's and women's sections, each with various baths, 6 steam rooms, 18 porcelain tubs, hot and cold showers from spring No. 1, hot air, massage, waiting and cooling rooms, mineral water fountains, toilets, cots and easy chairs, 20 dressing rooms, and larger private rooms for groups. The top floor, for "amusement or exercise," was used as a gymnasium or for dancing or other large gatherings. The photograph below includes Walbridge, second from the left. (Both, author.)

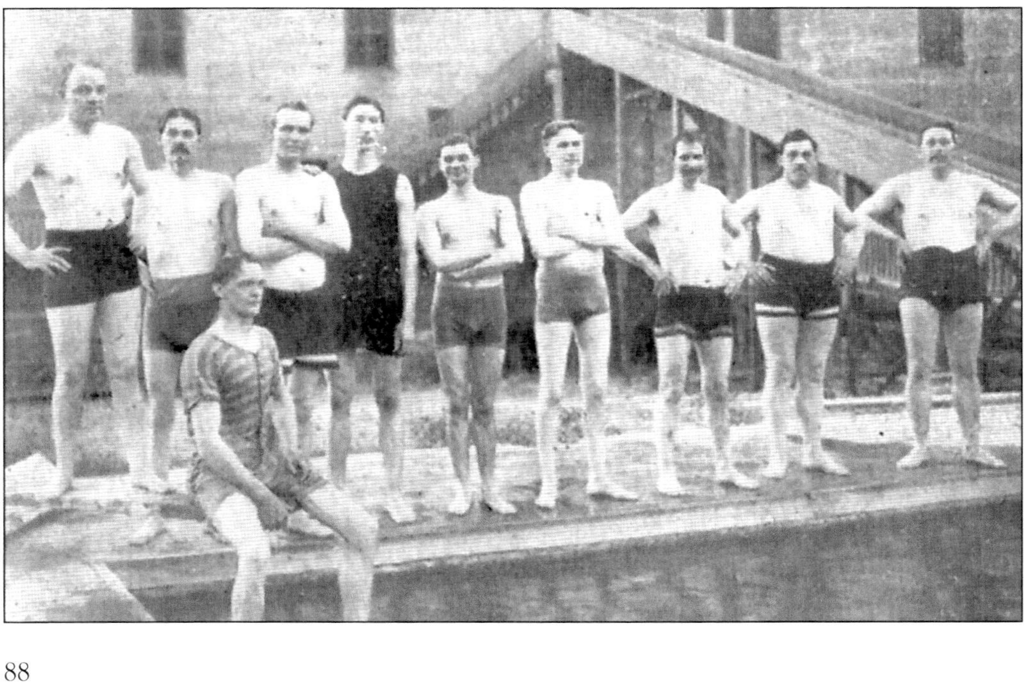

Eight

The End

During the weeks that followed his loss of consciousness, various doctors gave Walbridge various diagnoses but finally agreed the cause was either locomotor ataxia, probably caused by untreated syphilis, or Bright's disease, a kidney affliction.

He did recover temporarily, but, during a December trip, he was stricken with paralysis and taken to a hospital in Sacramento, where he died on Christmas Eve 1913. Ironically, Walbridge's own promotional pamphlets claimed a sure cure could be had for both diseases at Tuscan Springs.

Shortly after Walbridge's death, a Maud Cloutier—a domestic from Anderson, near Red Bluff—appeared, claiming Walbridge was her father and demanding half his estate. Martha Walbridge contested the claims, and court battles stretched on.

The eruption of Mount Lassen in 1915 must have seemed an eerie harbinger when, early on August 22, 1916, Martha was visiting her brother Al Dennis at the Walbridge Garage and Dr. J.A. Owens burst in to announce he had seen smoke again toward the resort. When she was unable to reach the tavern by phone, Martha's brother drove her there only to find everything but the concrete bathhouse in smoldering ruins.

Porter Frank Atkinson said, around 9:45 a.m., he had been working in the office when a girl rushed downstairs yelling that the hotel was on fire. He ran upstairs just as the skylights collapsed and hurried back downstairs, alerting the guests and gathering the money and records from the safe.

It was assumed that the fire started from a spark in the chimney on the eastern roof after an employee burned trash early that morning. Losses for the hotel were estimated at $75,000, and the paltry insurance payout went directly to the mortgage holder. By 1917, Martha had paid off the mortgage and was planning to rebuild again when, in 1919, the courts awarded Cloutier half the estate, totaling $54,000.

Martha then moved to Sacramento, where she died quietly on July 15, 1921, at age 57, without a husband, children, or a will. It seemed the land would languish forgotten until an Oakland attorney with a funny name decided to resurrect the past.

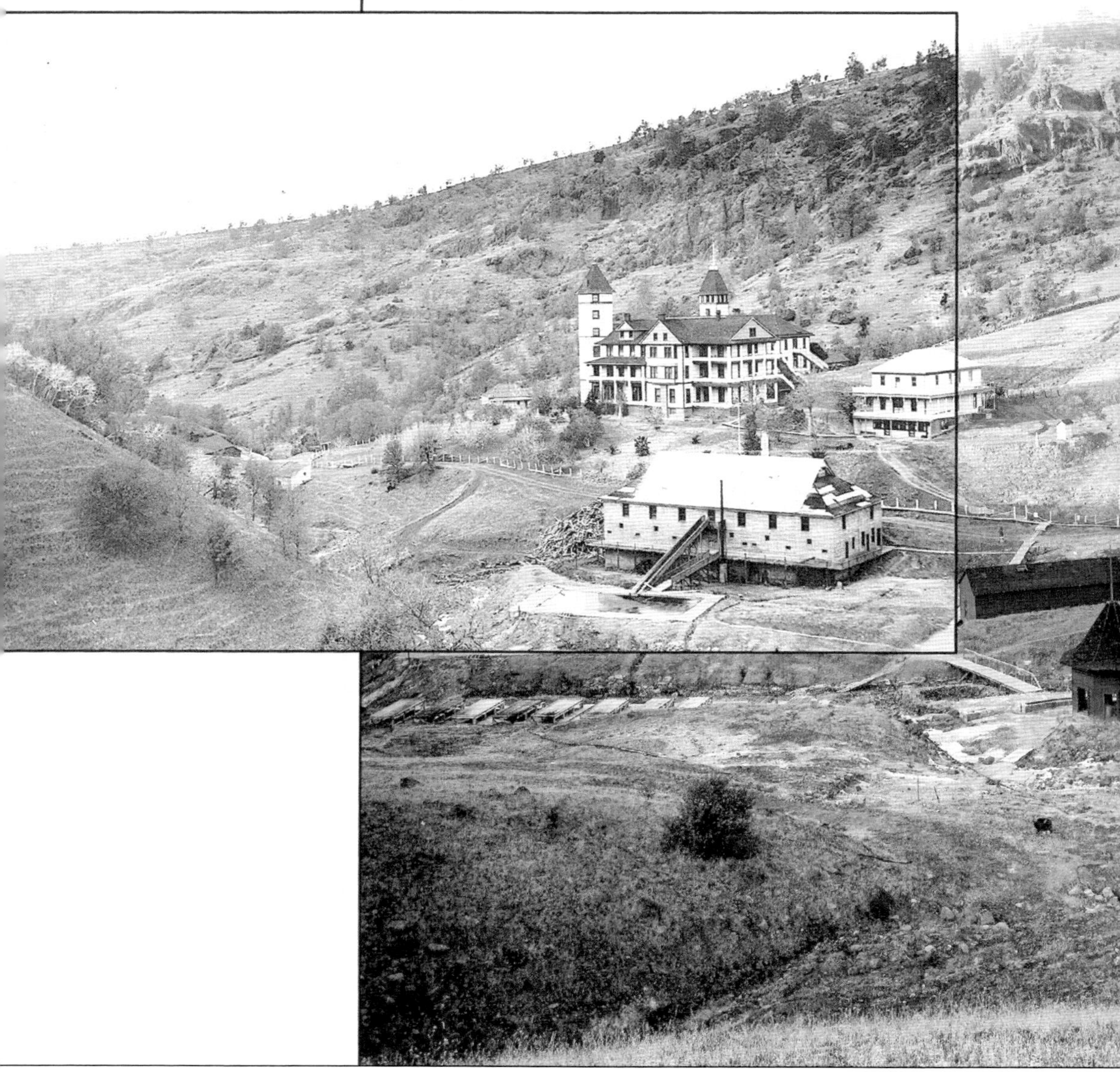

In 2013, the author discovered the final portion of a long-lost panorama of the Tuscan Springs resort. The photographs could have only been taken after 1905, when Walbridge rebuilt the bathhouse that had burned the previous year under the management of Frank J. Hellen and the Tuscan Mineral Springs Corporation. The new bathhouse was constructed entirely of cement and concrete so as to be fireproof. Work on the roof still seems to be in progress in the center

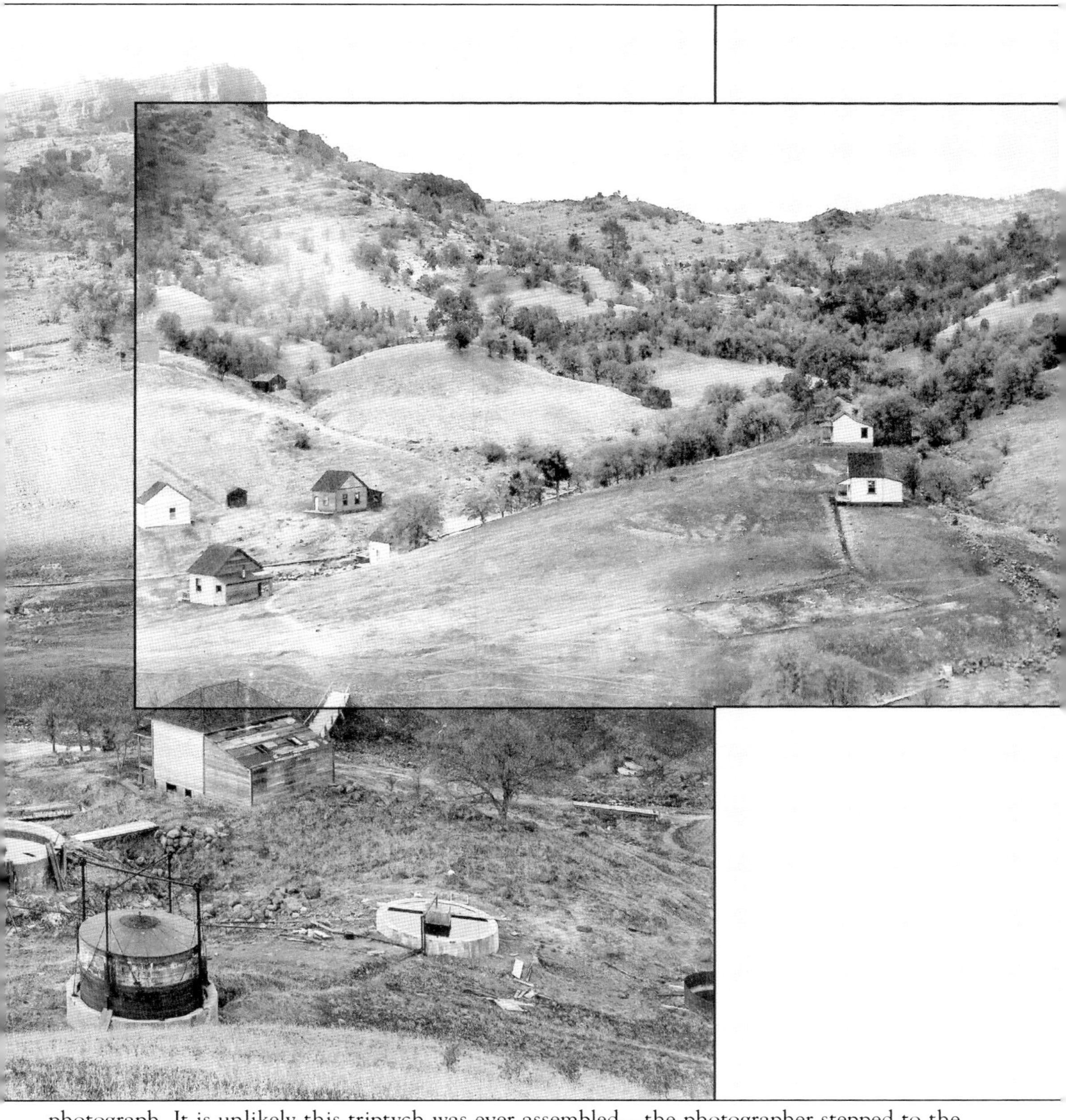

photograph. It is unlikely this triptych was ever assembled—the photographer stepped to the right before shooting the final photograph (on right), making darkroom alignment of the images impossible. However, 20th-century technology makes it a simple matter to finally see the entire resort in end-to-end detail. (Author.)

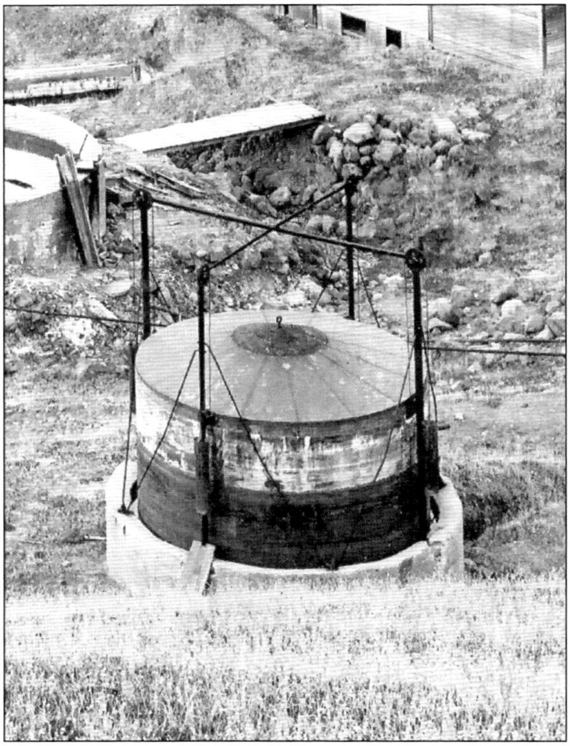

At left is a detail from the previous photograph, showing the resort's gasometer, which collected, stored, and pressurized natural gas to provide lights and heat. It works as illustrated in the drawing below. A long pipe was inserted into the gas source, and a large cylindrical tub was built around it and filled with water. Into this was inserted a smaller, weighted container (like an upside-down cup), held level by framing. As gas filled the container, it would rise, and when the spigot to the furnaces was opened, the weight of the bell would cause it to sink back into the water, forcing the gas through another pipe. (Both, author.)

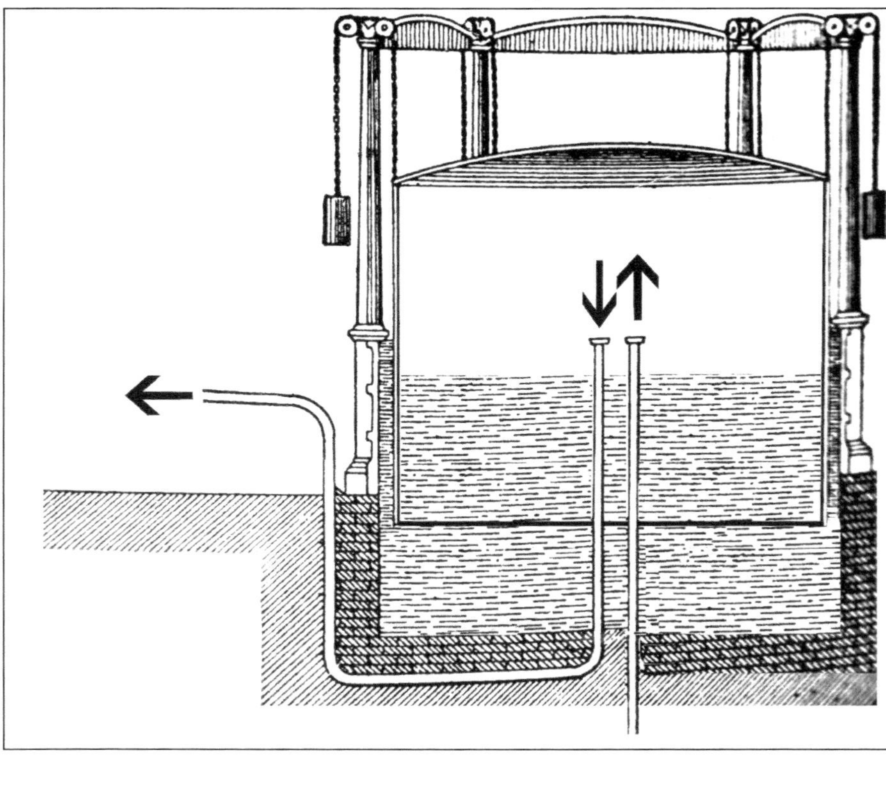

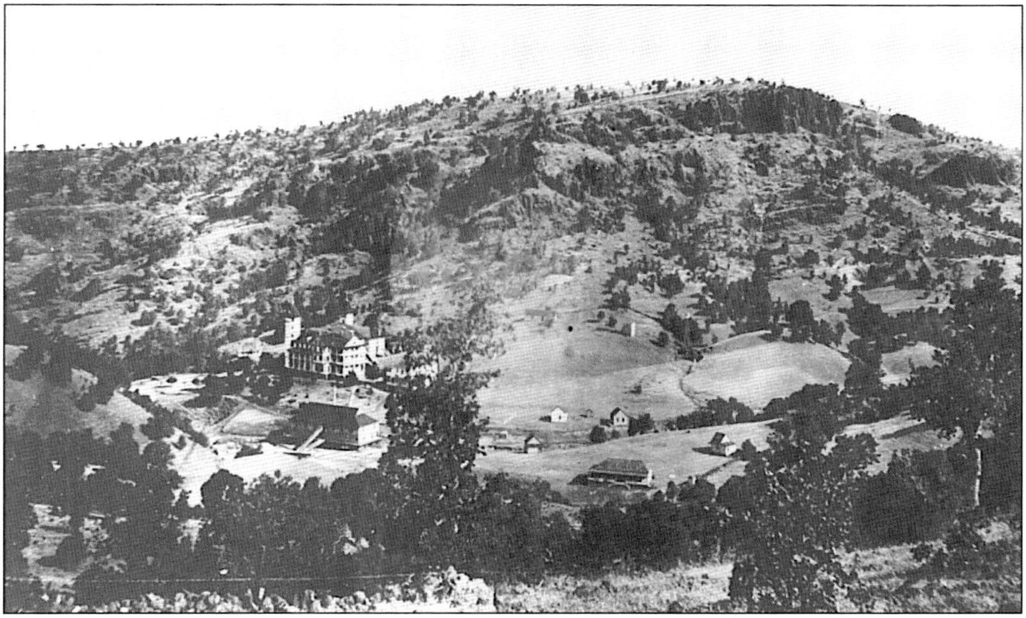

Though Kodak released its famous Brownie camera in February 1900, making photography more affordable for everyone, the majority of the images of the resort available today survive only because they were printed in magazines or promotional materials. Private photographs are very rare. One notable exception is a collection of a few shots by Rufus Cook, a 16-year-old Boy Scout from San Francisco who took photographs with his Brownie on a family trip to the springs in September 1907. The image above is from that collection. The view below shows the resort from the southwest. (Both, author.)

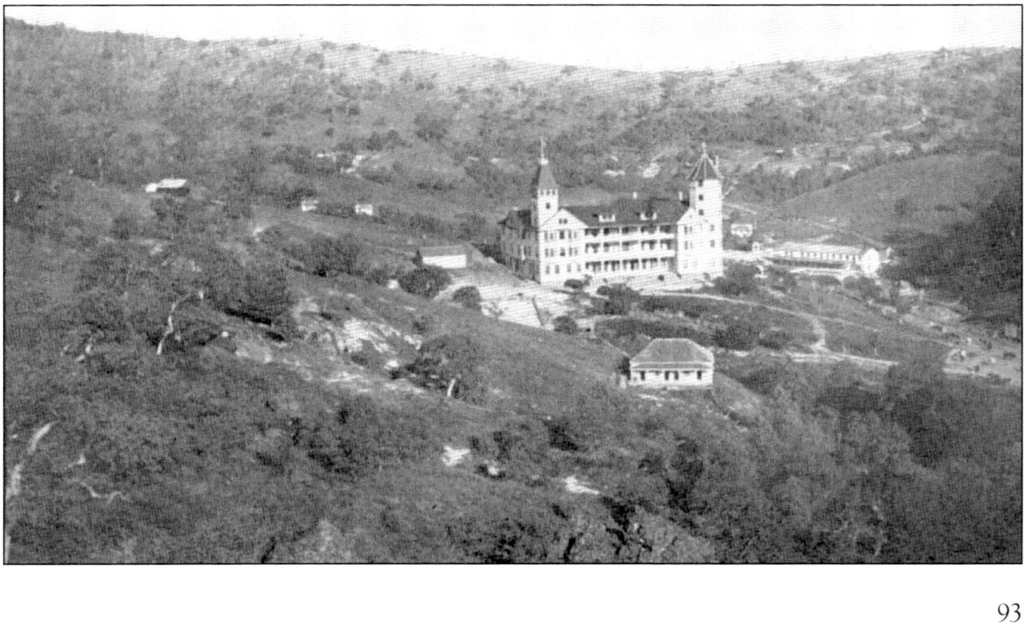

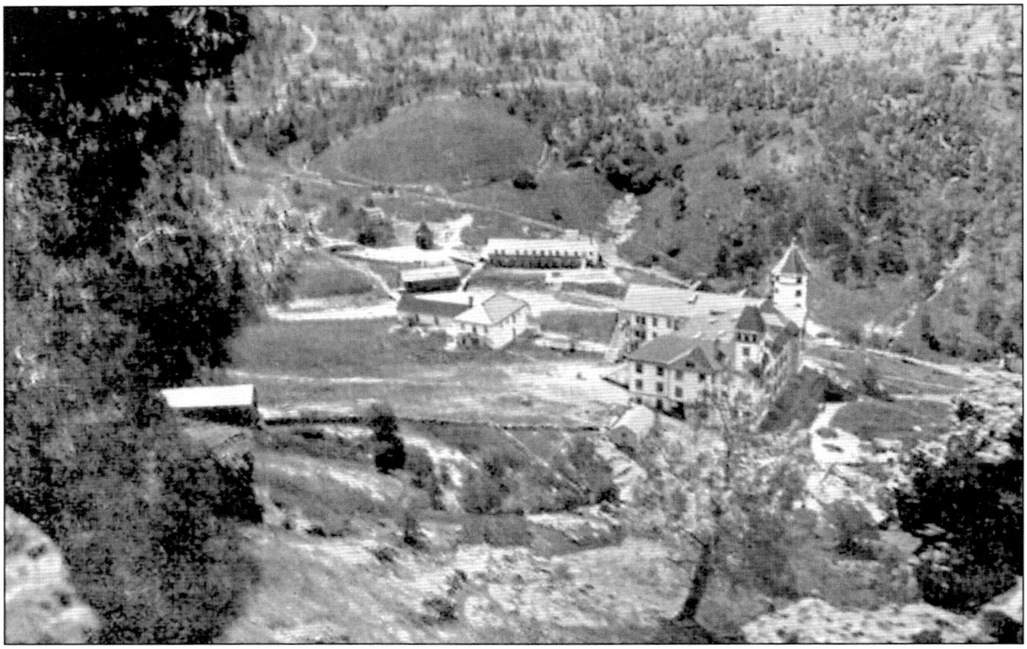

Above, the mortarless, hand-fitted stone walls that Walbridge hired Tehama County's Chinese workers to build can be seen winding around the resort. Many whites in Red Bluff resented the Chinese laborers, who would work longer hours for far less pay. For these walls, for example, they would have been paid approximately 15¢ (about $4 today) for every 16.5 feet completed. The Chinese residents of Red Bluff were compelled to keep to themselves within a two-block area along the river known as "Red Bluff Chinatown," just across from the Sierra Mill. The photograph below is a view of the resort from the southeast through the trees. (Both, author.)

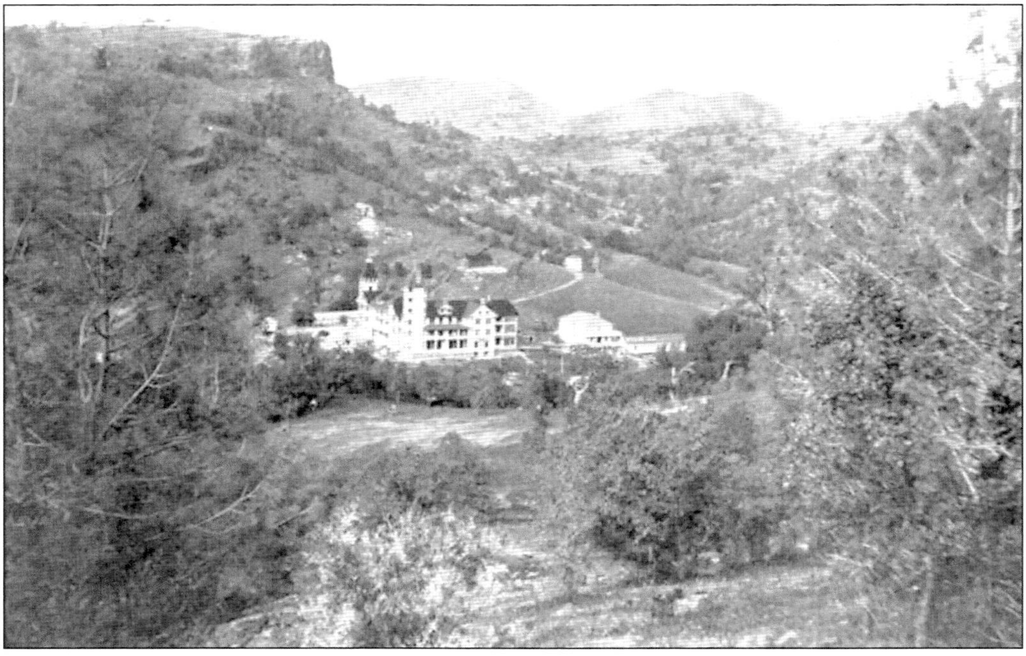

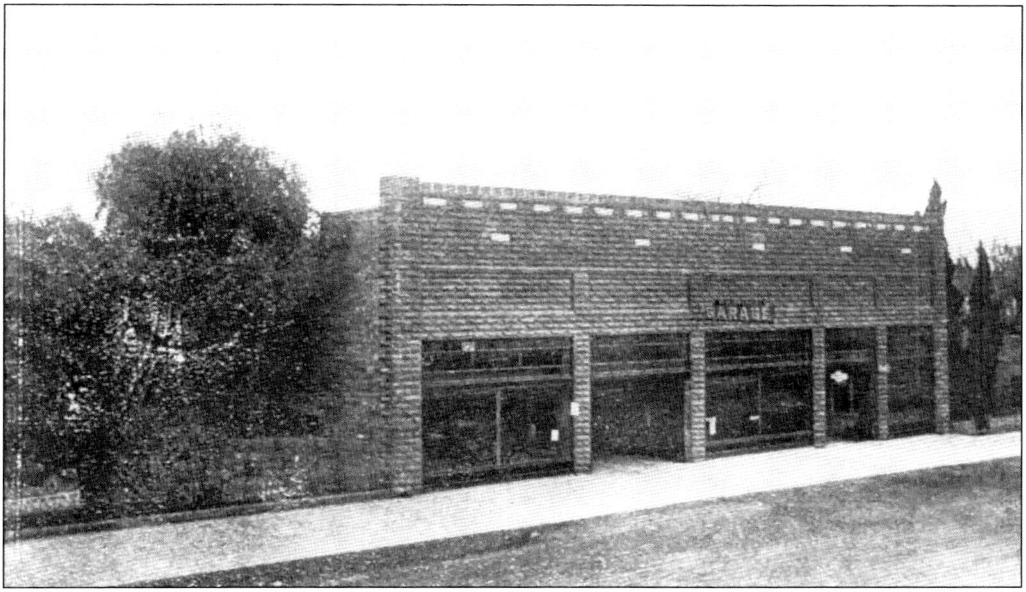

In 1911, Edgerton Walbridge tore down his Tuscan Springs Stables behind the Bank of Tehama County on Main Street and constructed the Walbridge Garage to service the increasing number of local automobiles and his own growing fleet of autostages, at least one of which can be seen in the photograph below. The business, just three blocks from the Southern Pacific depot, specialized in Studebaker, Flanders, Apperson, Grabowky, and Schacht automobiles and claimed to be "one of the best equipped on the Pacific coast." Walbridge, who built everything in stone, cement, and concrete after 1905, stressed in advertisements that the building was "absolutely fireproof." (Both, author.)

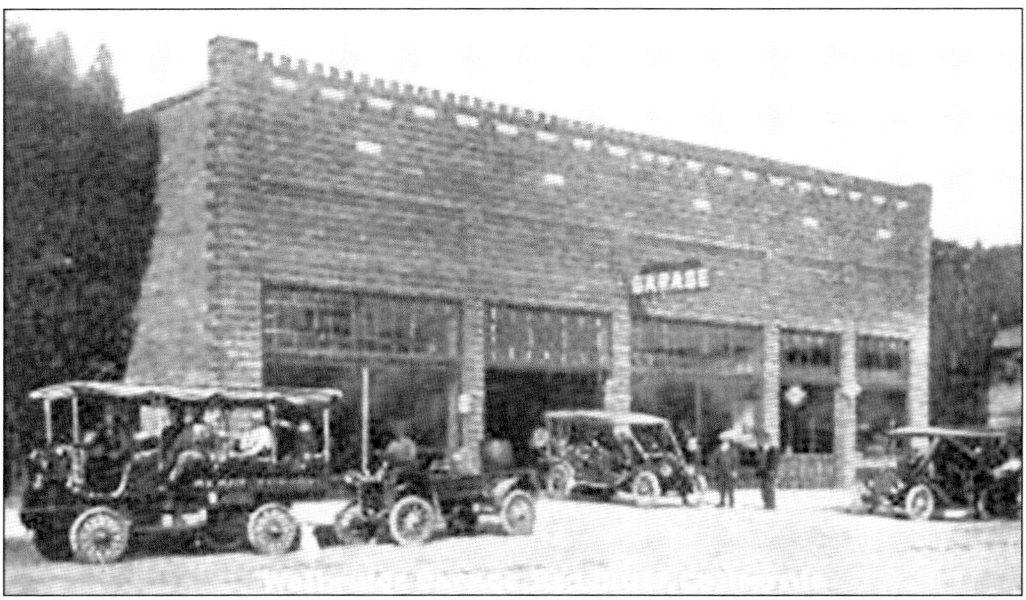

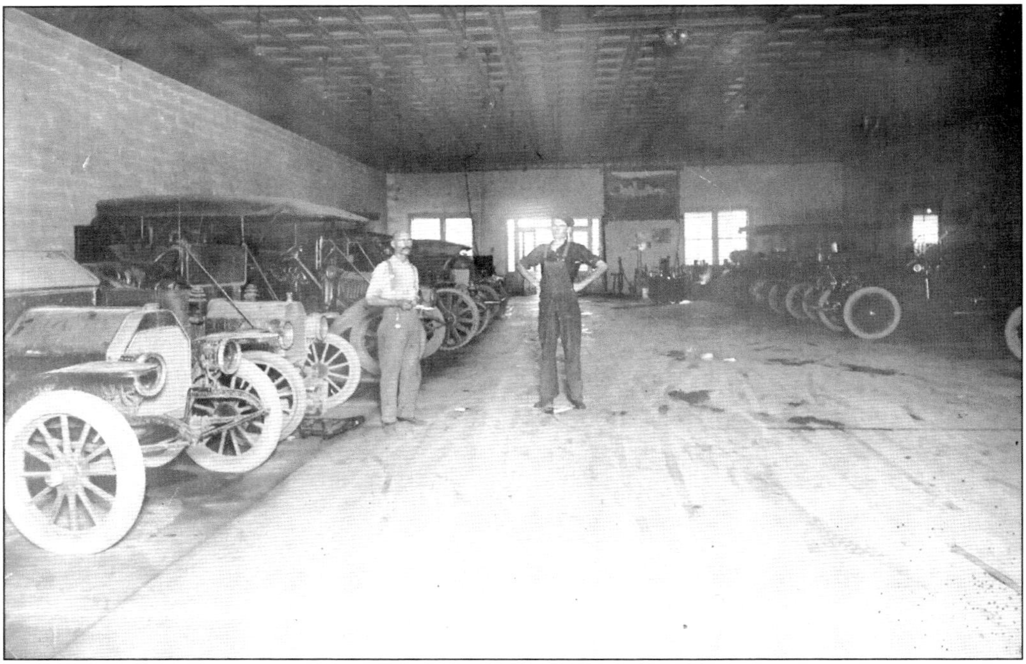

The above photograph shows the interior of the Walbridge Garage around 1913, the same year its owner died. Hanging on the back wall can be seen the large painting Walbridge had displayed at the state fair. One of the men pictured is likely Walbridge's brother-in-law and garage manager, Al Dennis. To the right of this large bay was a reading room where ladies could pass the time while waiting for the family automobile to be repaired. The photograph below shows downtown Red Bluff from the center of Main Street in front of the garage in about the same year. (Both, author.)

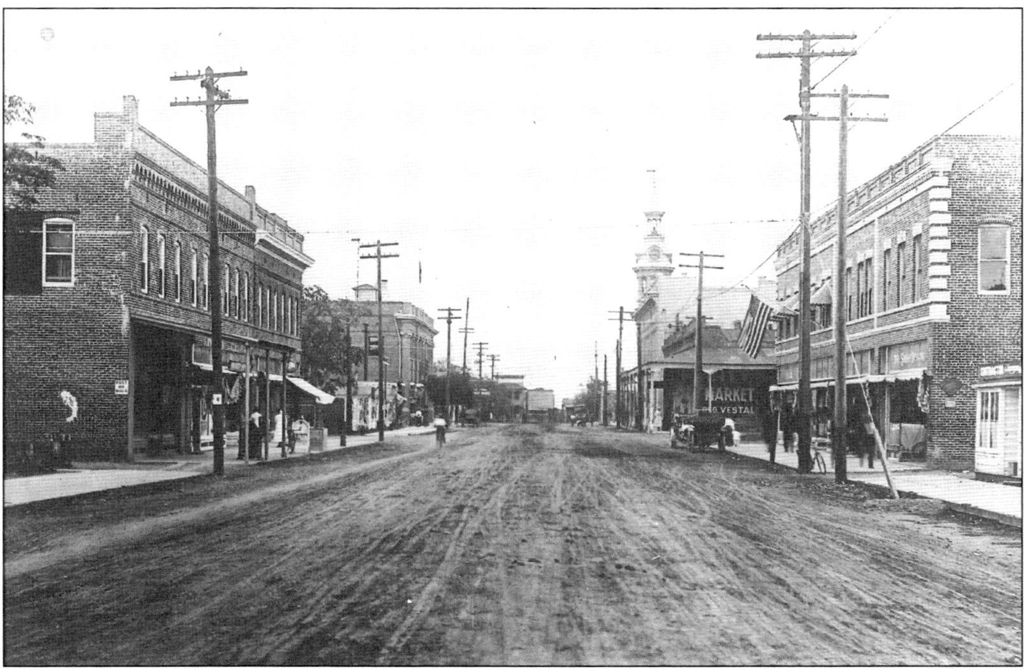

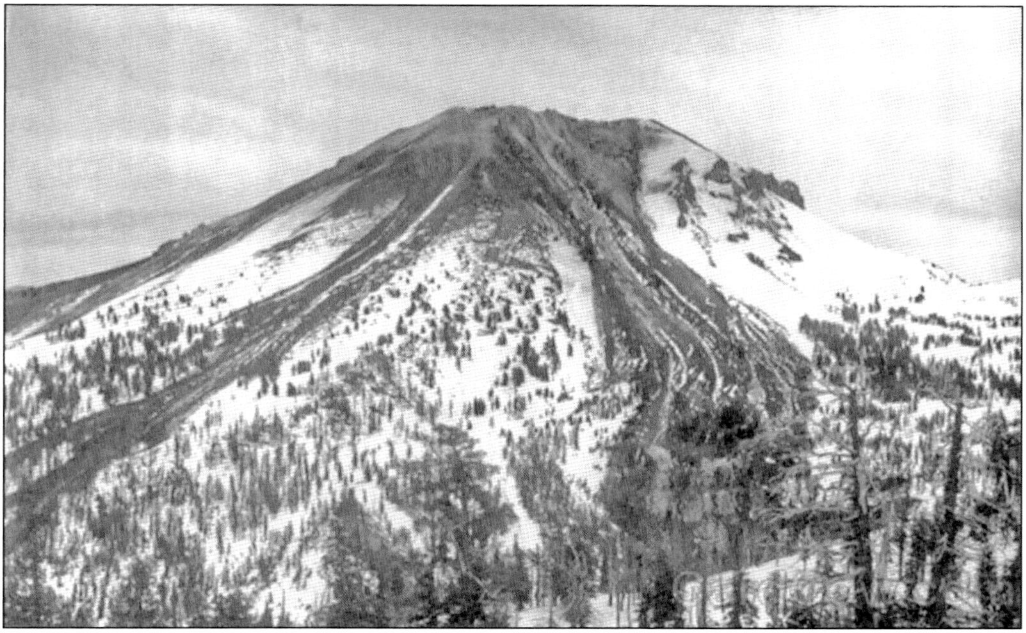

Within five months of Walbridge's death, events just 28 miles from Tuscan Springs caused many to fear for the future of Northern California. On May 30, 1914, Mount Lassen suddenly awakened with an enormous blast of steam. More than 180 such explosions continued for the next year, and on May 14, 1915, lava began to flow. On May 20, a new crater erupted, causing avalanches and flooding in nearby communities (above). The climax came two days later when Lassen became the first volcano to erupt in the United States during the 20th century. Smaller eruptions (right) continued into 1917.

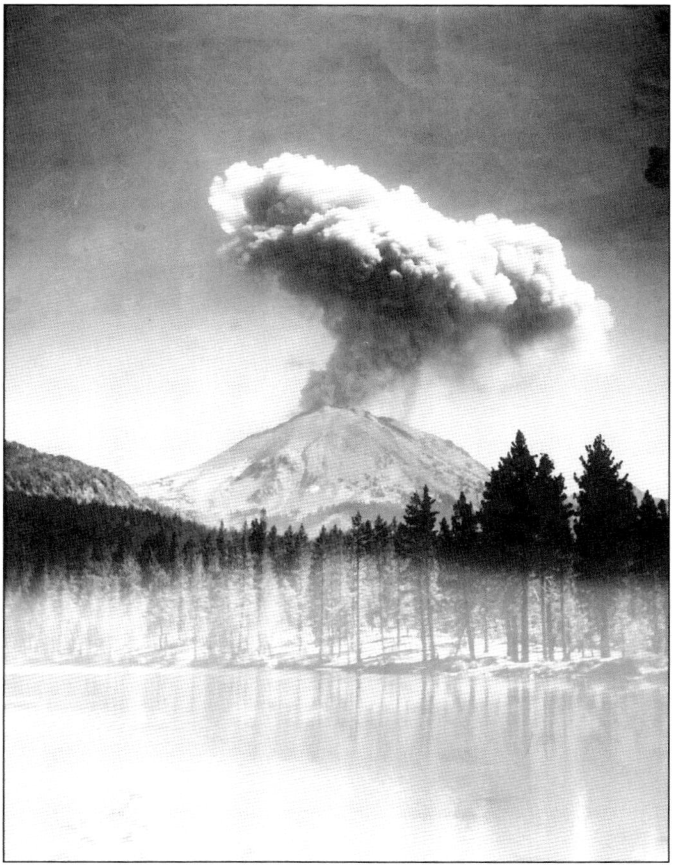

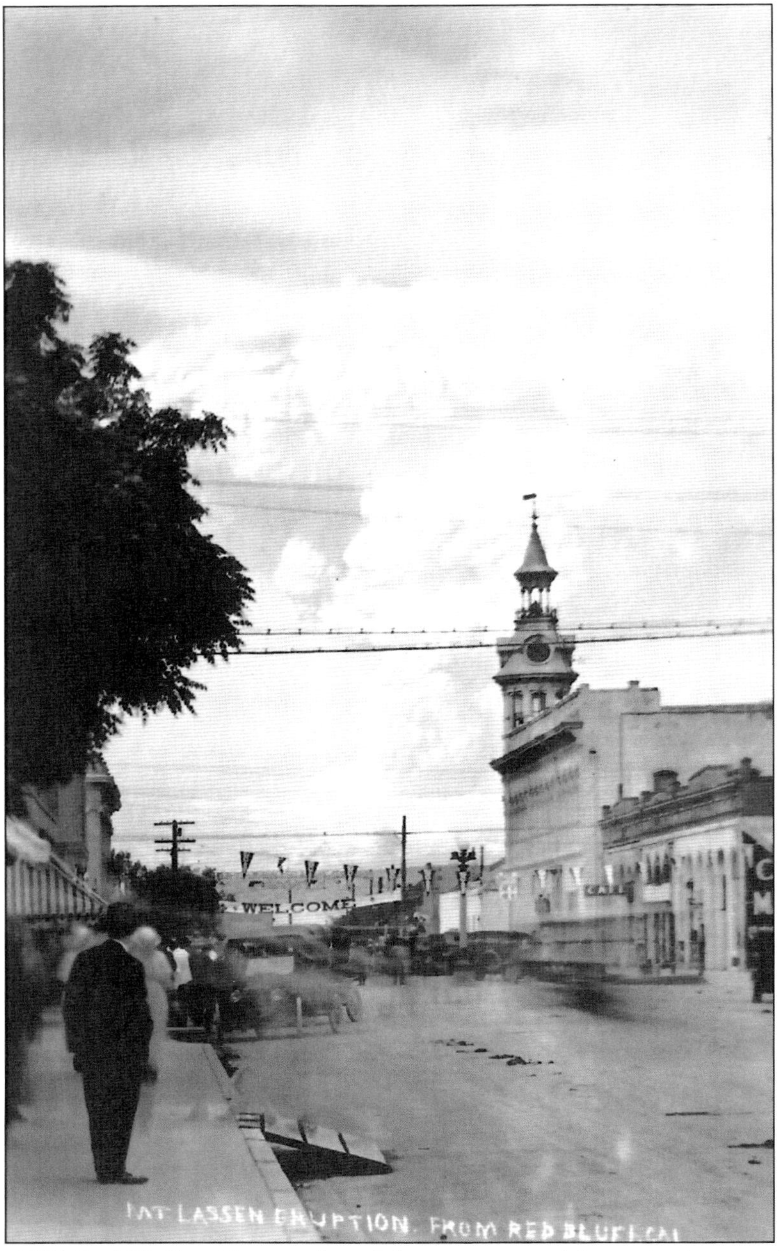

On May 22, 1915, Red Bluff residents gathered downtown to celebrate the long-awaited paving of Main Street. Flags and banners waved a welcome to out-of-town guests for the special event, a band played, food was eaten, drinks were served, and townsfolk danced. Suddenly, late in the afternoon, the ground began to shake, and an enormous explosion stopped the festivities as Lassen Peak (Mount Lassen) sent a column of gas, smoke, and debris shooting 30,000 feet into the skies. The eruption—which deposited volcanic ash in a 200-mile radius and completely covered the tavern and other buildings at Tuscan Springs over the next week—was visible from as far away as Eureka, 150 miles to the east. This photograph was taken several blocks from the downtown celebrations, the view looking east on Walnut Street.

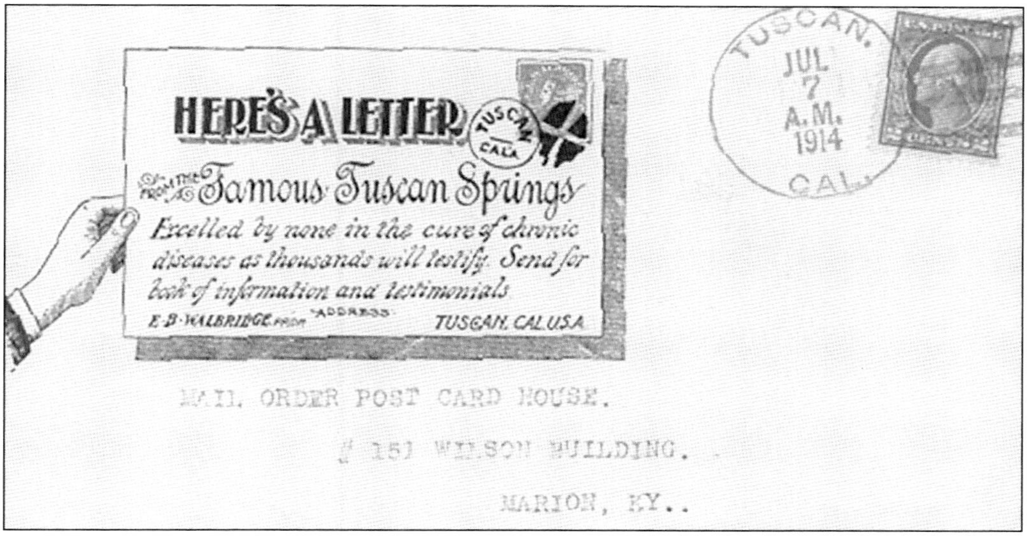

This envelope was mailed from the Tuscan Springs Post Office on Tuesday, July 7, 1914, just one week after Lassen began erupting and three weeks before World War I. The letter does not survive, but it was likely an order for replacement Tuscan Springs postcards from a lithograph importer in Kentucky. Both the front (above) and the back (below) of the envelope heavily advertise the springs, reflecting a new business trend of the era. By this time, every scrap of paper that left the grounds was branded with at least one resort logo. The 20th century had finally arrived at Tuscan Springs. (Both, KGHM.)

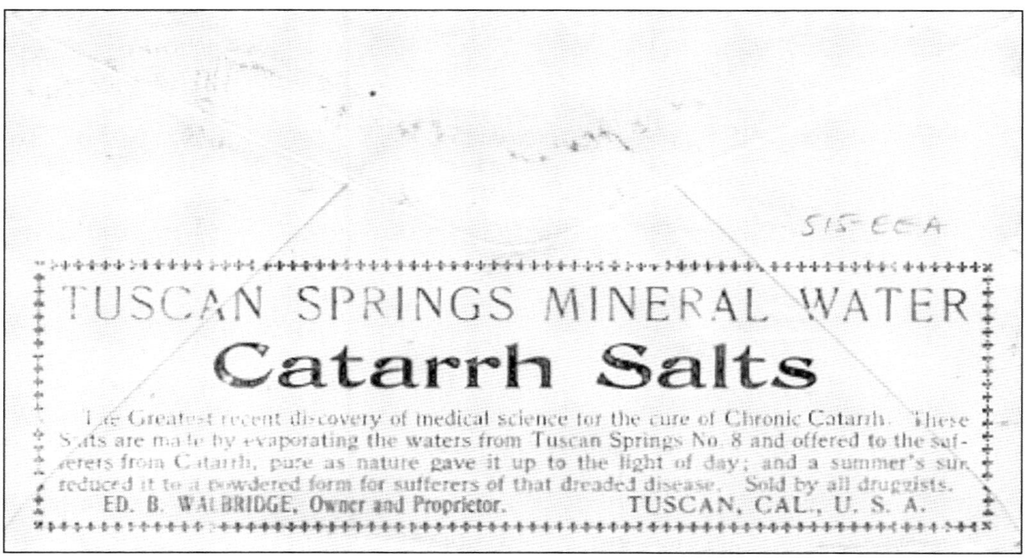

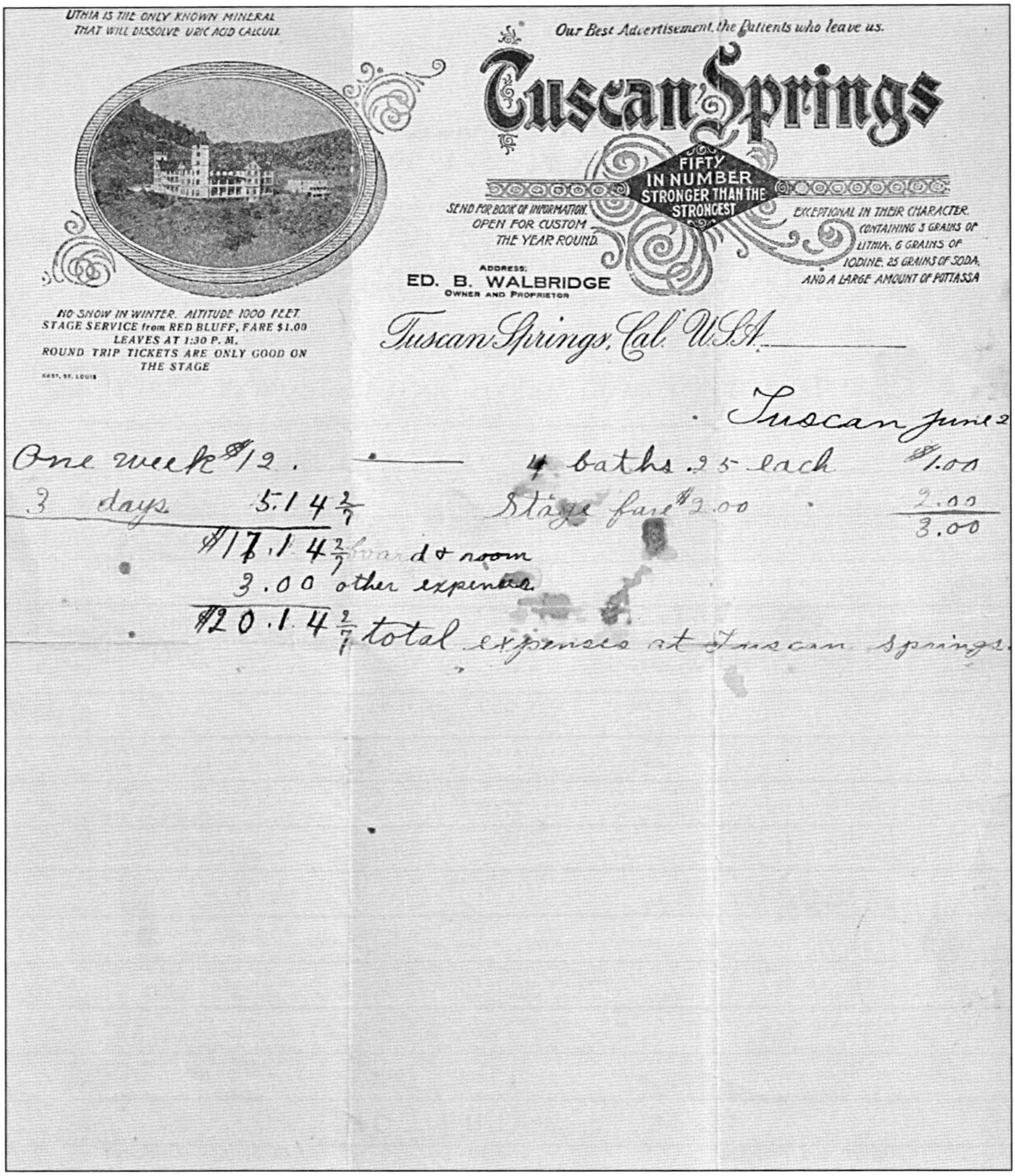

LITHIA IS THE ONLY KNOWN MINERAL THAT WILL DISSOLVE URIC ACID CALCULI.

Our Best Advertisement, the Patients who leave us.

Tuscan Springs

FIFTY IN NUMBER STRONGER THAN THE STRONGEST

SEND FOR BOOK OF INFORMATION. OPEN FOR CUSTOM THE YEAR ROUND.

EXCEPTIONAL IN THEIR CHARACTER. CONTAINING 3 GRAINS OF LITHIA, 6 GRAINS OF IODINE, 25 GRAINS OF SODA, AND A LARGE AMOUNT OF POTTASSA

ADDRESS: ED. B. WALBRIDGE OWNER AND PROPRIETOR

NO SNOW IN WINTER. ALTITUDE 1000 FEET. STAGE SERVICE from RED BLUFF, FARE $1.00 LEAVES AT 1:30 P. M. ROUND TRIP TICKETS ARE ONLY GOOD ON THE STAGE

Tuscan Springs, Cal. U.S.A.

Tuscan June 2

One week $12. — 4 baths .25 each $1.00

3 days 5.14 2/7 Stage fare $2.00 2.00

3.00

$17.14 2/7 board & room

3.00 other expenses

$20.14 2/7 total expenses at Tuscan Springs.

This handwritten receipt was jotted about 1906, and interesting details about the visitor can be gleaned from it. For example, the guest probably arrived by train and took the autocoach to the springs, arriving around 2:00 p.m. on June 12. He or she requested one of the most expensive rooms in the tavern (not on its sunny side or near the stairs or kitchen) and stayed for 10 days—enjoying only four fancy baths within that time—before leaving by autocoach on June 22. A person of some disposable wealth, this guest probably visited for reasons more recreational than medical, and was quite pleased with the visit, staying longer than the typical few days. The total for the visit was $20.14 ($530 today), a large sum in those days, when American wages averaged 22¢ an hour. (KGHM.)

Nine

THE BEGINNING

Van A Neher so disliked his middle named, Ashe, that he had it legally changed to the letter A. That is just one interesting facet of this divorce attorney who was himself married and divorced five times and who waited to become a lawyer until late in middle age, when most men look toward retirement.

What is most interesting, though, is that shortly after passing his bar, Neher was approached, by chance, to represent a claimant in a dispute over some property called Tuscan Springs—the very resort he had visited as a child with his mother, who claimed the waters had cured her inflammatory rheumatism. The deeper he delved into the case, the more apparent it became that the property could be a fantastic business opportunity and a great way to honor the memory of his mother. Neher spent about a decade chasing shards of the property through the courts before finally collecting all the pieces in 1947.

He commissioned blueprints for a $1.3 million resort, which—fully aware of the resort's fire history—he would build only of steel. The problem was that, between World War II and the escalating problems in Korea, the government had placed strict regulations on metals that might be needed for military purposes. So Neher concentrated on fundraising—selling natural gas, water, and minerals from the springs as well as $1 stocks—generating half the needed capital in just a few years. But, when the Korean War began, all steel was indefinitely restricted. By the time the conflict ended, many investors had pulled out. Neher died of a heart attack in 1955, his dream unrealized.

The property transferred to his son Van H. Neher, who passed away in 2006, and then to his grandchildren, who had already found their own lives and careers far away from Tuscan Springs.

Since the 1980s, the family has listed the land for sale several times, and serious interest has been shown by the Hilton Hotels chain and "prominent sports figures," according to Robert Neher, but the next Veatch, Bradley, or Walbridge has yet to appear.

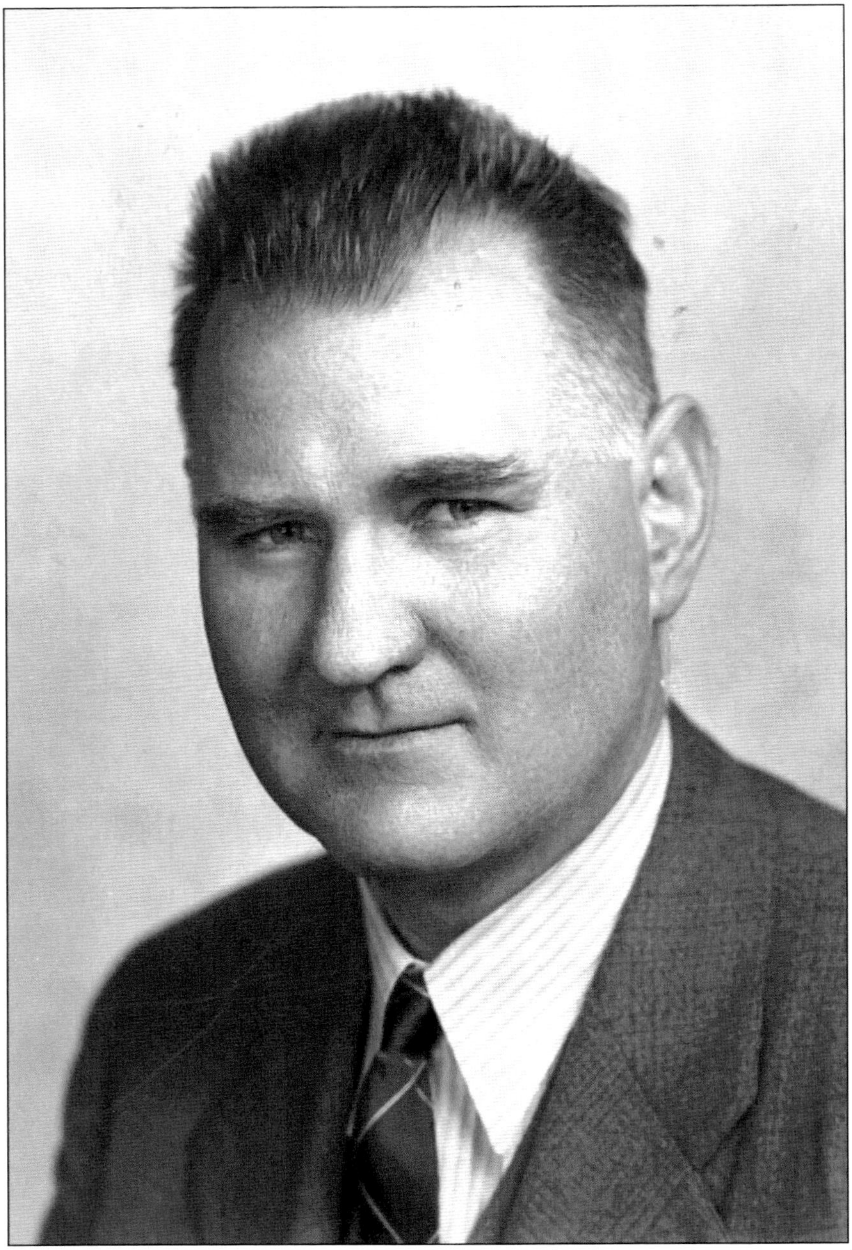

Van A Neher—a former railroad brakeman, schoolteacher, and insurance salesman—visited Tuscan Springs as a child with his mother, who claimed the waters cured her inflammatory rheumatism. Not long afterwards, the resort burned, and she was never able to return. Years later, when Neher had passed the bar and become an Oakland attorney, he was asked to represent a claimant in a land dispute over the same property and found himself involved with the resort. The idea of reopening the springs eventually consumed him, and he spent many years chasing the property fragments through the court system until, in 1947, he publicly announced his plans to construct a new hotel, bathhouse, and other recreational facilities built entirely of steel. He intended to reopen Tuscan Springs 30 years after it had been destroyed. (Neher.)

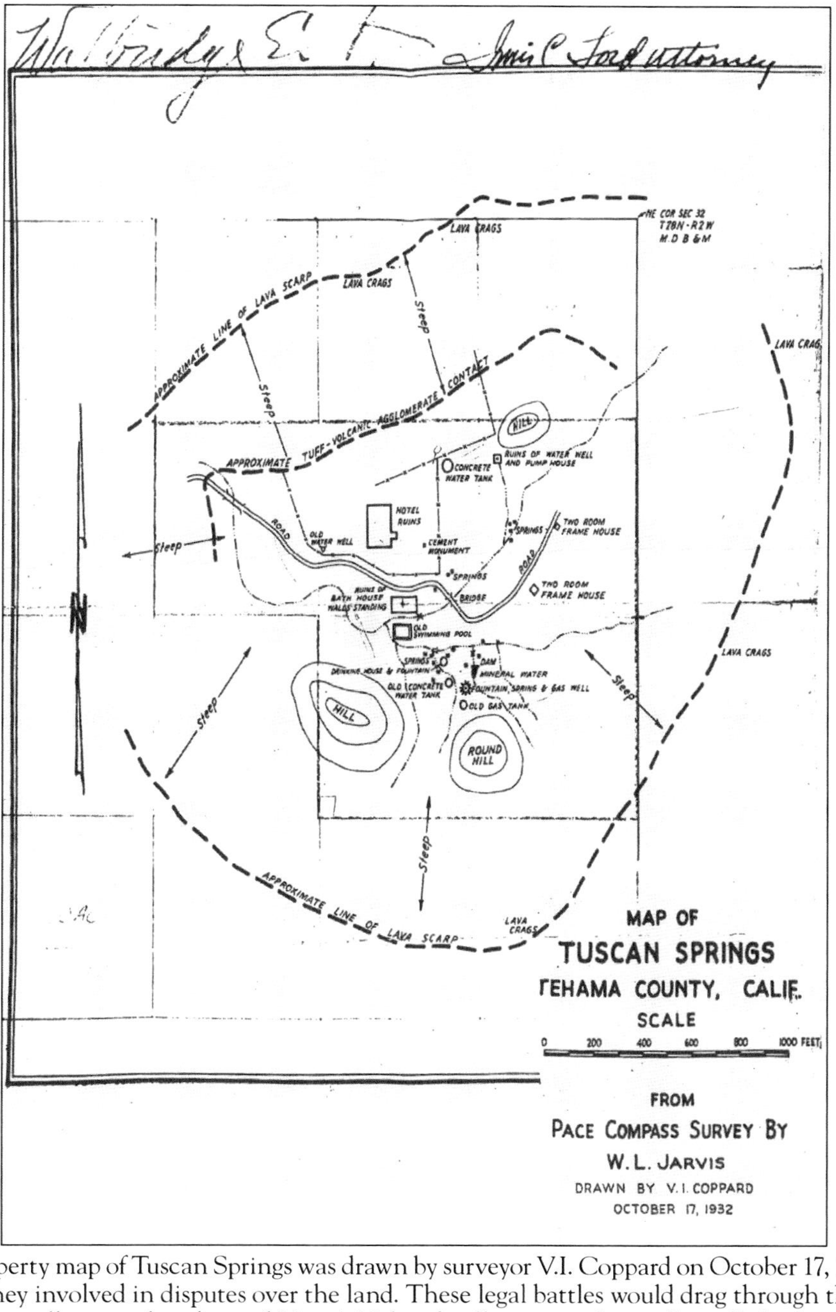

This property map of Tuscan Springs was drawn by surveyor V.I. Coppard on October 17, 1932, for an attorney involved in disputes over the land. These legal battles would drag through the court system for well over a decade until Van A Neher finally managed to collect all the lots in 1947. Soon thereafter, he began fundraising efforts to generate the money needed for construction by selling $1 stocks and products from the springs, including water, salts, and natural gas. Interest in reviving the springs was very high as most adults could still remember when the facility was operational, and Neher quickly gained investors during the prosperous and optimistic years following World War II. Created within 16 years of the final fire, this map is one of the best references for the arrangement of the resort features. (Author.)

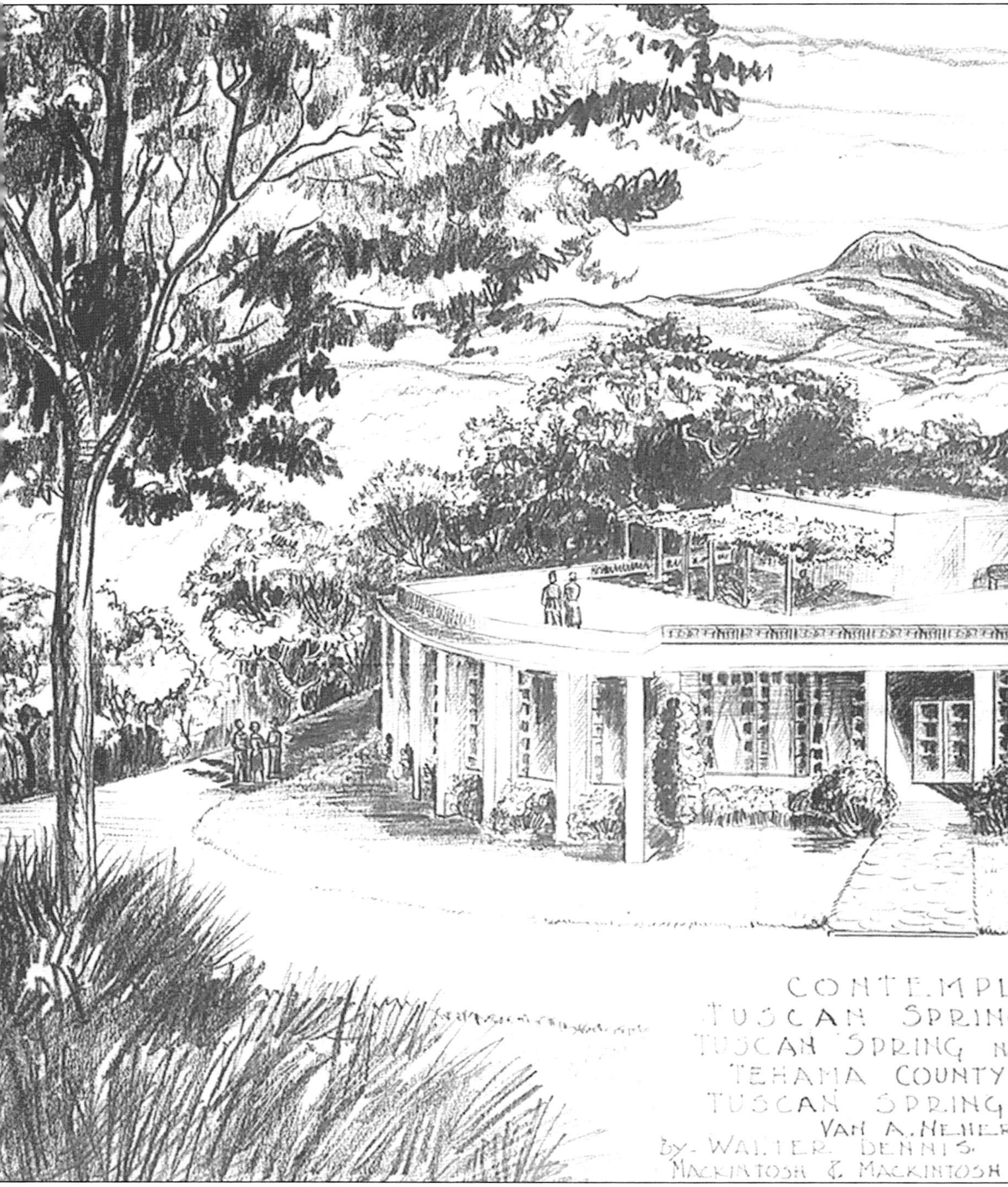

Before beginning his fundraising efforts, Neher had engineers create conceptual drawings to illustrate his vision to investors. The centerpiece of the planned resort was this two-story hotel, which could accommodate 200 guests. It sported a rooftop lounge and all the modern conveniences available around 1950. Neher originally estimated the resort would cost $750,000, but a later estimate

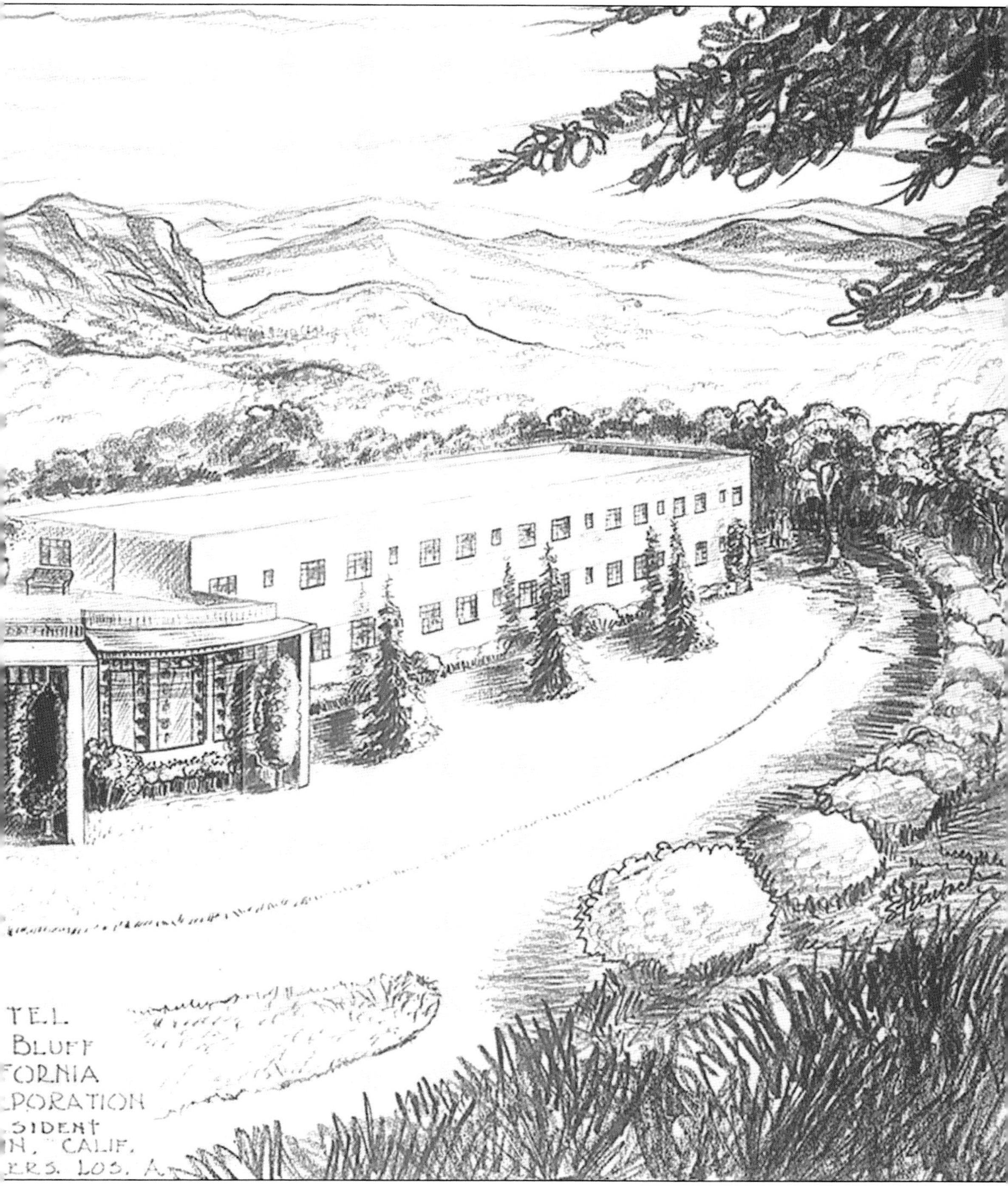

came in at $1.3 million. The main stumbling block, however, was that the federal government had strict rationing on steel at the time. However, being fully aware of the resort's relationship with fire, Neher refused to compromise. (Neher.)

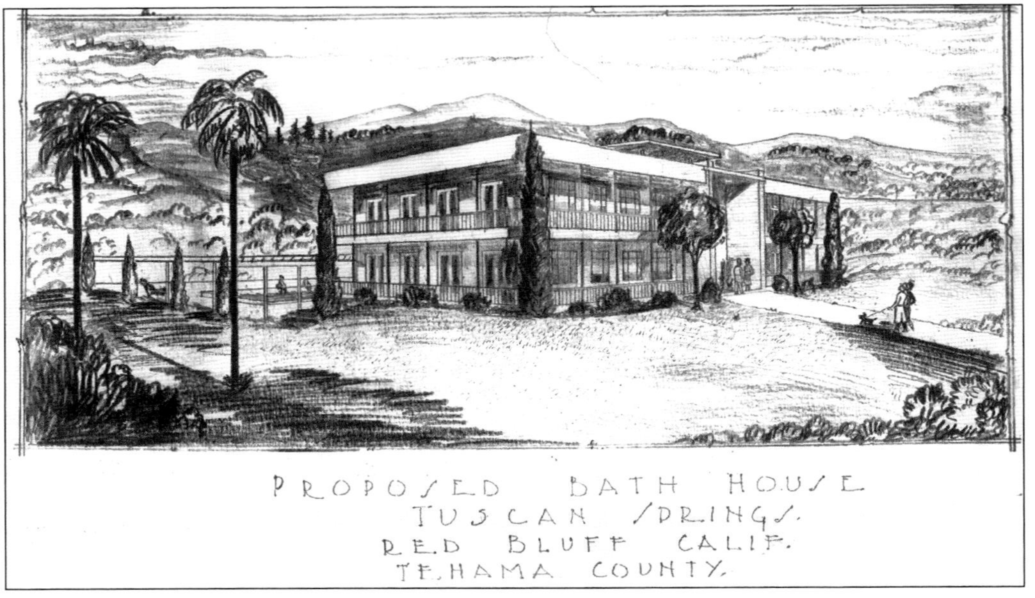

These are two variations of conceptual drawings for the proposed bathhouse commissioned by Neher around 1950. One shows a building of two stories (above), and the other, one of three stories (below). Both include a swimming pool. The same year he had the plans drawn up, Neher also had all of the spring waters analyzed by chemical laboratories in San Francisco and Berkeley. Their scientists determined that there were 57 distinct types of mineral waters on the property—ranging in color from crystal clear to milky white, yellow, pink, violet, and black—each rich in distinctive mineral combinations. (Both, Neher.)

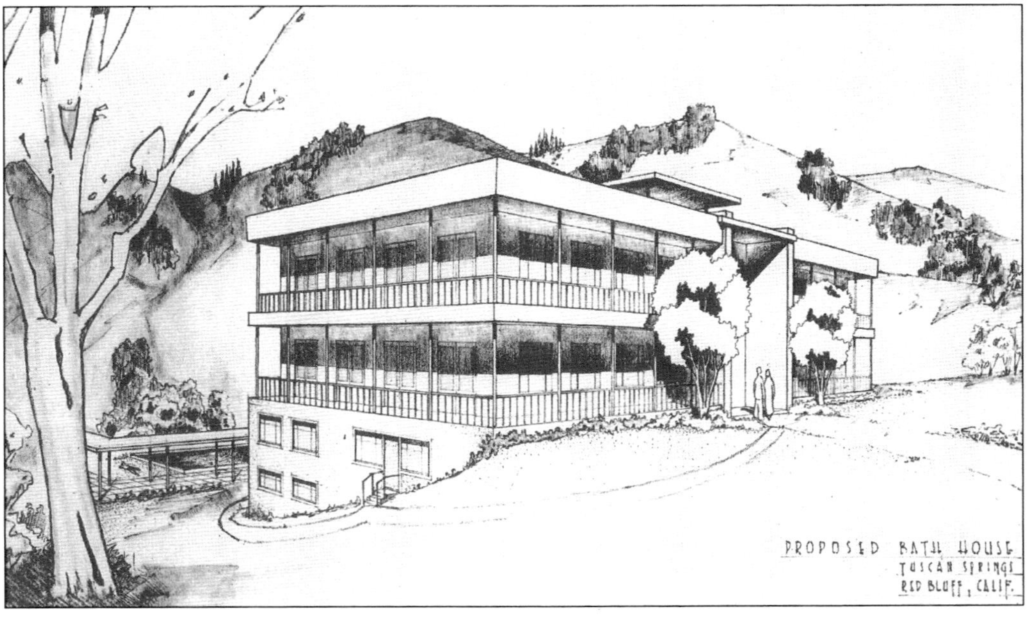

As part of his massive fundraising efforts, Neher began bottling and selling several of the springwaters at a depot in Red Bluff. The bottle of water pictured at right (with its wraparound label seen below) was prescribed for the relief of itching caused by poison oak. The label specifies that the water in the bottle is for external use only and instructs the afflicted to "apply to the affected area with a soft cloth." The label also claims more than 100 springs on the property, "although only some 25 [are] of sufficient flow to be commercially profitable." (Both, author.)

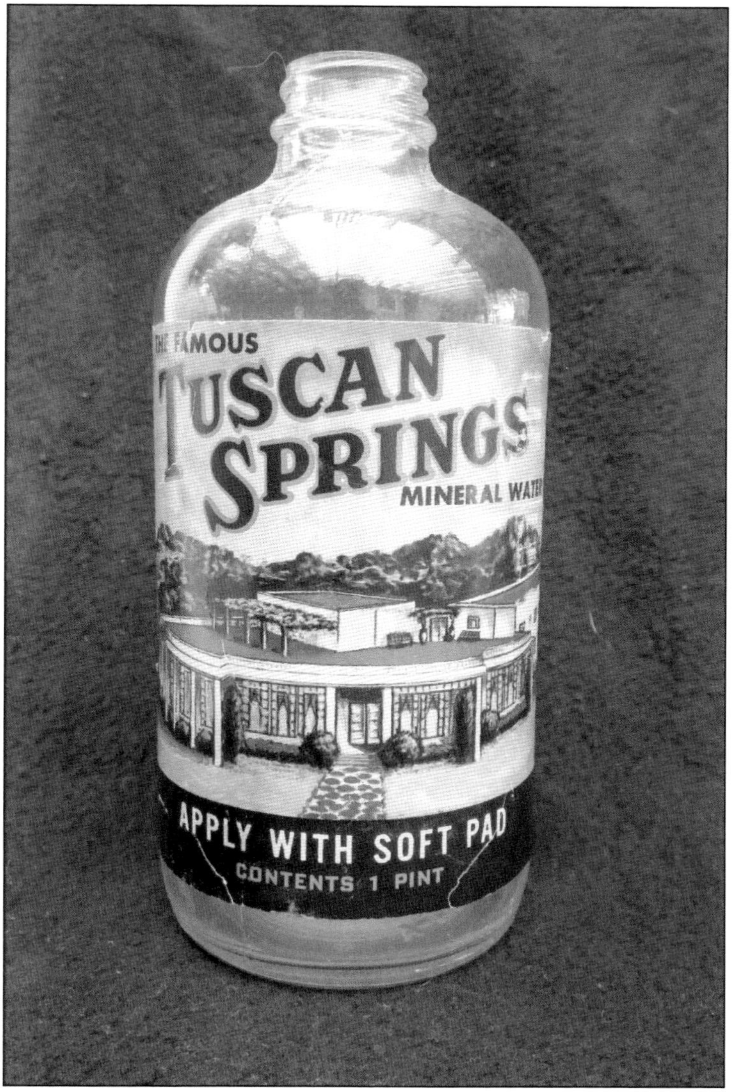

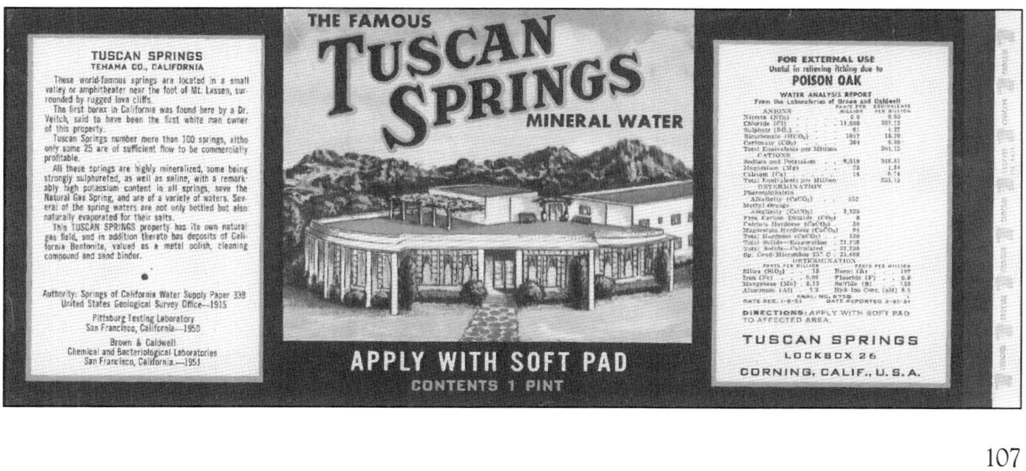

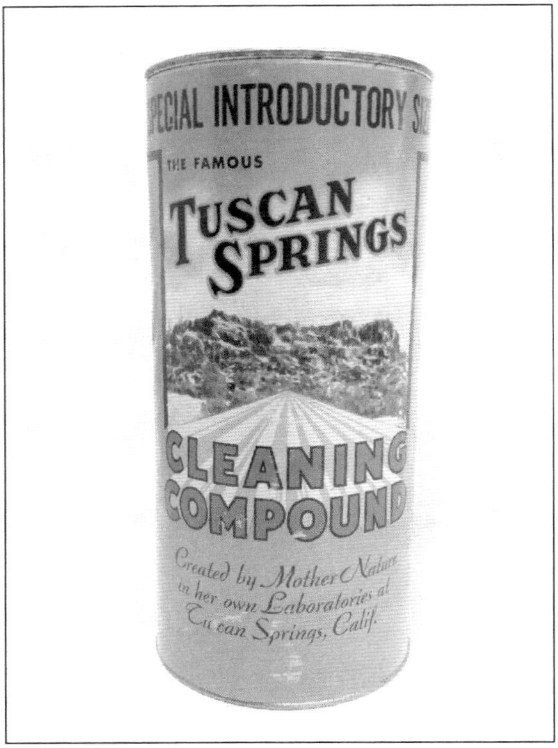

Other products Neher offered for sale to raise funds for his new resort included a cleaning compound (left), a silver polish (below), and a scouring compound (not pictured), all of which were created from select pulverized rocks on the property. Some contained California bentonite, commonly used in metal polish and cleaning compounds and as a sand binder. Neher's product were composed mainly of silica, but also contained varying quantities of alumina, iron oxide, and lime. He also had plans to produce a tooth polish, toothpaste, shaving soap, and shaving creams for sale, but these products never materialized. (Both, author.)

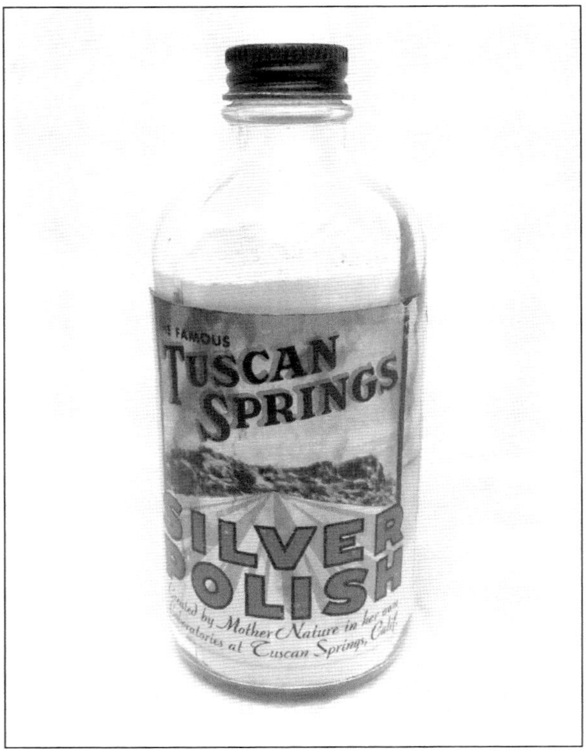

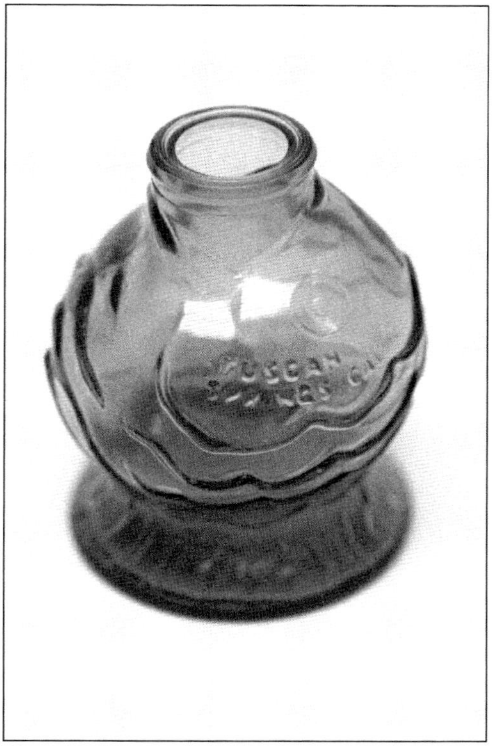

Neher's son Van Herbert Neher later designed and sold these bottles—which are often found today in antique shops and online, labeled "reproductions"—for the Wheaton Company in the 1960s. They bear little resemblance to any bottle ever used for Tuscan Springs products. In the photograph at right is a colored, fish-shaped bottle with "Tuscan Springs, CA" embossed on one side and "Catarrah [*sic*] Cure" on the other. It is actually an approximation of the famous fish bottles used by Dr. Fisch's Bitters, popular in the 1860s, 1870s, and later. Apart from the embossing, it had no relation to Tuscan Springs. (Both, author.)

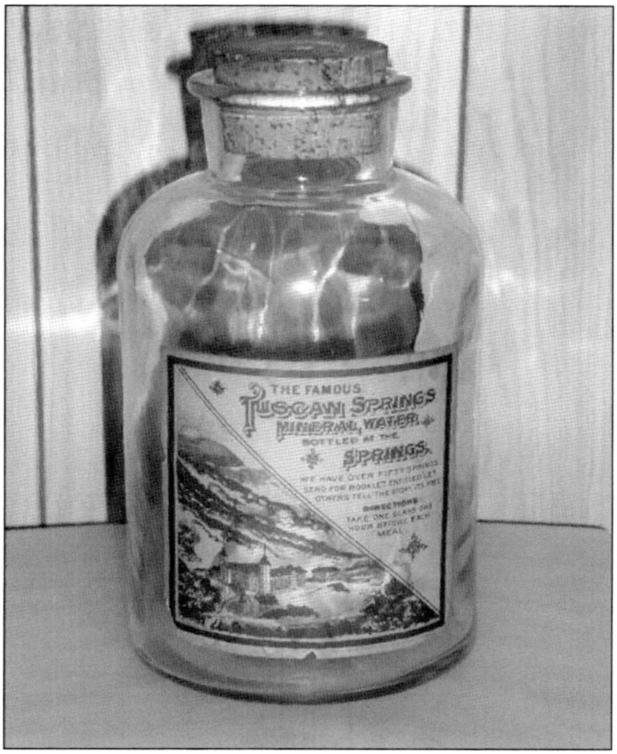

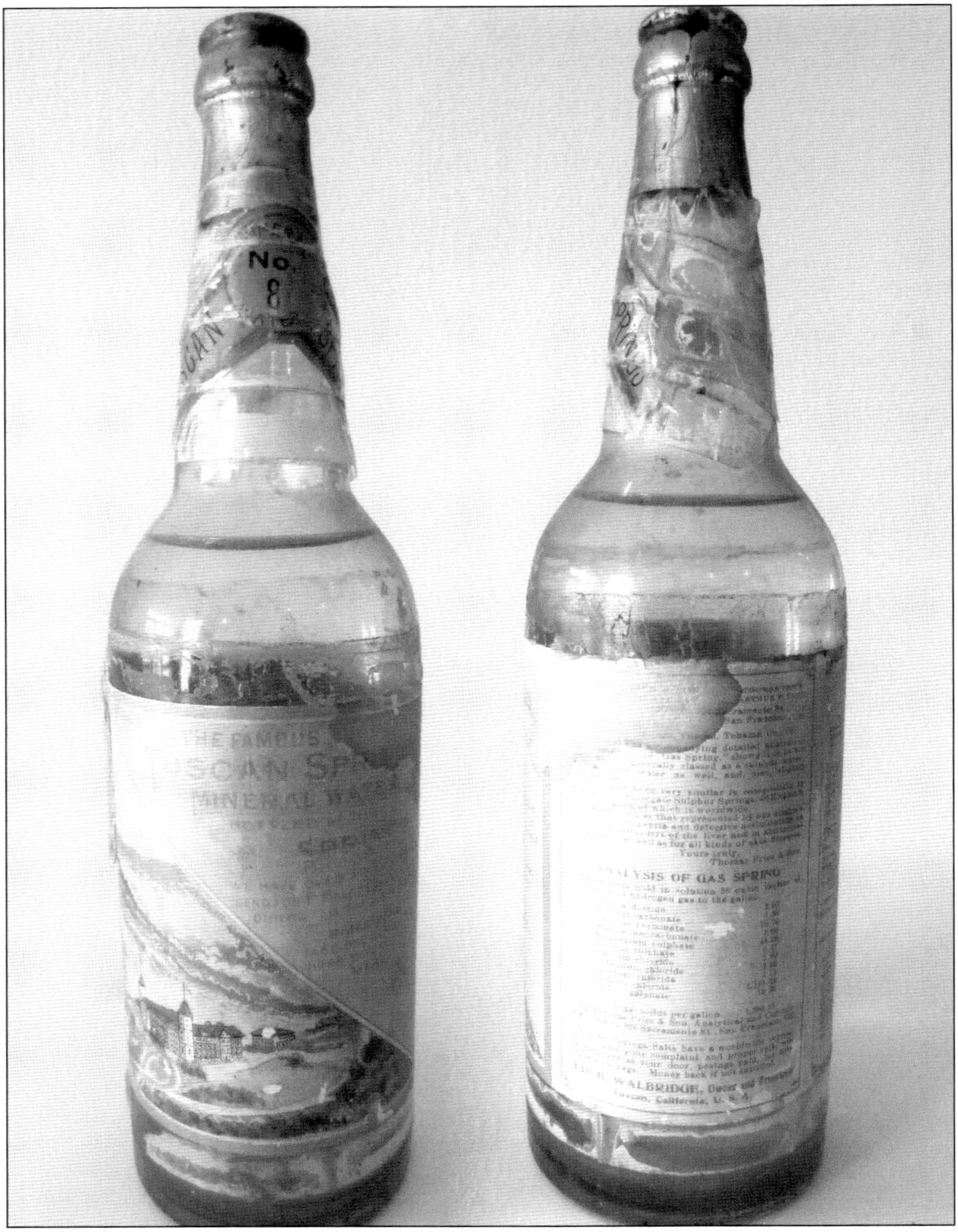

This is an actual bottle (front and back) of Tuscan Springs mineral water, which was sold by Walbridge starting around 1899. Corked like wine and sealed with wax, this particular product was filled from the "gas spring," which was also tapped to provide lighting and heat. The analysis printed on the back identifies the water as containing mostly sodium chloride, calcium carbonate, magnesium sulphate, sodium sulphate, magnesium carbonate, and calcium chloride, as well as "58 cubic inches of sulphuretted hydrogen gas per gallon." The analysis, by Thomas Price & Sons out of San Francisco, recommends drinking the water for help with dyspepsia, liver problems, constipation, and skin diseases. The only known surviving bottles are still full of springwater and belong to the Nehers. (Neher.)

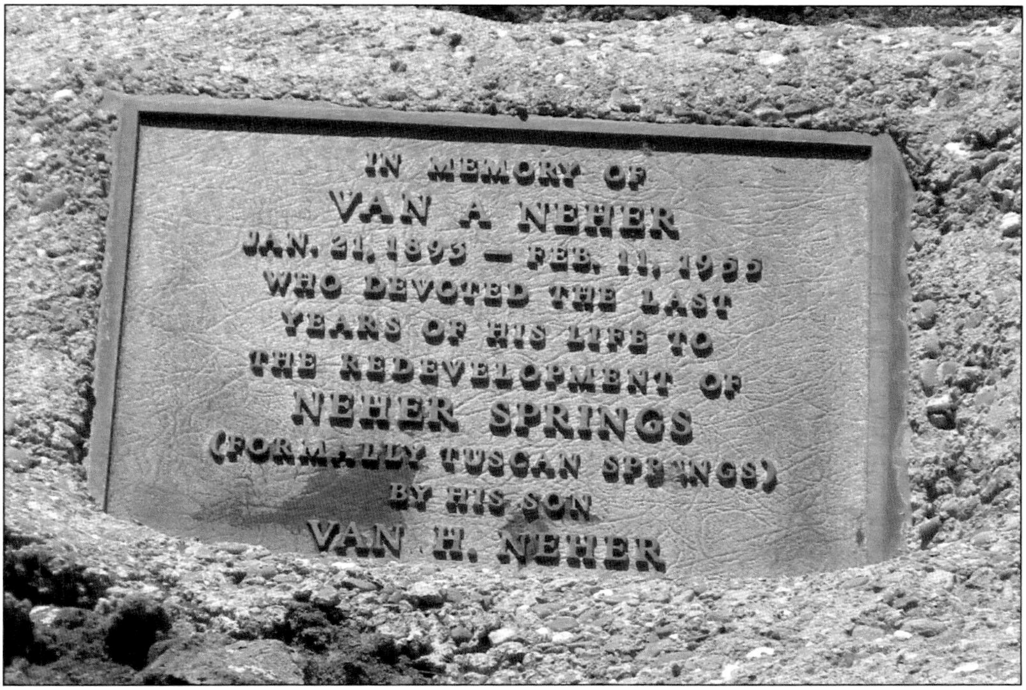

Van A Neher died of a heart attack in 1955 before he could realize his dream, and the land passed to his son Van H. Neher. The younger Neher was not as strongly motivated to develop the property into a new health resort, though he did explore the possibilities at various times. He passed away in 2006, also of a heart attack, having previously transferred the land to his children, twins Robert and Richard, Leni, and Van H. Jr. The ashes of both men were scattered from a northern cliff at Tuscan Springs, and memorial plaques for both were installed. (Both, Neher.)

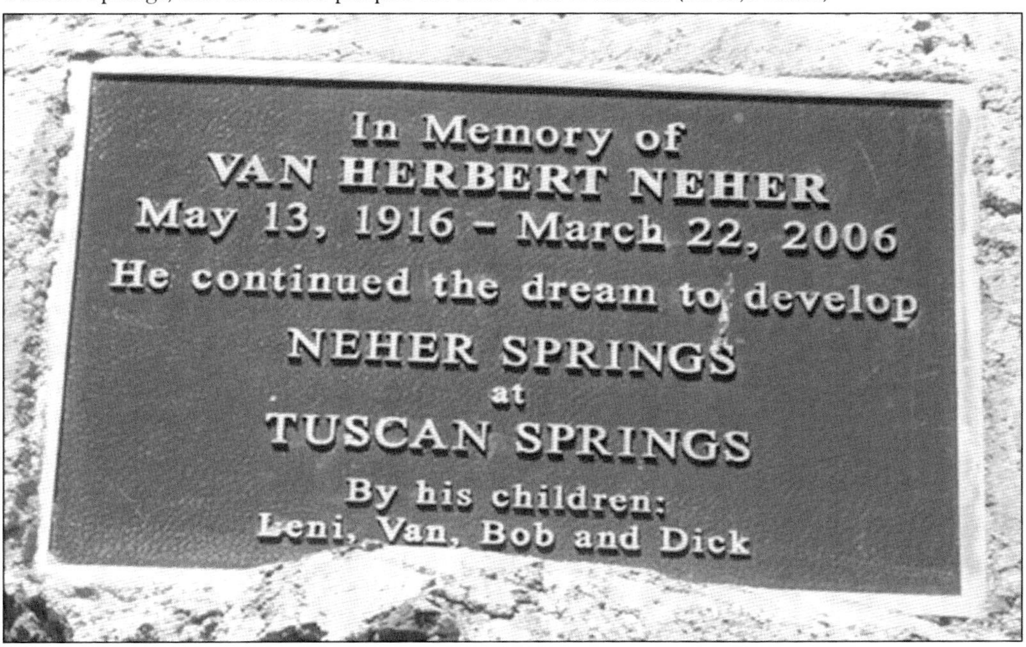

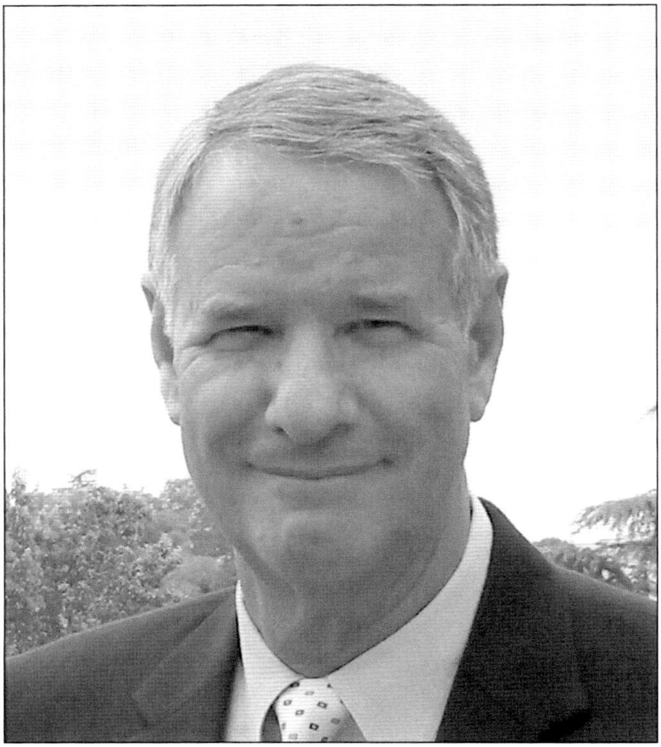

Twins Robert (left) and Richard (below) Neher, along with their sister and brother, are the current owners of Tuscan Springs. By the time they inherited the property, they had careers, families, and lives far from Northern California. They have examined many possibilities for the land over the years, including harvesting the natural gas or building a family retreat, and have even met with Hilton Hotels representatives and "prominent sports figures." However, nothing has ever developed. Most of all, according to Robert, they would ultimately just like to see their grandfather's dream realized and a new resort raised from the ruins. (Both, Neher.)

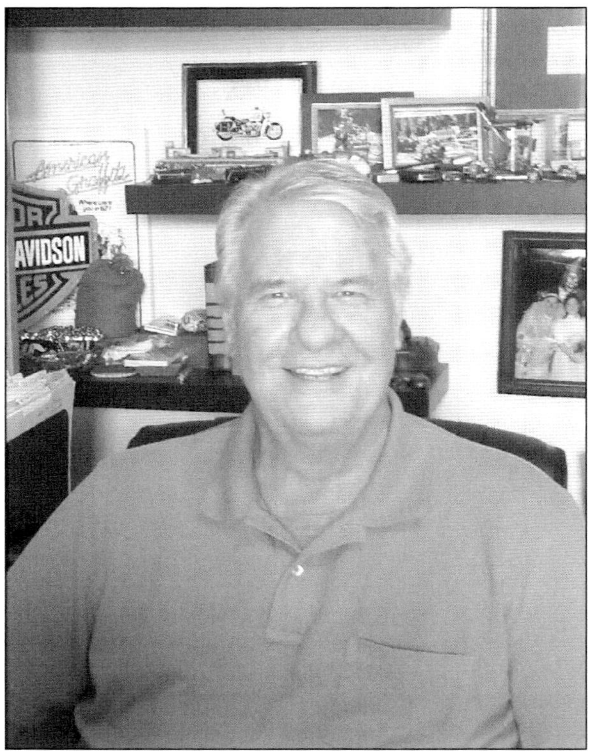

Ten

O Brave New World

From the Gilded Age to the Information Age, Tuscan Springs looks much the same today as it did when Veatch first set foot there in 1854. It is still like stepping into a storybook, only now, the "story" is less about what it might become and more about how it must have been.

For 60 years, the popular resort was the repository for countless dreams of wealth, health, and hope. And, while it did apparently provide genuine miracles from time to time, it was frequently more bust than boon for those expecting a sure cure or fast fortune. The only thing as good as gold, as they say, is gold, and like the elusive nugget, Tuscan Springs sometimes rewarded patience but seldom recognized greed.

A century later, the land has remained relatively undisturbed, visited only by hard-core historians or the casually curious. Tuscan Springs had its day, some say, and people no longer believe in that sort of thing—the world has changed. Then again, perhaps the times are not that different after all.

"Neurasthenia Americana" was a catchall term describing the struggle to keep pace in a swiftly spinning world increasingly overwhelmed by change, technology, and noise. Today, that is called stress, and the afflicted turn to prescription drugs, performance enhancers, and energy drinks to ease the same symptoms, just like the patent medicines of old. And each year, thousands still "take the waters" at resorts throughout the country, which have survived and thrived into the 21st century and brag better-than-ever business. So perhaps it is not too far-fetched a fantasy, in the end, to think that the world might once again embrace the famous Tuscan Springs.

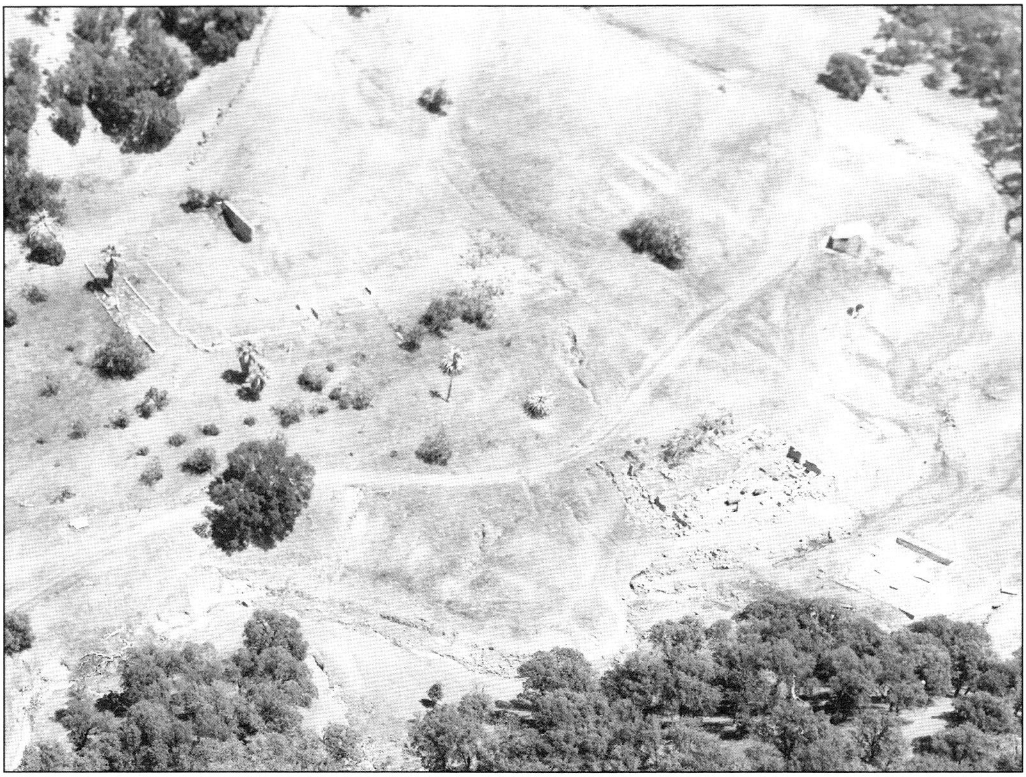

These shots, taken by the once well-known Red Bluff photographer Francis Bayles in 1964, show bird's-eye views of the resort ruins. The image above, taken from almost directly over the resort ruins, shows the main trail through the property. The tavern foundation can be seen at the upper left, and the last standing cottage is located at the top right. Vestiges of the Chinese walls can still be spotted here and there. The image below, with a view from the southeastern corner, shows more dramatic detail of the area around the pool and bathhouse. Toward the bottom right, remnants of the gasometer can be seen. (Both, Bayles.)

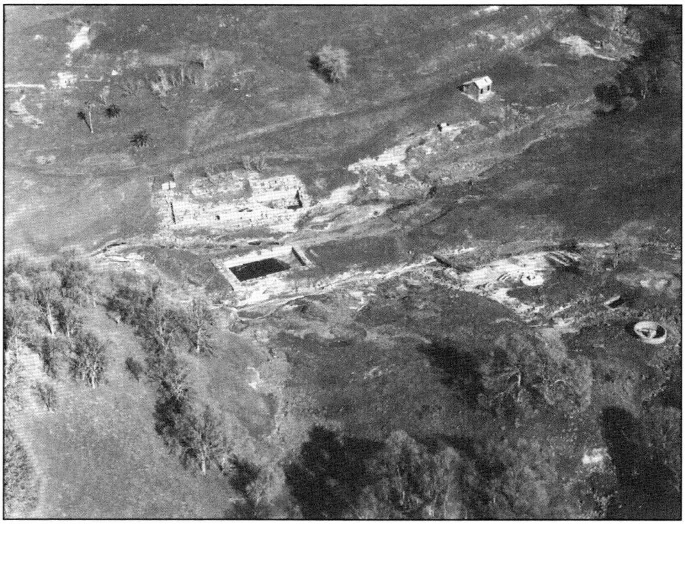

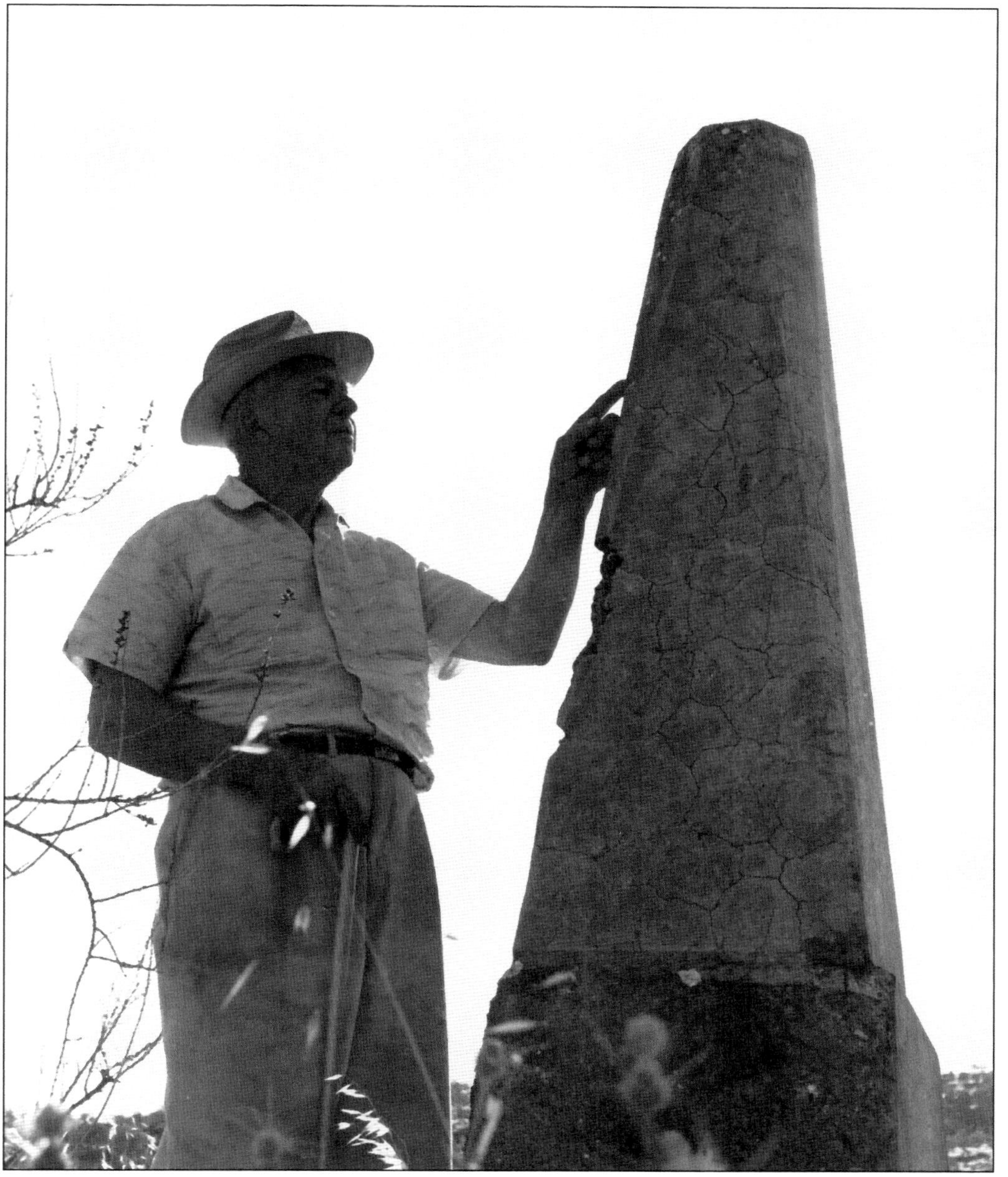

In this 1964 image, David Bayles examines the monument built at Tuscan Springs for Van A Neher after he passed from a heart attack in 1955. It was installed by his son Van H. Neher, who graduated from the University of California, Berkeley, in 1938 and worked for the federal government in Oakland before joining the Navy as a radar officer on a destroyer in the Pacific. After the war, he became a traveling salesman for the Walt Disney Company, the Wheaton Company, and then for an artificial-flower–manufacturing business. In later years, he would open his own artificial-flower company. Though he respected his father's dreams for Tuscan Springs, from the far end of the country, he was simply unable to devote to the project the time and resources that would be required to make it succeed. (Bayles.)

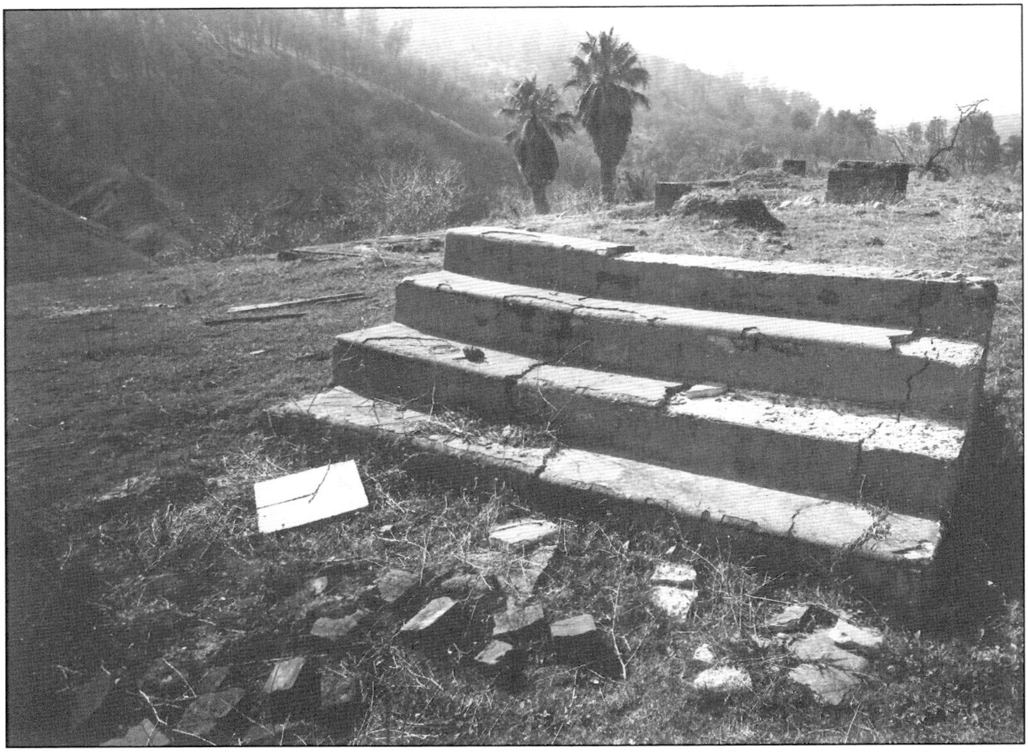

The photograph above shows the front steps to the great tavern Walbridge constructed in 1900. The one below shows the foundation, steps, and column. The palm trees seen were planted when the last hotel was built and will not be found in any photographs from before 1900. It was something of a craze in Tehama County after the 1890s to plant palm trees around large businesses and homes, calling to mind the more exotic locations seen on postcards and insinuating that the area was so unique that "anything and everything could grow there." The palms remain there today. (Both, Bayles.)

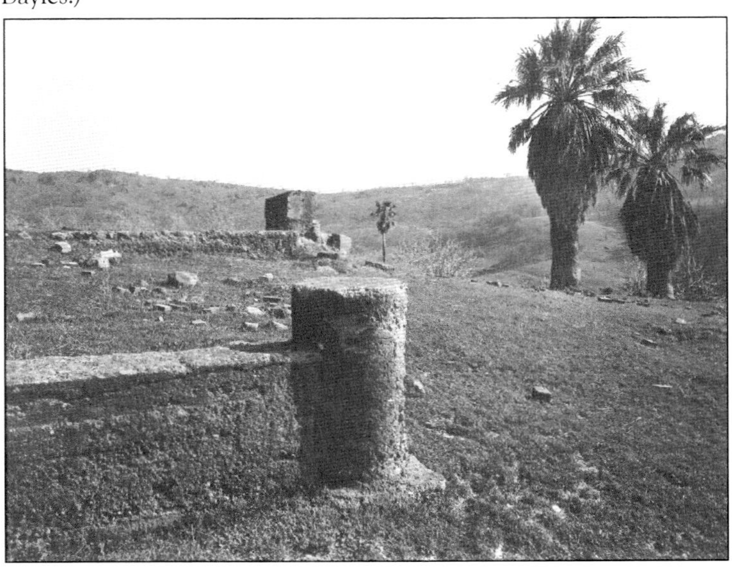

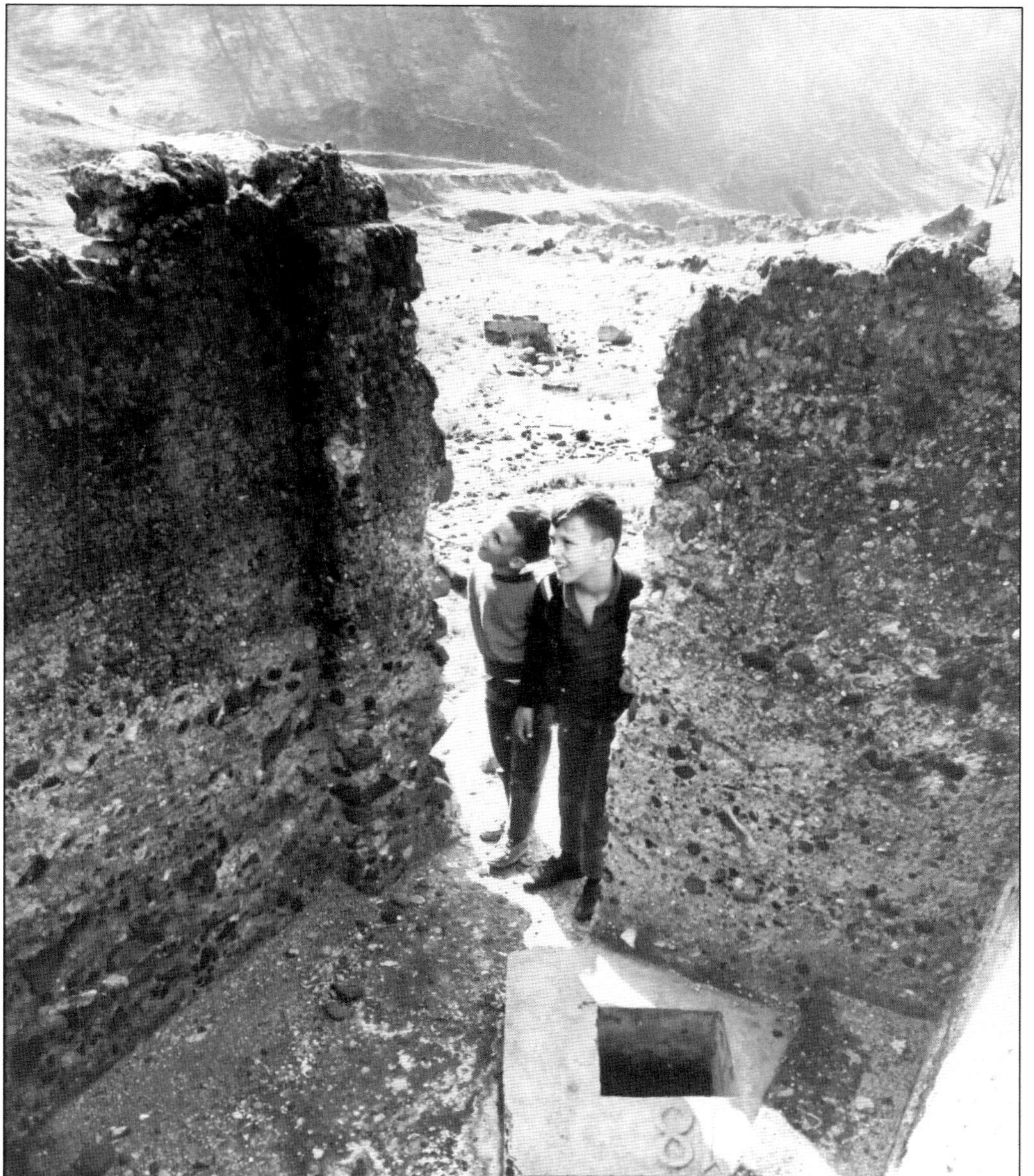

The Bayles children are seen here exploring the roofless drinking house of spring No. 18. These structures were built to protect a spring from debris and to offer patrons a shaded area to sit and sip from the waters. Some were very crudely made of stone and mortar and may have been built at the same time as Walbridge's walls. The exact afflictions thought to be treated by spring No. 18 are unknown, but nearby are springs 15, the "bowels spring," and 17, the "constipation spring," if those are any indication. (Bayles.)

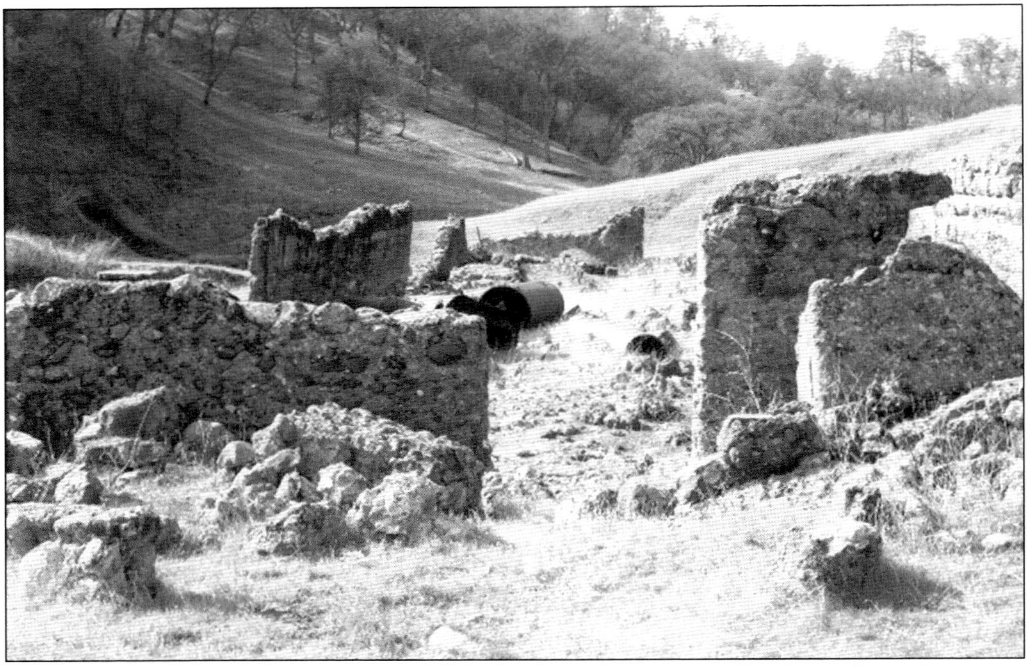

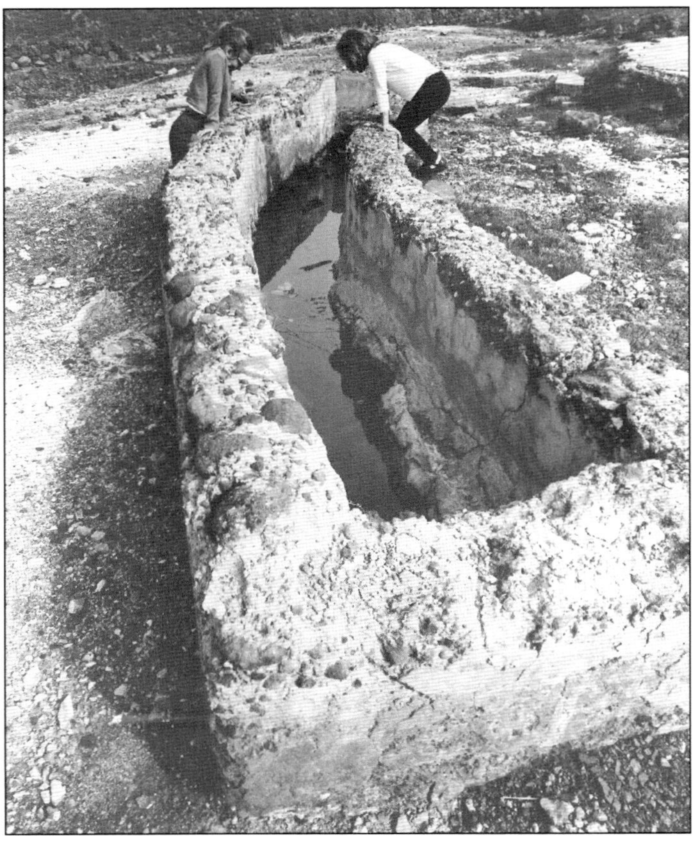

The image above shows the ruins of the famous bathhouse that Walbridge had built entirely of concrete and cement in 1905; it was intended to withstand any future fires that might befall the resort. Fireproof though it may have been, it, too, eventually fell to the ravages of rain, wind, and time. Just beyond that entrance, however, countless thousands of guests at Tuscan Springs once found relief in its therapeutic mud baths, steam baths, hot plunge bath, saunas, and showers. The left photograph shows a trough-like portion of the bathhouse foundation. (Above, Massie; left, Bayles.)

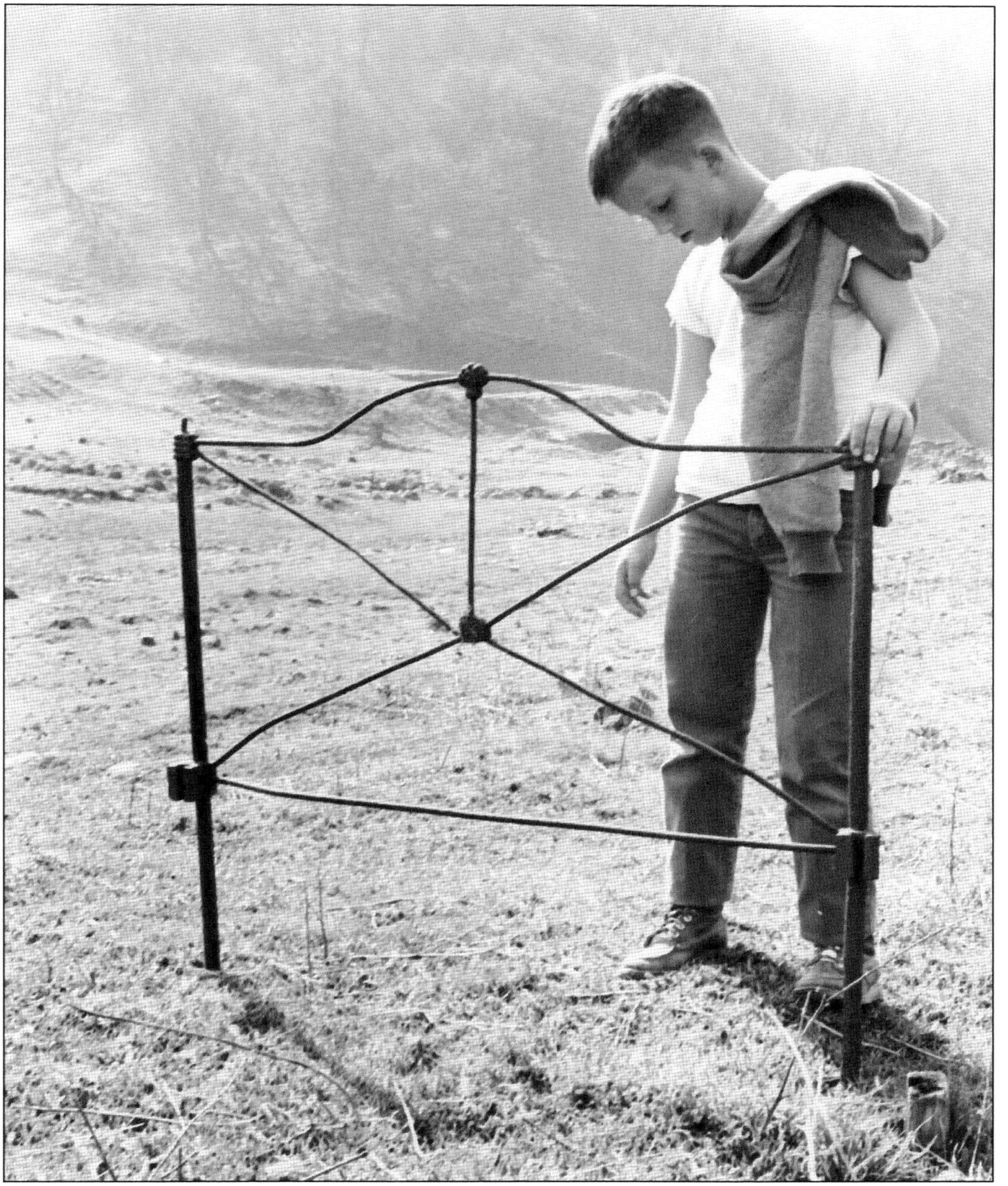

The crude, rust-crusted portion of an old iron bed frame being examined here by one of the Bayles children was not from one of the rooms in the tavern but from one of the cottages scattered throughout the property. The cottage beds were simple, small, and functional, while the brass beds used in the rooms of the tavern were much larger and sturdier. They were also of a much more elaborate design. This frame, like all of the other artifacts once found at Tuscan Springs—including stray coins, dishes, bottles, silverware, tiles, and fixtures—has long since disappeared with the many curiosity seekers and treasure hunters who have found their way onto the property over the years. (Bayles.)

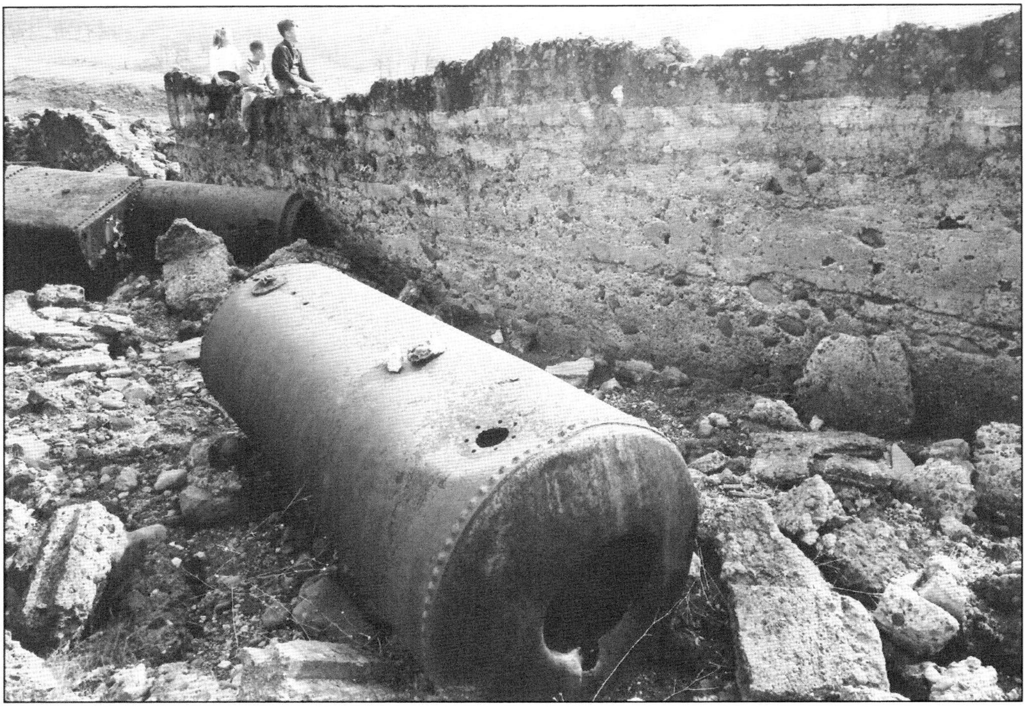

These two photographs show the hot-water furnaces that were kept in the ground floor of the bathhouse to heat the bathwaters, steam rooms, laundry facilities, and the hot plunge bath. They were fed natural gas directly from the gasometer, which also piped to the tavern to provide heat and lights. It may have been a furnace very similar to these but faulty—or possibly bad piping to them—that caused the fire that gutted the bathhouse just after its complete renovation in 1904. (Above, Bayles; below, Massie.)

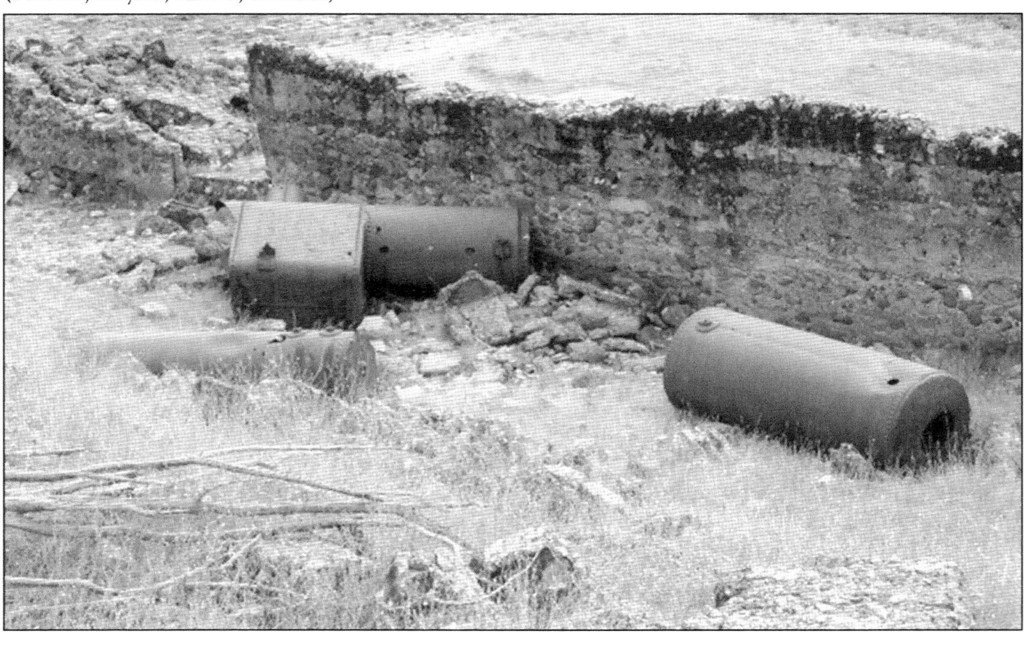

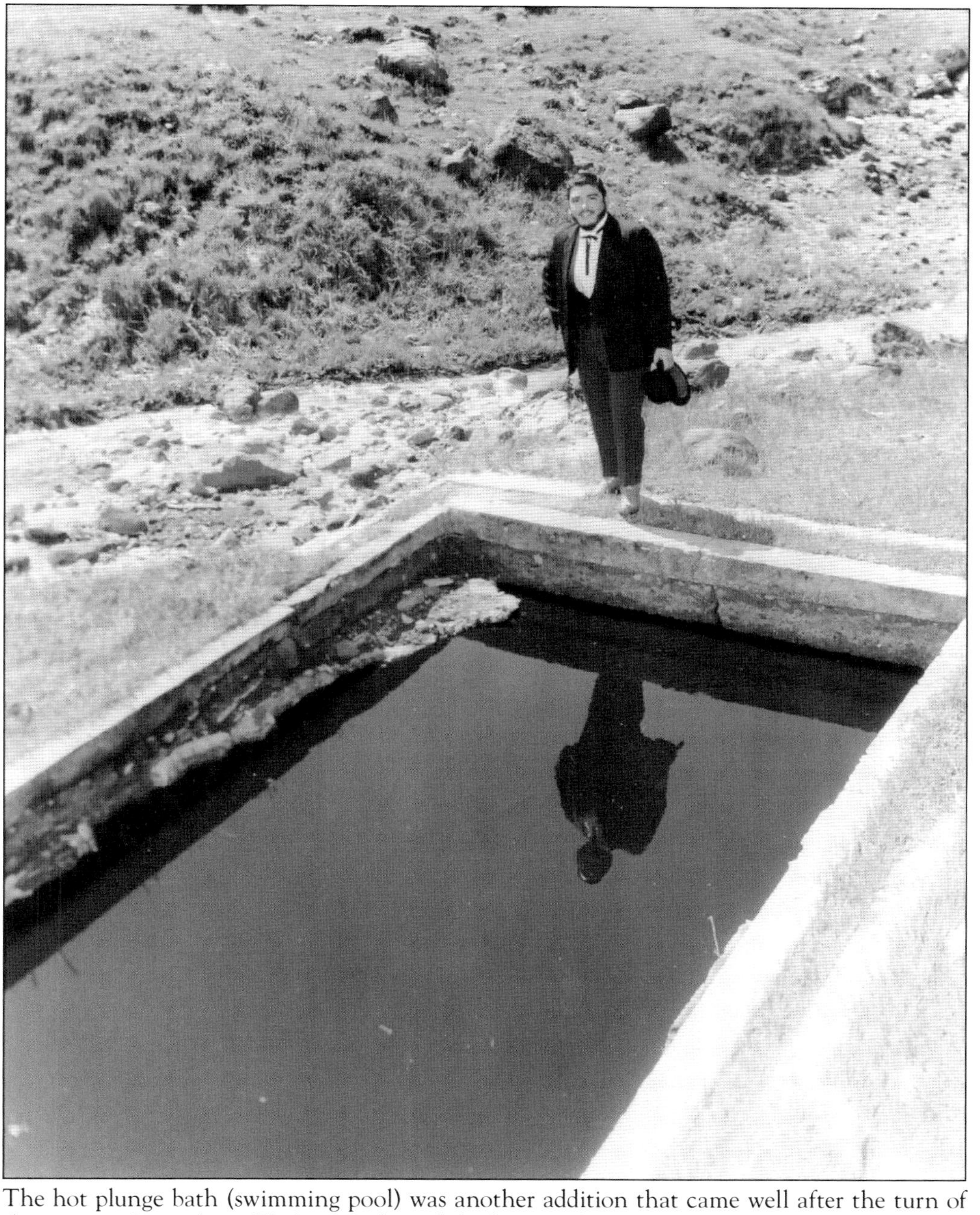

The hot plunge bath (swimming pool) was another addition that came well after the turn of the century. It was kept filled not with cool, fresh water, but with mineral waters from different springs at different times of the year (or according to whichever springs were most productive at the time). "The water is so dense [with minerals], with a very little exertion one can float with ease," Walbridge advertised in his promotional materials. In 1904, the pool was said to be 60 feet long, with a depth ranging from 5 to 15 feet. (Bayles.)

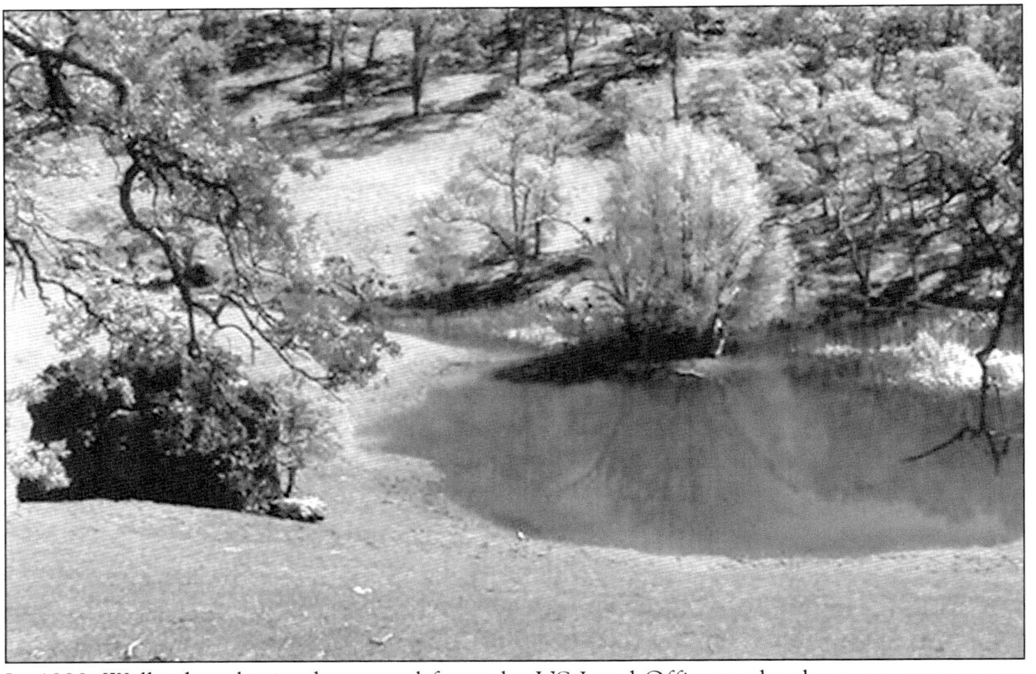

In 1899, Walbridge obtained approval from the US Land Office to develop property next to Tuscan Springs into an artificial 12-acre lake. Set in a natural rock basin, the lake was installed in short order and was stocked with a variety of fish and ducks. But, within just a few months, a fire destroyed most of the resort, necessitating immediate repairs and construction, and the lake was likely abandoned. The feature was never again mentioned in the papers. Trees and shrubs have long since reclaimed the basin, as can be seen here. (Both, Massie.)

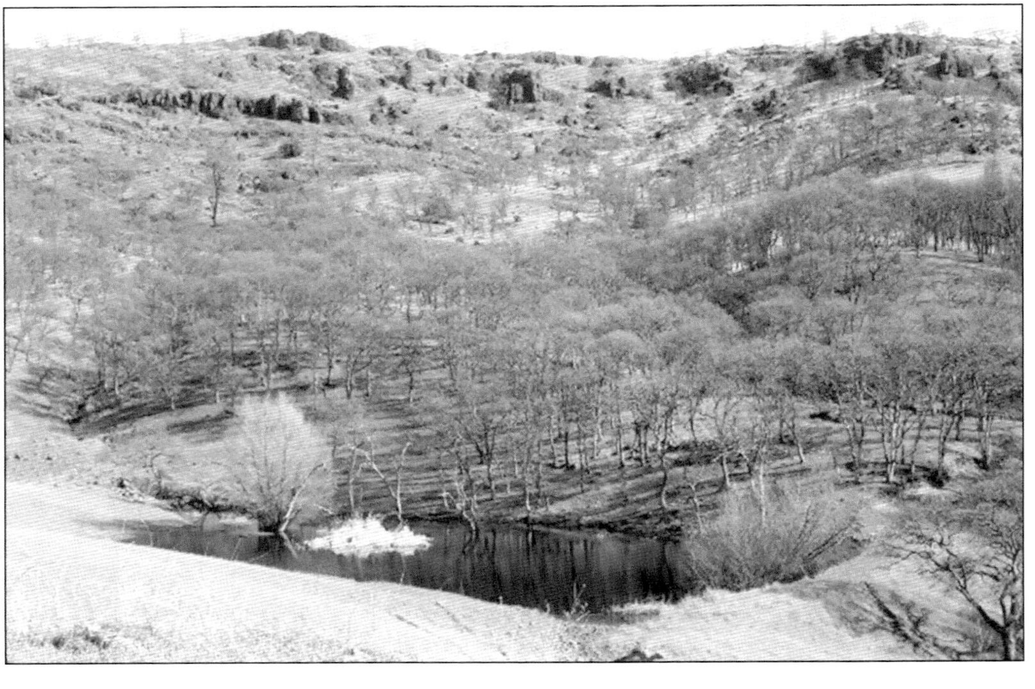

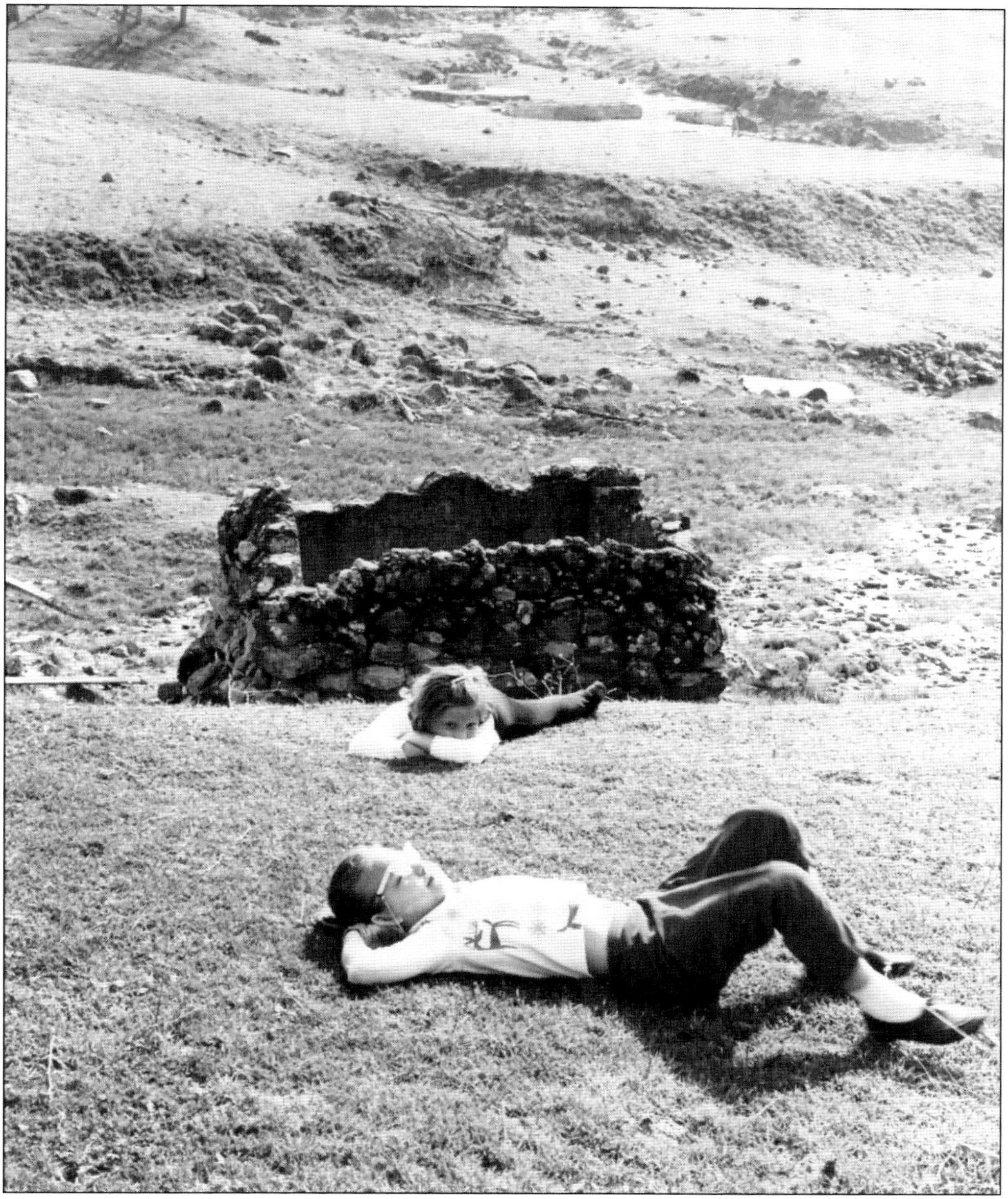

The Bayles children are seen here relaxing after a long afternoon of exploring Tuscan Springs in March 1964. The drinking house for spring No. 18 can be seen in the background. Exactly 100 years before this photograph was taken, Dr. John A. Veatch was lucratively harvesting borax from his new source in Lake County, and Dr. William Olendorf, the disgruntled owner of Tuscan Springs, had not the slightest idea of what to do with the property and was ready to unload it at a bargain to the first person who expressed the slightest interest. (Bayles.)

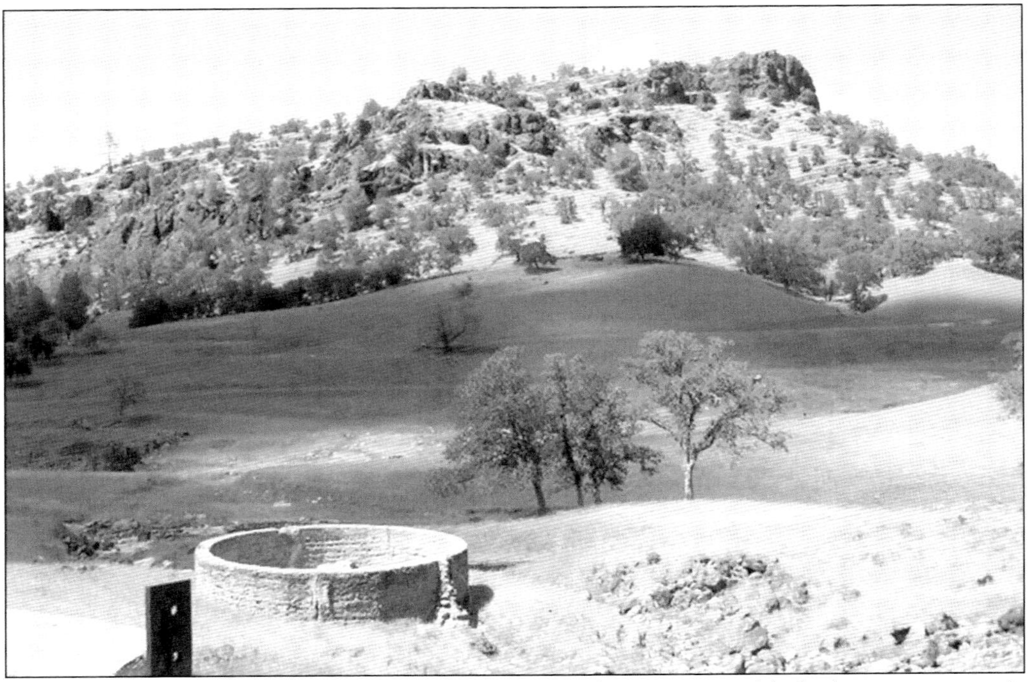

These photographs show some of the spring tubs. These tubs were not used for bathing, as commonly thought, but for special purposes such as gas harvesting, bottling, and drinking. "These springs are unsurpassed on this Coast," writes Walbridge about the springs in the 1903 promotional pamphlet, "for the cure of rheumatism, dropsy, salt rheum, tetter, paralysis, dyspepsia, neuralgia, mercury in the system, catarrh . . . fever and ague, St. Vitus' dance, poison oak and female complaints. They are also a dead shot on piles!" (Both, Massie.)

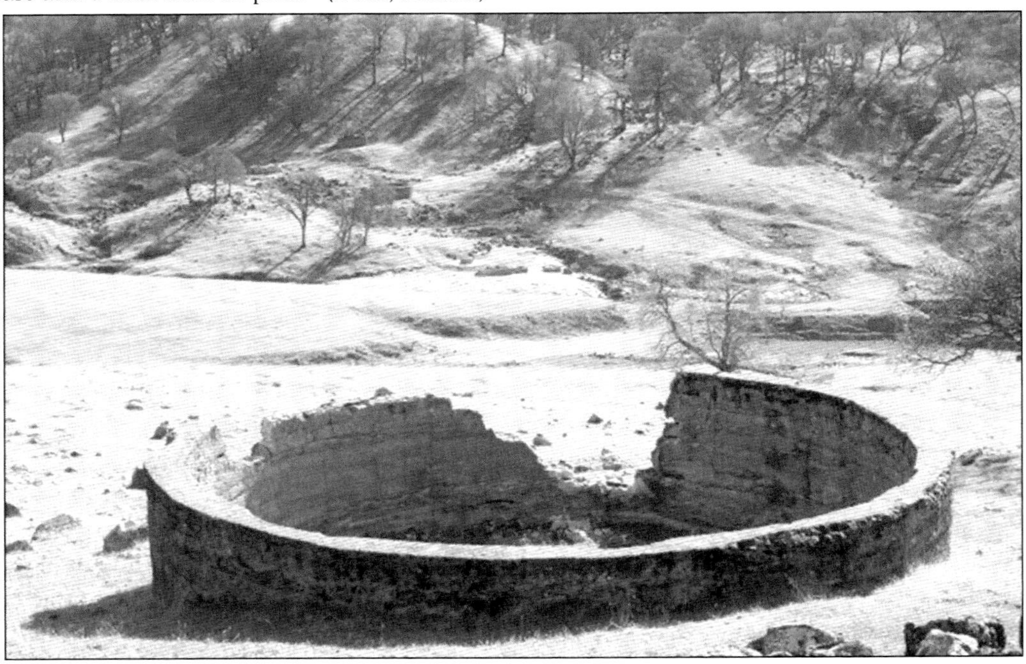

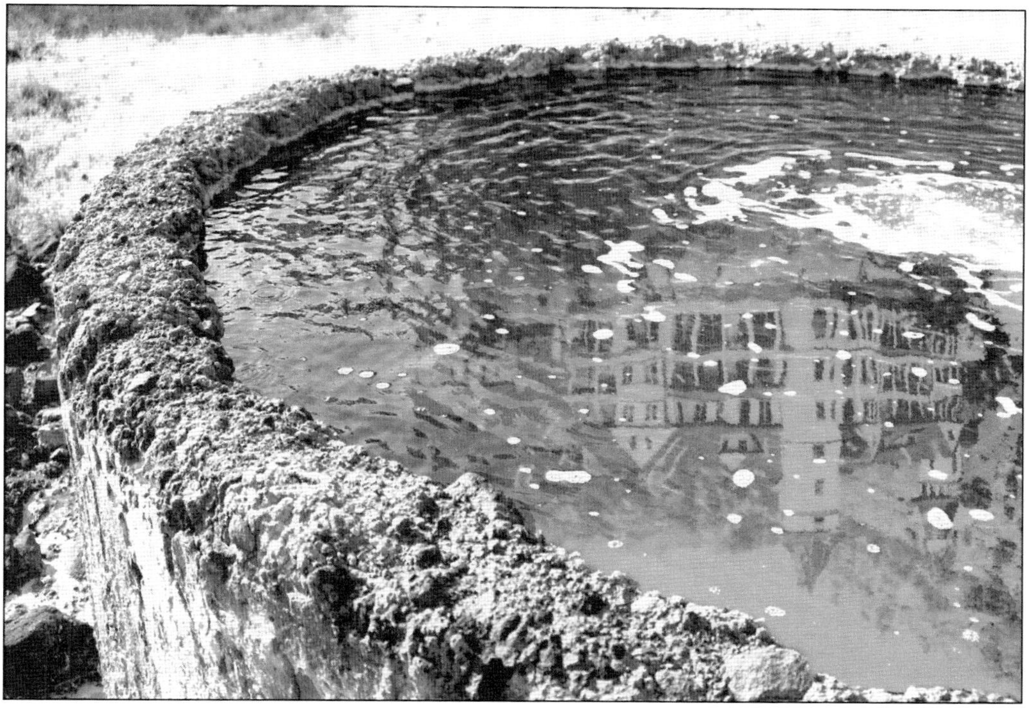

Seen above is a photograph illustration created for a 1996 public tour of the resort ruins in conjunction with the premiere of *The Famous Tuscan Springs*, a stage play. In it, an image of the tavern in its prime is reflected in the waters of the last active spring on the property today. The waters that bubble from a central source in this tub can still be lit on fire from the natural gas content. Below is what remains of the last cottage, which stood for around 100 years before finally collapsing in the 1990s. (Both, author.)

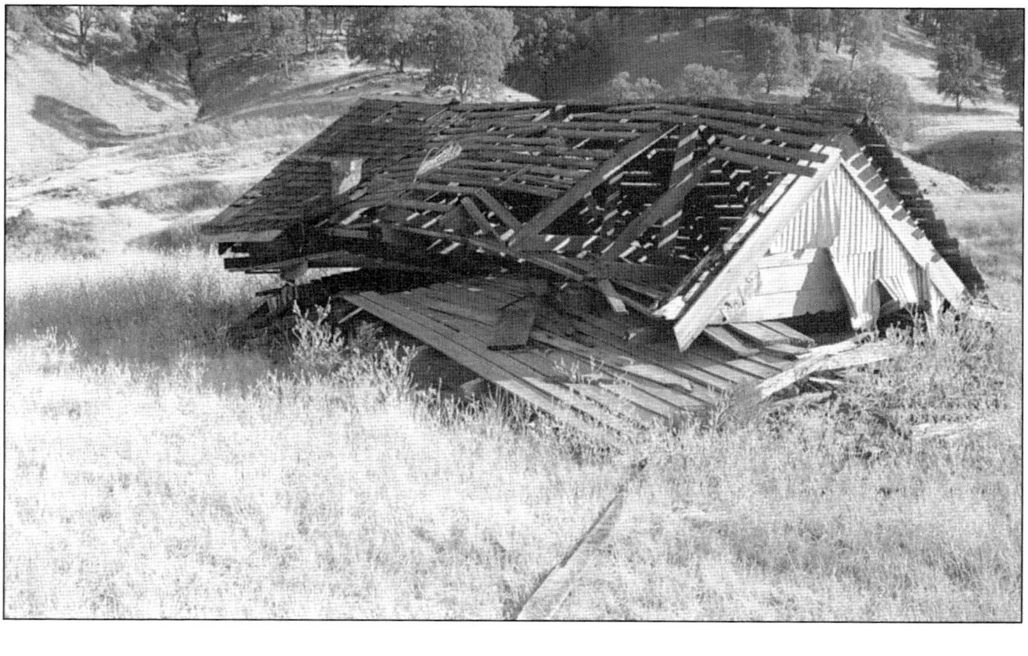

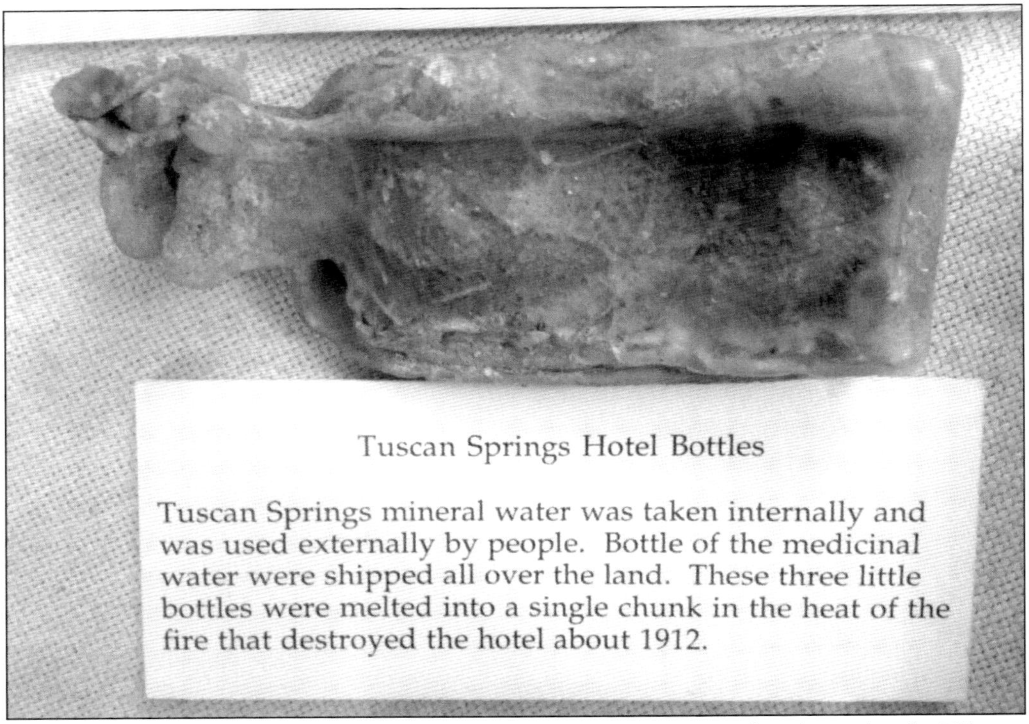

Above, these three bottles are among several unique Tuscan Springs artifacts housed at the Tehama County Museum. Found in the tavern's ruins, they were fused together in the heat of the great fire that destroyed the resort in 1916 (not 1912, as labeled). These may have been mineral salts or patent medicine bottles. Below, a model at the museum is a faithful scale representation of the final tavern at Tuscan Springs, built in 1900. It was researched, built, and donated by Mercy High School students Mark Heffernan and Matt Rodriguez in 1990. (Both, TCM.)

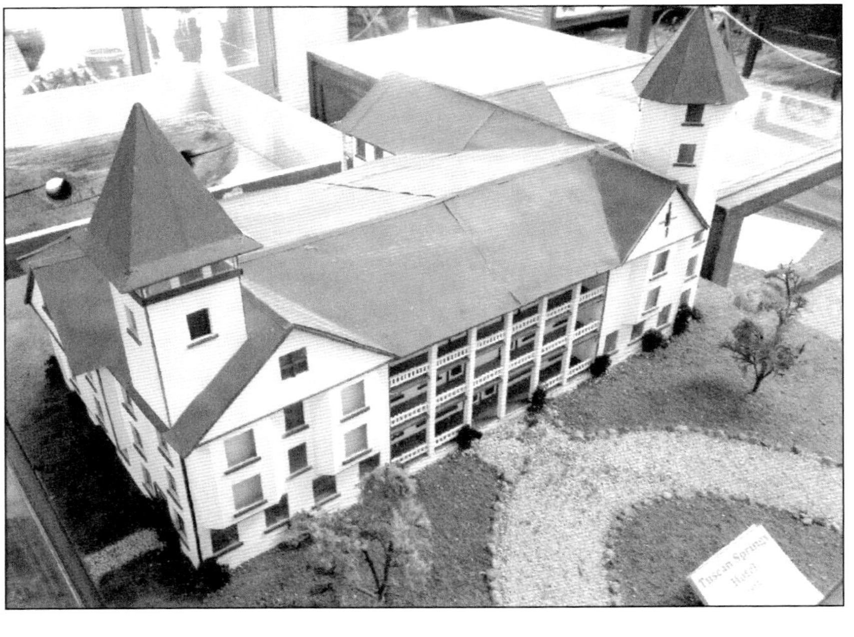

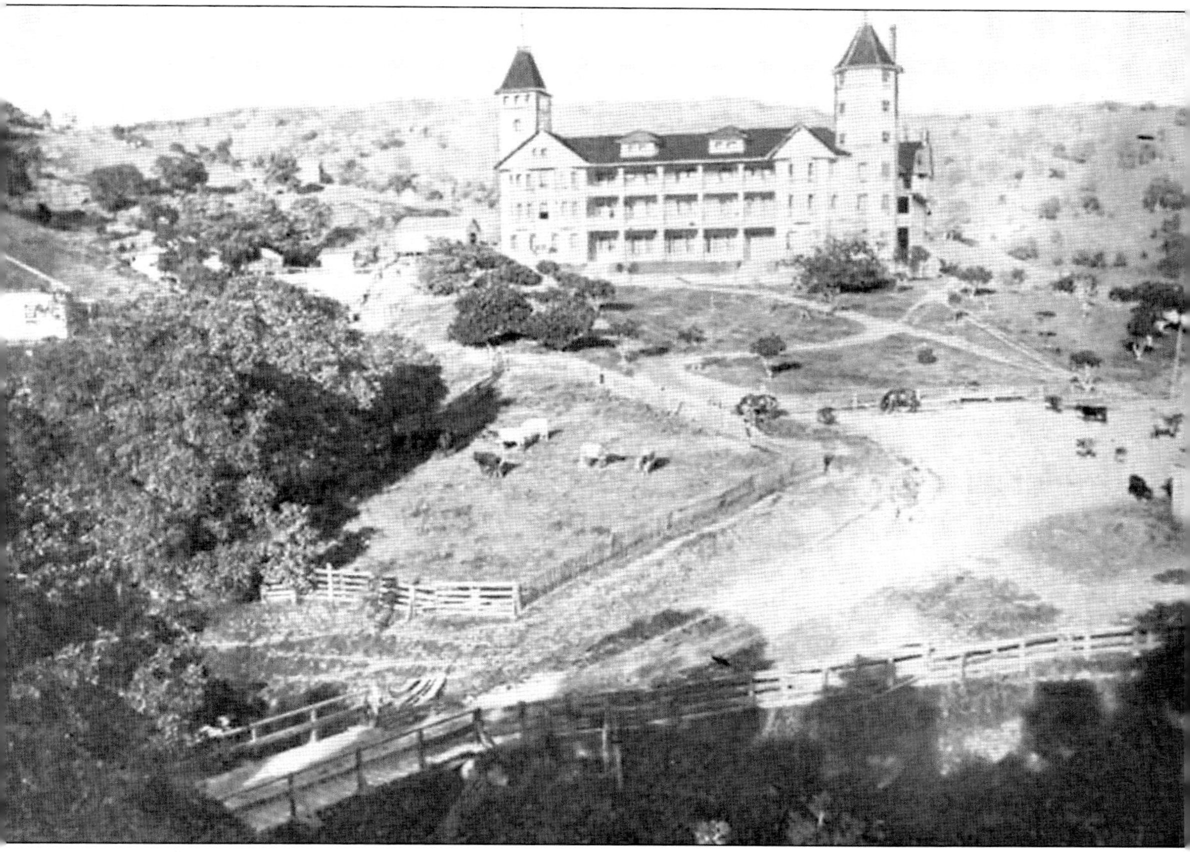

"Trusting I have not wearied you, gentle reader, I will bring this little book to an end, and take this opportunity to thank my past patrons for their kind words, knowing full well a healthy patient leaving Tuscan Springs is a visible advertisement that needs no word of explanation from me and is far more beneficial than I am capable of expressing myself in these few lines in my poor way. Again thanking you all for your liberal patronage, I am, / Yours Respectfully, / E.B. Walbridge" (1903).